SCM STUDYGUIDE TO SCIENCE AND RELIGION

In memory of
Howard
constant friend
and inspiration

SCM STUDYGUIDE TO SCIENCE AND RELIGION

Footprints in Space

Jean Dorricott

scm press

© Jean Dorricott 2005

British Library Cataloguing in Publication data

A catalogue record for this book is available
from the British Library

Acknowledgement is made to the following for permission to use
copyright material:

Rebecca Elson, 2001, *A Responsibility to Awe*,
Oxford Poets, Carcanet Press.

The Authorized Version of the Bible (The King James Bible),
the rights in which are vested in the Crown,
are reproduced by permission of the Crown's Patentee,
Cambridge University Press.

New English Bible © Oxford University Press and
Cambridge University Press 1961, 1970.

0 334 02975 9

First published in 2005 by SCM Press
9–17 St Albans Place, London N1 0NX

www.scm-canterburypress.co.uk

SCM Press is a division of
SCM-Canterbury Press Ltd

Printed and bound in Great Britain by
Biddles Ltd, www.biddles.co.uk

Contents

Introduction   xi

Part 1 Exploring the Universe   1

1 Two Footprints – Super Bangs and Starter Packs   3

The First Footprint – Super Bangs   3

Pyrotechnics, balloons and crunches – universe evolution   5
From the sublime to the ridiculously tiny – subatomic particles   9
Other idiosyncrasies   12
A mysterious yet reasonable universe   17

The Second Footprint – Starter Packs   18

Life emerges   19
Variety   27
Conclusions   35

Ideas for Discussion   36

References and Further Reading   37

2 The Third Footprint – A Conscious Universe   40

Degrees of Awareness   41

Interaction with the environment   42
Recognition of others and response   42
Selfconsciousness and creativity – I'm only human   54
Conclusions   64

Ideas for Discussion   65

References and further reading   67

3 The Fourth Footprint – Deal Justly, Love Mercy   68

First Possibility – Laws are Given by the Gods   69

Second Possibility – Laws are Developed by Humans through Experience   70

Third Possibility – Laws are Intrinsic to the Universe   71

Insect societies – 'I will die to protect my colony'   72
Vertebrate societies – 'We will share the common
   crust, the common danger'   73
The primate world – chimpanzees – 'I know just
   how you feel and I am going to use that knowledge'   81
Primate world – humans – 'We will encode laws'   88
Conclusions   93

Ideas for Discussion   94

References and further reading   95

4 The Fifth Footprint – I Heard the Voice of God   96

Religious Tradition and Practices   97

Comparisons   97
Sociology of religion   99
Beauty and mystery   104
Suffering, death and miracles of healing   105

Religious Experiences   108

Spirit as bias   109
Emerging spirit   110
Religious experiences   116

Conclusions   118

Ideas for Discussion   119

References and Further Reading   120

Part 2 Science and Religion   123

5 Remember the Ancestors   125

Hunting, Fishing and Gathering   126

Fire   127
Wise men   127

Farmers   129

Wandering Tribes and Ziggurats   133

Building cities   133
Nomads in Palestine   134

Sea People and Assyrian Hordes 136

Iron Age 136
Writing the Old Testament 137

Greeks and Romans 140

Philosophy and technology 140
Riots in Palestine 142

Decaying Empire 144

Islam and Muhammad 145

The European Middle Ages 147

Feudalism 147
Scholars 150

Ideas for Discussion 152

References and Further Reading 153

6 First, Enquire Diligently 154

Renaissance and the Birth of Modern Science 155

Books and broomsticks 155
Vegetable lamb meets natural philosophers 157

Eighteenth Century – Enlightenment 161

The rights of man – sometimes 162
Ill fares the land 163
A furnace seal'd 164
Friendly societies and religious societies 165
A long shining fly 166

Nineteenth Century – Industrial Revolution   168

The old farmhouses are down   168
'If I am out of work . . .'   170
Bind up the broken-hearted   171
Descent with modification   174

Twentieth Century – A Relative Era   176

Green revolution   176
Social revolution and suffragettes   178
Spiralling DNA   179
Worldwide Church   180

Ideas for Discussion   181

References and Further Reading   183

7 Re-Imaging a Faith   185

Loss of Belief   185

Loss of Status   186

Responses   187

Only God can reveal himself to us   187
Scientific models have some relevance   188
The universe reaffirms God's self-revealed nature   188

How Not to Use the Bible – Creationism   189

Fruitful Discussion – Divine Action   190

How does God act within the universe?
    General and Special Divine Action   190
Defining miracles, natural law and their relationship   191
Four possibilities for Special Divine Action   193

'Teach us to order our days rightly that we may enter the gate of wisdom' (Psalm 90.12) – Christian Teaching   198

What is in the teaching?   199
Some difficulties   201
Scientific perspectives   203

A Positive Revolution – Feminism   204

A Divided Church – Homosexuality   205

Ideas for Discussion   207

References and Further Reading   209

8 The Samson Effect   211

Technology – Solution or Problem?   212

Tackling Current Issues   213

Population   213
Energy and use of resources   216
Medical advances and concerns   228
Human futures   237
Things that we don't know we don't know   238

Ideas for Discussion   241

References and Further Reading   243

Index   245

Introduction

During winter storms the ancient cliffs of north-east Yorkshire collapse into the North Sea. Among its stones are many fossils of plant and animal life that once lived in vast swamps, but the strangest are footprints of long-dead creatures that munched and wallowed among them, leaving great hollows that filled with mud of a different colour. These natural casts show the imprints of giant claws as well as smaller footprints, and palaeontologists from Sheffield University locate, study and preserve them with photographs and measurements, before the sea erodes them beyond recall. Series of footprints provide some of the most interesting information. From footprint size and depth and the distance between strides, the scientists can calculate the height of the animal at the hip and its speed of travel.

What animals were they? As you pace the footsteps, you, a creature whose ancestors have been around some 4 million years, are treading in the tracks of dinosaurs which lived about 160 million years ago.

Just as the dinosaurs left footprints we can analyse, so the universe leaves clues about itself that we can try and interpret. There are a number of different theories about our universe, necessarily covering many disciplines, and no-one can be expert in them all. So this book presents one approach rather than a definitive view, and tries to include sufficient information for the reader to disagree. The ideas for discussion, websites and booklists at the end of each chapter are designed to present other views and give a wider background.

Part 1, 'Exploring the Universe', examines the scientific interpretation of our position in the universe as we understand it today. Probably all cultures developed such stories, but as their scientific understanding was very limited we view their explanations today as pleasant or grotesque tales. The rainbow is not the sacred bridge to Valhalla where souls of brave warriors feast for ever with the gods. Balder the beloved was not slain by an arrow of mistletoe, nor did Athene, Zeus, Hera and Poseidon argue together over the outcome of the Trojan War. The strong central core of scientific knowledge based on thousands of years of technological experience provides a firm base for the scientific account.

Part 2, 'Science and Religion', explores the historical relationship between religion and science/technology since the Stone Ages. It includes the development of Christianity, and the cross-currents between scientific discoveries and religious beliefs and doctrines. Christianity is used as a test case because it is the religion that will be best known to most readers. It has a long, complicated relationship with science, and by studying it we can apply our insights to other religions. The book ends with a consideration of some of the problems facing our world today and how religion and science together can provide a fruitful and constructive approach.

If we are searching for some way of interpreting the universe, we need a term to describe this fundamental quality. 'God' is too loaded a word, with its connotation of a male person who is totally other than the universe and actively interferes with the way it works. It is also not a term acceptable to all religions. Part 1 refers to Reality, the undeniable truth embedded in the universe as firmly as the height of the dinosaur is embedded in its fossilized stride.

Many scientists approach their subject with a feeling of awe and wonder. 'Wow, isn't it amazing that you can put your feet into steps made by a dinosaur whose family tree went extinct long before your ancestors trod the earth? This is miraculous – it opens our minds to search for the deeper Reality.' We shall use this version of 'miracle' in the first part of this book, and in the second consider the religious interpretation – 'miracle' is an event which goes against natural laws and displays the power of God, such as the resurrection of Jesus from the dead.

Part 1

Exploring the Universe

1

Two Footprints – Super Bangs and Starter Packs

THE FIRST FOOTPRINT – SUPER BANGS

Stand and look at the sky on a clear night. If you are fortunate enough to live away from the glare of street lighting, then the beauty of stars, planets and moon are even more fabulous. And fables have indeed been invented about them for thousands of years. They are homes of mysterious gods. Their enigmatic influence affects cycles of menstruation, seedtime and harvest. They are set there as guides for merchants and armies. The ancient Greeks watched their rhythms and deduced that God moves all things as something loved. At the beginning of the fourteenth century Dante the Italian poet wrote of the love that moves the sun and the other stars.

Now we know that as we look at the stars we are looking back into deep history (Figure 1.1). The speed of light is so fast that on *earth* it appears instantaneous, but in the vastness of space the time factor comes into play. Here distances are so great we measure them as the distance travelled by light in a year. M2 in Aquarius is one of the finest globular clusters in the sky. We see it as it was 50,000 years ago, long before recorded human history began. The *universe* itself is thought to be some 16 *billion* years old. The further we can see, the further back we are looking in time.

The existence of the universe raises huge questions. All through recorded history people have tried to understand why it is here – the whole caboodle,

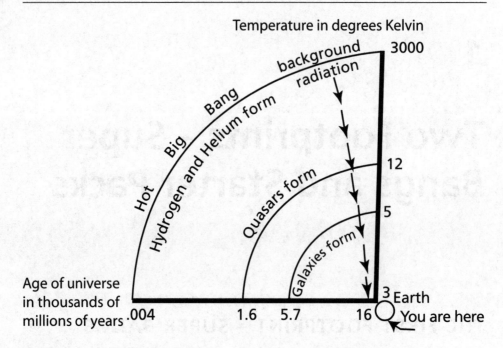

Figure 1.1   Looking back in time: You are here.

stars, trees, humans. What does it all mean? Is there a meaning behind this great cosmos?

Before we can answer these questions we need to look more closely at what we know about the universe. We will delve into some of its mysteries as we understand them today and then we shall be in a better position to think about any meaning it might have.

Billion	1,000 million.
Cosmos/universe	Used synonymously to include everything that exists.
Earth/world	Used synonymously to describe the planet Earth only.

- **Pyrotechnics, balloons and crunches – universe evolution**
- **From the sublime to the ridiculously tiny – subatomic particles**
- **Other idiosyncrasies**
- **A mysterious yet reasonable universe**

Pyrotechnics, balloons and crunches – universe evolution

- Beginnings
- Elements
- Anthropic principles and multi-universes
- Endings

Beginnings

There is no period *before* the universe, because time itself did not exist then. In the extremely early universe as we currently understand it, all our usual physical concepts break down. Using mathematical calculations it appears that the material of that universe was highly compressed into a space of atomic dimensions. It expanded *exponentially* and rapidly in an unstable vacuum-like state. The energy of this state transformed into thermal energy, the universe became extremely hot and the Big Bang followed, a firework of immense proportions. As it exploded and cooled, space/time began.

One analogy of the expanding universe is that of a balloon being blown up, though we have to remember there is nothing outside this strange balloon and that there is no period 'before' it began its growth. If you put dots on the flat balloon to represent galaxies, then as it is blown up the dots 'see' one another moving away.

There are a number of convincing arguments for the hot Big Bang and expanding universe. Background white noise, the relics of that initial explosion, comes from all directions and hampers the current Search for Extra Terrestrial Intelligence (SETI), which listens to sounds from space with radio telescopes. In 1990 the Cosmic Background Explorer satellite (COBE) detected microwave echoes of that initial explosion. We know that galaxies are moving away from us by measuring the spectra of light they emit.

However, some measurements suggest our universe actually has no beginning or end, but exists in a steady state. Our data about this vast, hugely complex body is bound to include confusing items, providing us with endless fascination.

| Exponential | A state of growth where the logarithm of the original state increases linearly with time. |

Elements

All the different elements like hydrogen and iron developed out of the hot Big Bang. The first ones were the lighter elements like hydrogen and helium.

The astronomer and poet Rebecca Elson, who died in 1999, felt it important to explain to others outside her field just how awe-inspiring she found her work. She writes of the child walking down the street with a helium balloon, 'a little piece of pure Big Bang bobbing at the end of her string'.

As the universe continued to cool and expand, gravitational forces condensed matter into the first generation of galaxies and stars. Nuclear reactions in these stars produced the heavier elements. Astrophysicists are now able to calculate very accurately what materials were manufactured inside stars and then scattered by *supernovae*. Second-generation stars are 99% hydrogen and helium, and the heavier elements eventually condensed round them as planets. The most common planetary elements are hydrogen, carbon, oxygen and nitrogen (CHON). The composition of our earth is not unique, so it is likely that if there are life forms on other planets then they too will be based on CHON.

We like to claim we are stardust. Well, there is also the mysterious dark matter, one of the most intriguing problems in astrophysics. It seems to hold galaxies and galaxy clusters together by its gravitational pull. Some calculations on the distance of supernovae from earth suggest there may be a dark energy – anti-gravity stuff that drives the galaxies apart. If these calculations are correct, then our universe is 70% dark energy and 25% dark matter. Ordinary matter like the galaxies, stars and ourselves may be just universe sediment.

Supernova, pl. supernovae	When a massive star finishes its career, it collapses in a huge explosion, blowing much of its material away and spreading abroad heavy elements.

Anthropic principles and multi-universes

Life is dependent on the initial physical conditions of those first pyrotechnics, for had the proportion of hydrogen to helium been different there would either have been no water, or the heavy elements would have been locked up inside the stars. If the nuclear force that holds atoms together had been stronger, then carbon, essential for life, would have been converted to oxygen as it formed. The importance of such initial conditions has given rise to the *anthropic principle* – the natural laws of the universe are fine-tuned so that our own existence (intelligent self-conscious life) becomes a possibility. Is this design by an external 'mind'?

Before we get too excited about this, we have to remember there may be large numbers of universes and ours is in the subset of those capable of producing complexity and consciousness. In some theories, exponentially expanding parts of the universe are thought to continually spawn other exponentially expanding parts – many inflating balloons producing new balloons which in turn produce more new balloons. In this scenario we live in an eternal, self-reproducing inflationary universe.

Anthropic principles	The weak anthropic principle (WAP) is based on the way the universe has developed from its beginnings (its laws and slight irregularities). These have been essential for the production and evolution of life. The strong principle (SAP) claims that the universe *must* have the properties which allow intelligent life to come into existence, and once it exists it will not die out. SAP has been

criticized by many scientists. It is sometimes quoted
by theologians to support intelligent design with
humans as the ultimate goal of creation.

Endings

If the universe has a beginning, then the chances are it will have an end.
According to the *second law of thermodynamics* decay is inevitable. One
scenario is that our universe will start to collapse and everything will be
compressed into a Big Crunch. Physicists generally agree that atoms themselves will erode away into smaller particles. But we can't be absolutely sure
that regions beyond our current horizon limit are like parts of the universe
we can see. The current limit was set up by the Hubble Space Telescope in
March 2004, when it returned deep-space pictures of the very early universe,
about 700 million years after the hot Big Bang. There could be new supplies
of energy beyond this that only come into play as the universe collapses.
A Crunch is not certain. But we can breathe a sigh of relief because we shan't
be around to see it happen. It's billions of years away.

Second law of thermodynamics	The amount of disorder (entropy) increases in an enclosed system like our universe. Order can be increased in small localities by an input of energy, such as our sun provides, but this energy supply will eventually fail. This is one of the most important laws in physics.

From the sublime to the ridiculously tiny – subatomic particles

- Strangely charming
- Newton and uncertainty
- Entanglement

Strangely charming

Figure 1.2 shows a very simple interpretation of the current standard model of quantum theory.

Quantum theory can only be explained mathematically. It is counter-intuitive, based on theoretical physics and research, like that at *CERN* outside Geneva, Switzerland. Here the Large Electron Positron (LEP) accelerates subatomic particles round a 27km circle at very high speed onto target nuclei, and records the interactions.

Quantum mechanics studies these interactions, and has shown there is no real distinction between effects traditionally described as waves (e.g. light) and as particles (e.g. electrons). The smallest particles currently thought to exist fall into two groups, quarks and leptons. The electron is the best known of the latter group. Quarks come in six 'flavours' including 'strange' and 'charm'. 'Up' and 'down' quarks are the most common and are the constituents of the neutrons and protons that make up atomic nuclei.

CERN   Conseil Européen pour la Recherche Nucléaire

Newton and uncertainty

Newtonian physics describes the regularities of the world we live in. When you undo a nut with a spanner, the turning effect of the force depends on the size or weight of the force and the perpendicular distance from the force to

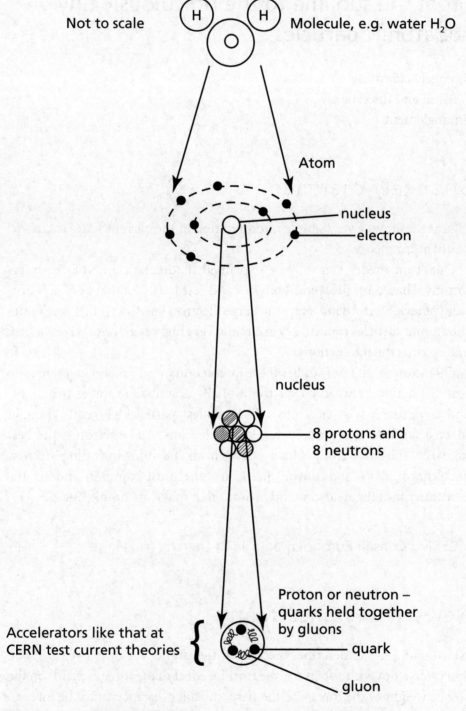

Figure 1.2 Quantum theory – current standard model.

the pivot – so you use a longer spanner to give a greater turning force and make the job easier. Calculations about the force required are straightforward.

The world of the very small is not deterministic in this way. Uncertainty, first described by Heisenberg in 1927, exists at a deep level. The Heisenberg Uncertainty Principle finds that certain pairs of quantum properties cannot both be defined at the same time. This uncertainty is nothing to do with inadequate measuring apparatus but is a fundamental property of the quantum world. The more accurately we measure the position of an electron, the less accurately we can determine its momentum. Conversely if we measure its *momentum* it becomes difficult to determine location. There is similar uncertainty when considering energy and time. It is possible to predict the time taken for half a group of radioactive atoms to disintegrate, but not the moment when one particular atom disintegrates. Here we are calculating probabilities, because it is not possible to measure the actual event.

The many worlds approach assumes that a new world arises for every quantum measurement-like interaction (the theory does not require there to be an actual measurement). We could be dead in one of these bifurcating worlds and alive in the other. We would never know we are dead in one world because no two worlds can communicate.

Momentum	momentum = mass × velocity

Entanglement

Information can be studied as formally and mathematically as the rest of the material world. It takes time to travel and nothing can travel faster than the speed of light. Yet in the quantum world, when the spin of one of a pair of protons is measured, the spin of the other is instantaneously determined as equal and opposite to the first, however far apart they have travelled. It appears that information is travelling faster than light and, unlike other physical laws, its speed does not decrease with distance. 'Spooky action at a distance' is what Einstein called this weird theory about the quantum world. He never liked it. It was verified by experiment in 1997, using detectors

30 km apart. It raises interesting ideas. Since classical physics does not allow instant cause and effect, then possibly space is not as we currently suppose.

This phenomenon is already in use as a technological tool, as in quantum cryptography where information is passed without the possibility of eavesdropping. Money has been transferred securely by researchers at the University of Vienna.

Entanglement is also linked to *teleportation*, but while quantum teleportation is real, teleportation of large objects is far more problematical. It currently lies only within the realm of science fiction. Claims made by some people to perform action on large items at a distance by willpower or charms (psychokinesis and magic) have not been verified. (See Chapter 4, 'Into the Ganzfeld').

Physicists say we need to radically rethink our ordinary world-views, for matter does not behave as we've always thought it did. This weird world of quantum physics is not the only challenge, for the theories underlying relativity and chaos are equally formidable, and we shall look next at these. Together they pose problems for other disciplines such as theology, further discussed in Chapter 7, in 'Fruitful Discussion – Divine Action'.

> **Teleportation** Travelling through time and space by merely reappearing at a distant location.

Other idiosyncrasies

* What is the time, relatively speaking?
* Chaos, ruler of the Evil Empire
* Prophecy and prediction

What is the time, relatively speaking?

Time is a concept that has exercised many minds, from Zeno of Elea in the fifth century before Christ's birth to Augustine and Kant. No doubt it has puzzled most people throughout human history. For some, time is circular, for others it does not exist and for others it's an arrow or time-line. Time passes in discrete minutes of 60 seconds. It also lags when you are waiting for exam results and speeds up when you are happily engaged with people you love.

Time presupposes change and movement and has given rise to the opposite concept of eternity. The poet Henry Vaughan lived from 1622 to 1694, through the violence of the English Civil War and the new discoveries in the heavens by Galileo. Drawing on the events of this period, he pictured eternity as peace – 'a great ring of pure and endless light, all calm as it was bright, and round beneath it, Time in hours, days, years . . . like a vast shadow moved'. In his thought, to be out of time is to be in changeless eternal perfection. When death ends our human time, we pass into the blissful light of God.

Practical problems of space travel have made us aware today that properties of space and time depend on the frame of reference of the observer. *Space/time* and matter are interdependent. Space/time in Einstein's *theory of general relativity* is an indivisible block in which past, present and future exist together, solid and static. In such a block universe all future events exist and are possibly knowable, much as Henry Vaughan seems to have imagined.

This universe is pictured as a smooth four-dimensional fabric with gravity being the result of its curved shape. Here the attraction of the sun's gravity for planets is imagined as marbles rolling on a rubber sheet that is weighed down in the centre. But we also know that the maximum speed at which anything can travel is that of light, which gives us the concept of order in time.

Because time is linked with space, people moving through space relative to one another find it difficult to agree what 'now' means. Relativity first aroused interest in the nineteenth century with the increased speed of rail travel. Robert Louis Stevenson wrote of the child's delight as the 'painted stations whistle by'. The child wonders at the snatched pictures of other lives moving at slower speeds, 'each a glimpse and gone for ever!' Our twentieth-century ventures into space include more practical problems. Engineers must solve the difficult adjustments of satellite clocks in the Global Positioning System (GPS).

Yet does time exist? Some physicists believe that our experience of time as passing is due to our physical make-up in three-dimensional space. In multidimensional space, time may be non-existent. Could time be bent into a loop? We know that clocks run slower closer to earth's gravitational field than they do far out in space. If something with mass or energy can distort nearby space and time in this way, then perhaps time could be bent back on itself, making a type of time machine. Some theoretical physicists are looking at this possibility.

Space/time appears frozen, yet we experience past, present and future. Combining these observations is one of the major conundrums of physics today with implications for quantum mechanics and general relativity.

Space/time	Four dimensions, three of space and one of time.
Theory of	The relationship between space/time and matter,
general	linked by gravity. Einstein showed there is no
relativity	difference between acceleration and gravity.
	(Theory of special relativity is contained in the
	famous equation E(nergy) = m(ass) × c², where c is
	a constant identified with the speed of light.)

Chaos, ruler of the Evil Empire

Chaos, the collapse of the current world into total disarray, has been a human theme for centuries. In many ancient myths it is the primal monster which destroys beauty, reason and happiness, and the gods must continually battle with it to keep creation on track. Everything decays, moth and rust destroy our accumulated wealth. John Milton, writing in his epic *Paradise Lost* about battles in heaven after the upheavals of the English Civil War, named the ruler of deepest hell Chaos.

It is only since the 1970s that scientists have begun to consider chaos as a process of becoming, where under certain conditions entropy itself becomes the precursor to order. Chaos theory is now a mathematical discipline including several models.

Early experiments plotted increasing water flow of a dripping tap onto a three-dimensional graph and found patterns of order within disorder. Here random data is pulled into patterns. Sometimes simple deterministic systems like *algorithms* can develop a quite new complexity. Many algorithms show only dull patterns, but the Mandelbrot set has an infinitely deep structure, a repetition of structures on finer and finer scales. These intricate and beautiful designs have been used by artists. The fundamental equations which govern our universe are of the Mandelbrot type, bringing about endless novelty and complexity. Mathematical design is built into the structure of the universe. Living things use mathematical progressions to produce amazingly beautiful artifacts like fern fronds.

Share price fluctuations and predator–prey relationships involving sudden population crashes are examples of chaotic systems. Slightly different initial conditions can lead to radically different outcomes.

Chaos theories indicate we live in an unpredictable, open-ended world, unlike the deterministic block universe where the future is potentially knowable. Quantum theory too suggests that unpredictability is inherent in the universe.

> Algorithm   A precise series of actions to solve a problem. Algorithms often have steps that repeat until a problem is solved. See Figure 1.3 for an example.

Prophecy and prediction

Scientists are aware that predictability itself is surprising. We can calculate exactly where an object must be placed in relation to a particular convex lens (a magnifying glass), so that it will be magnified to a certain size. We can repeat this endlessly and the result is the same. This is the basis of the clockwork universe concept.

This is not the whole picture, as some futures are basically unpredictable. When there are a number of interacting components even the largest computer cannot resolve the resulting complexity. There's that hypothetical butterfly dreaded by all weather announcers. As the small effect of its fluttering wings is multiplied, a system may be tipped into a different state and a hurricane occurs in the south of England. As for the solar system! It is a dynamic system which can and will exhibit chaotic behaviour. We cannot

By using a special form of numbers called *complex* numbers, a beautiful pattern is created which is called the Mandelbrot set. The algorithm to create these patterns is very simple:

For each point in the picture:
Step 1   Select a complex number, c.
Step 2   Set z = c and n = 0.
Step 3   Calculate new numbers using the formulas

$$n_{new} = n + 1$$
$$Z_{new} = z^2 + c$$

Step 4   If $|z_{new}| > 4$ or $n_{new} > 1000$ go to step 7.
Step 5   Set $z = z_{new}$ and $n=n_{new}$.
Step 6   Go to step 3.
Step 7   Plot a point on the graph choosing a colour depending upon the value of n.

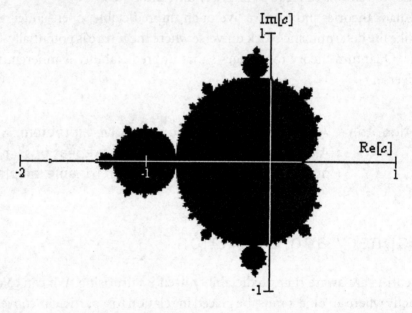

Figure 1.3   Algorithm.

even calculate just how unexpected its behaviour may be, as its distant past is hidden from our mathematics. Yet it is only mildly chaotic, or the mathematician Kepler would never have been able to formulate laws in the early 1600s that predict its state accurately over short human timescales.

So the predictable deterministic world is also non-deterministic and unpredictable at many levels. Only if we could know all forces of nature, overcome the 'fuzziness' in knowing the location and momentum of any subatomic particle, could we hope to calculate past and future. But there is a basic uncertainty underlying the universe at the quantum level, so this knowledge is for ever beyond the reach of intelligence. Still, in a totally deterministic universe there would be no free will, so the inherent unpredictability also gives us freedom of choice. (More in Chapter 3, under 'Primate world – humans').

A mysterious yet reasonable universe

- Mysterious
- Reasonable

Mysterious

In the 1920s we thought that the Milky Way, our galaxy, dominated the universe and other light patches were smaller satellites. By the 1990s we knew we had underestimated the size of the universe by several orders of magnitude, and that our galaxy is an average one among many. We had also worked out a reasonably accurate age for the universe lying between 13 and 16 billion years – which doesn't sound very accurate!

Yet whatever we learn about the universe, it will always remain mysterious. Since science is based on laws deduced from repeatable events (probability) and the evolution of the universe cannot be rerun, then our best understanding will always be uneven. Certain laws may well remain hidden.

There are many difficulties when we try to relate the quantum world to ours, yet the two are intimately entwined. Perhaps the laws of quantum theory can't be applied to humans because we operate at a different level of reality. What quantum theory *has* taught us is that we cannot perceive 'matter' and the 'material world' as we used to. Matter is localized energy and includes not only atoms and molecules but also light, gravity, electrons and information.

The universe and the minutely small particles that make it can only be understood mathematically; analogies and models break down. This makes it even more difficult to grasp ideas connected with cosmology, relativity and quantum theory. It also makes it easy to build false links between, say, the hot Big Bang and a God who says, 'Let there be light!' Cosmology is not religion.

Reasonable

The universe is reliable. It does not suddenly play magical tricks on us by changing the rules indiscriminately. As far as we can tell, its law and order extends throughout space. On planet earth living things have evolved 'knowing' they can rely and act on this stability. It delights our senses with its beauty. It is endlessly dynamic, a mysterious shape-shifter whose movements and patterns we can only dimly interpret.

The universe is blind. It does not have aims or morals, so the events that occur are neither just nor unjust.

Yet it leaves an unusual footprint. It is intelligible, and this is one of the strangest things about it. How is it that intelligent beings have evolved who can stand 'outside' it and make some accurate predictions about its behaviour? Is it just our minds that impose order on experience, much as observation forces an either/or on particle activity in quantum theory? In that case, where does our ability to make order come from?

What other secrets might it hold?

THE SECOND FOOTPRINT – STARTER PACKS

Imagine yourself watching the unfolding of the universe. As it bursts into life and expands, the supernovae throw out new elements around them and some of these condense into an obscure planet around a very ordinary star in an average galaxy. Not an event worth noticing as you watch the immense firework displays across space.

So you might not even check out the little planet as it cools and forms oceans where strange shapes wriggle and writhe. Slowly its grey and ochre rocks become covered with green material of all different shades and tints. Dinosaurs trot across the ground and birds fly in the lower atmosphere.

But if you turn from the pyrotechnics in space and look more closely at this pinhead of a planet, you will begin to realize a second miracle has taken place, an event beyond your imagining. Because how could anyone guess that out of non-living stardust, obedient to physical and chemical rules, Life will emerge – a completely different development from anything that has gone before?

So what exactly is *Life*, this mysterious force that energizes plants, fungi, bacteria and animals on planet earth? How did Life start? Why is it so full of variety?

Life/living things/ life forms/ creatures	These terms include all life on earth and any we may one day find beyond it. Living things are generally categorized in five Kingdoms: Monera (e.g. bacteria, blue-green algae), Protista (e.g. seaweed and single-celled creatures like amoebas), fungi (e.g. yeasts, moulds, rusts, mushrooms), plants (generally photosynthetic and green) and animals (e.g. jellyfish, eelworms, sea urchins, molluscs, squid, insects, spiders, reptiles, you. Please note the term 'animal' includes all these and many more.

- **Life emerges**
- **Variety**

Life emerges

- Definitions
- Evolution – life gets on its bike
- Evolution – does it have a goal?

Definitions

Life is complexity of a different order from the Big Bang. There are two remarkable things about life as we see it today. One is that all known living things are at root the same, which points to a limited and simple origin. And most of them are now very intricate.

What exactly is life? Easy. We all know that a hen is alive and the gravel she pecks at is non-living. Hens grow by synthesizing body parts out of food. They repel disease and mend wounds. They reproduce others like themselves. They die. Decomposers turn them into food for future lives. But what about viruses? They use the metabolism of their host to multiply, and when the host or its infected cells die their offspring are released. Some viruses exist in the free state as non-living chemical molecules and they can be crystallized and stored. They do not die. In 2002 a polio virus was synthesized from scratch in a laboratory. Was this the creation of life?

With care we can come to a working definition of a living thing. Its atoms are constantly changing, but its form remains constant. Its parts contribute to its well-being and reproduction. It has two important talents; it can replicate and it can metabolize nutrients for energy. It doesn't require an additional 'life force' but develops from the natural materials on the planet, following the same rules laid down in the early universe and subject to chance like everything else.

Evolution – life gets on its bike

The first diagram (Figure 1.4) explains the principle of evolution. Much of the evidence comes from the fragmentary fossil record which has very little information about changes in soft body parts, lifestyles or habitats. It consists chiefly of more recent skeletal remains (recent as in tens of millions of years).

Has there been enough time for complex life to evolve? If chance alone was expected to result in complexity, then the answer would be no. But chance acting together with the laws of chemistry and physics can do the trick. Slow transformations, each step of which can occur by chance, provide material

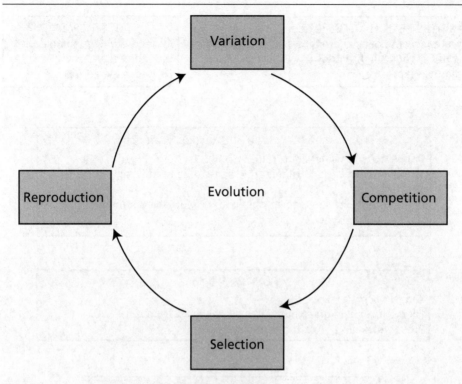

Figure 1.4   Evolution feedback loop.

for evolution to work on. Meanwhile many organisms enjoy their lives but don't pass on their genes. Extinction is gentle and slow, not savage. Mathematical calculations show there has been plenty of time for life to evolve to its present state since it first appeared some three and a half billion years ago.

Figure 1.5 shows how we think the starter packs took shape, and how they changed the primitive atmosphere. Modern meteorites contain a variety of amino acids, the building blocks of proteins, and so biological molecules almost certainly landed on the early earth. Experiments last century sparked electricity through a mix of those gases most likely in the early earth atmosphere, and amino acids were made. So these molecules could have arisen on earth and/or arrived in meteorites.

The mechanisms of life's origins are endlessly debated. The earliest living systems would have been very different from any life form today, and would be manufactured out of existing biomolecules, probably in the early seas, safe from destructive ultraviolet light.

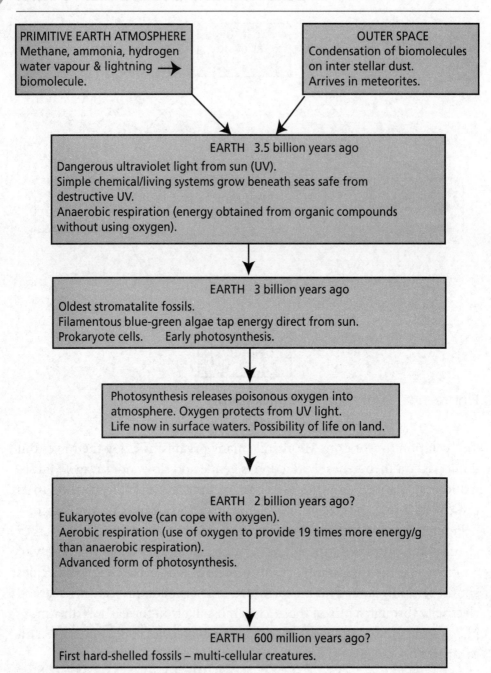

Figure 1.5   Starter Packs.
Early Evolution and Atmosphere Change.

The next step for life was grouping together in primitive 'cells', the first form of cooperative life. Nucleic acids and proteins must be held in some form of bag, a cell boundary. This must be sloppy, allowing the passage of some molecules both in and out, but capable of retaining those essential for life processes.

Today archaebacteria, a very ancient group, live in many places impossible for other life, such as total darkness near oceanic volcanic vents (smokers). Here they provide food energy for whole communities of clams, worms and crabs around the vents. Their ancestors may have been the first cellular life forms. Some of the earliest fossils are large structures called stromatolites, growth layers produced by simple filamentous *blue-green algae*. Similar algae are still working away, and you may see living stromatolites on the northern coast of Australia. They developed an early form of photosynthesis which added oxygen to the atmosphere, a gas which was poisonous to the life forms then in existence.

Bacteria live a long time, so could any of these be alive today? Live bacterial spores have been found in thousand-year-old sediment, but there were none alive in Tutankhamun's tomb in Egypt (three thousand years), so all our present bacteria have evolved from the ancient ones.

Early bacteria and blue-green algae, like their descendants, are *prokaryotes*. *Eukaryotes* evolved, able to cope with the oxygen atmosphere, and all other creatures like microscopic amoebae, plants, fungi and animals, are descendants of these. But bacteria did not disappear – there are still far more of them than of us (Figure 1.6).

About 600 million years ago soft-bodied multicellular sea creatures appear in a few rare deposits. Once creatures developed hard parts far more fossils are found. After the evolution of multicellular creatures, the next big step for life was the colonization of the hostile land about 400 million years ago and then the air. Colonization of space is at a very primitive stage!

So for the first three billion years of life, everything looked rather dull. But appearances are deceptive, and if one day we find similar boring situations on other planets we shall all be greatly excited. But could there be life on other planets? Life can exist between -5°C and 113°C, in solutions as acid as pH 0 and as alkaline as pH 10, and at pressures one thousand times above atmospheric; and some forms can survive for a thousand years. The next

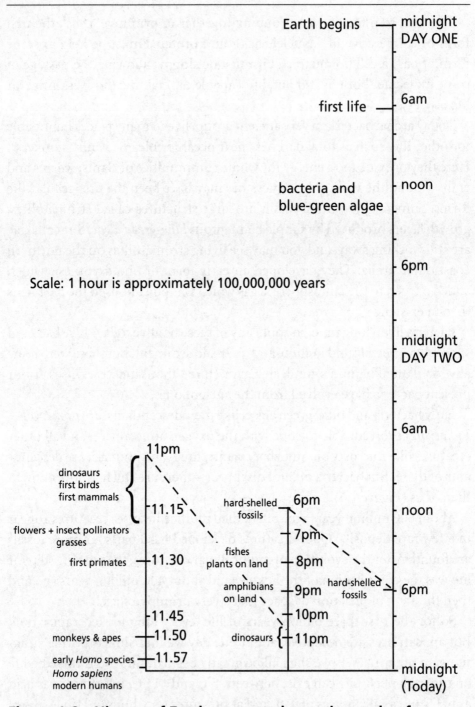

Figure 1.6 History of Earth expressed on a timescale of two days.

probe to Venus will probably test the Venusian atmosphere for some of these extremophiles.

Blue-green algae	Prokaryotes which grow successfully in low light conditions where other creatures can't thrive. Some can fix atmospheric nitrogen. Some species associate with fungi to form a composite plant – the lichens.
Eukaryote (eucaryote)	Their DNA (deoxyribonucleic acid) is enclosed in a membrane, forming a nucleus. They divide by meiosis or mitosis. They contain small structures such as mitochondria (used in respiration) and chloroplasts (used in photosynthesis and only found in plants). It is possible that these structures were originally prokaryotes that were assimilated by early eukaryotic cells.
Prokaryote (procaryote) bacteria and blue-green algae.	Small, one-celled or filamentous. Their single cell is not enclosed in a nuclear membrane. They do not have mitochondria or chloroplasts, but contain structures that perform the same functions.

Evolution – does it have a goal?

There is no evidence that evolution is anything other than a blind force. It doesn't aim to produce more complex creatures at the expense of the simple, for as far as we know none of the major divisions of life has been extinguished over time, even though some 99% of all *species* have become extinct. Evolution is neither a ladder of improvement nor a pyramid of relative importance with bacteria at the base and brainy creatures at the top, for all living things are unique in their own way. It is better pictured as a bush with many twigs, all depending on one another, so all equally important to life on planet earth.

We can see how blind evolution is when we notice how it progresses by extending and adapting original body patterns. The jawbone in ancient reptiles developed into mammalian ear bones, the hammer and anvil, so improving hearing and assisting survival. Certain dinosaurs developed feathers from their scales that were later adapted for flight, and their bird descendants colonized the air and feasted on flying insects. Adapting existing patterns without a fundamental rethink increases design faults, and humans like other animals have inherited patterns that are now a disadvantage. One is the position of our nose above our mouth which we inherited from our fish ancestor. This animal had a head opening to a chemical sense organ, and when our ancestors moved onto land it was adapted for breathing air. We are prone to choking because our food and air passages meet at the back of our throats and we stand upright – a real botched job.

All kinds of interrelationships affect evolution, from the very large, like environmental change, to the minutiae of the *genome*. Some key differences between many creatures lie not only in their genes but also in the areas of the genome which control timing, amounts and place. These regulating gene sequences are on the same strand of DNA as the gene they control. They are difficult to identify because they are not always near the gene they regulate, but some quite dramatic systems have been worked out. Certain genes order the early development of both fins in fish and limbs in four-legged animals. They have different regulatory sequences. In mammal foetuses these trigger the formation of feet and toes, not fins. So mechanisms controlling the genes, rather than the genes themselves, may account for some major differences.

As a species evolves, so do its competitors. Each acts to its own advantage and the whole community reaches a state where each species does reasonably well. But the collective behaviour of the system tends to drive species to extinction over the long term. Some species have beaten the system. Coelacanths have swum the oceans for 400 million years. Gingko trees grew alongside dinosaurs before grasses and brightly coloured flowers evolved.

Genome   The total genetic material within an individual or cell, depending on context.

Variety

The variety of life forms intrigues everyone. Earth teems with a medley of complex forms, so much more interesting than the surface of neighbouring planets. How did this variety come about?

Consider some of the basic problems living things must solve, whether they are simple or complex. They must acquire energy for growth, repair, protection and reproduction either from a source like the sun (plants) or by assimilating it from other bodies (fungi and animals). As members of a species increase they must tackle overcrowding and competition, which lead to famine and increasing disease. So they colonize new areas or cooperate with other species to make new niches. If they fail to thrive, opportunities are provided for other species to take over. Definitely a case of one man's meat being another's poison.

Problem-solving leads to growth and development. We shall look in more detail at some of these solutions, particularly those developed by plants because of their importance – we animals are so totally dependent on them. They preceded animals onto land, they can grow bigger and live longer, and they thrive in conditions where animals struggle.

Plants can do two things which animals can't – they harvest energy from the sun by photosynthesis, and they turn atmospheric nitrogen into the ammonia essential for manufacturing proteins. To be more accurate, some plants make oxygen-free homes for nitrogen-fixing bacteria. The bacteria can't work if oxygen is present as it stops the nitrogen-to-ammonia process. Members of the clover family have special white root nodules where bacteria live in symbiosis with the plant, and you can see them if you pull up any clover weed from a lawn. Leguminous plants – clover, peas, beans – all have this ability, which has been used by farmers for centuries to improve soil fertility.

Far back in time animals and plants shared similar ancestors, and some basic life processes are recorded in the genes of both groups. Some living things today still include both plant and animal characteristics. There are about twenty British species of tiny *Chlamydomonas*, a pear-shaped alga with a light-sensitive receptor and flagellum, able to swim and explore its home waters like an animal. It also has a large green cup-shaped chloroplast for photosynthesis.

- Growth and waste removal
- Tackling repairs and avoiding predation
- The number one question – why sex?
- Times of famine
- Storing information
- Competition and cooperation
- Dynamic relationships

Growth and waste removal

Plants use energy in growing from embryo to reproductive maturity and they must transfer food from leaves to the growing parts. The capillary system in *higher plants* is very delicate so phloem cell function is easily disrupted during experiments. But careful measurements using radioactive carbon show that a sugar molecule made in the top leaf of a tree of 100m, and travelling at the average speed of 100cm per hour, would take just over four days to reach the roots. Most plants sensibly supply food to roots from their lower leaves, while upper leaves supply flowers and growing leaves.

Many plants have some limited movement, for even anchored plants move leaves by unfolding them and turning them to the light, where they can capture energy like miniature solar panels. Some exceptional plant leaves move fast like those on sensitive mimosa and the Venus flytrap – an electrical response, expensive in energy use. Male spermatozoids in mosses and sea wracks actively swim to find the egg using tiny flagella.

Rather than move themselves to find a mate, most plants use wind, water or animals. This means they only have to spend energy on making protective coats for pollen and seeds. Many reproduce themselves by *cloning*. They thrust long whippy stems into the soil and grow a new plant at the tip (strawberry, blackberry), or they send up new stems from their roots. Some bracken stands on British mountains form very ancient clones. The original plant germinated at the end of the last Ice Age, and the underground stems have been spreading ever since. Today's plants are all similar clones and after 10,000 years the whole stand is still going strong.

Because plant metabolic rate is low, waste excretion is minor compared with animals. Much of their waste such as fallen leaves is decomposed by other creatures and can be reused by the plant later. This is especially important in tropical forests where soils are naturally low in nutrients. Soil becomes impoverished when the plant is eaten but the wastes aren't returned – a major problem for farmers and market gardeners who must replace nutrients by other means.

Clone	An identical copy of one parent.
Higher plants	Seed-bearing plants like conifers, flowering plants, grasses.

Tackling repairs and avoiding predation

Trees may lose a limb or be bodily uprooted, but they still grow new parts. After a willow tree has fallen, the broken branches digging into the soil can make roots, and so the tree remains alive. Plants produce all sorts of chemicals for healing and to deter pests and diseases. Cytokinins, a class of hormones that encourage cell growth, help heal wounds made by breakage or disease and predation. Plants generate ethene gas at the point of attack by insects, bacteria, fungi or viruses that kills the surrounding plant tissue and so isolates the disease. Against caterpillars and other grazers they have evolved foul-tasting leaves and spines. Some East African acacias have such long spines that they're used as toothpicks by local people, while wild cabbage releases cyanide to repel both fungi and grazers. We have bred out this unpleasant taste and naturally the cultivated plant has become a delight for powdery mildew and cabbage white caterpillars.

Species-specific disease can build up in the soil where the same plants grow year after year – animals have similar problems. Cattle in fields and deer on savannahs will pick up worms from other animals' dung.

Somehow plants send out alarm signals, possibly hormonal or electrical. When one plant leaf is attacked by a caterpillar, adjacent leaves prepare defence compounds. Neighbouring plants can also respond; this has been observed in studies of Sitka willows. The mechanism is a mystery – to us, not the plant!

The noxious chemicals that plants manufacture are also used by other creatures. Cinnabar moths have voracious caterpillars which reduce ragwort weeds to skeletons. They sneakily stockpile ragwort poison in their plump orange and black bodies. The colours announce I'm yuk! to birds, who will only try them once.

The number one question – why sex?

Why is sex, a major recombination of genes, so important in the kingdoms of plants, animals and fungi? Many of these can reproduce by cloning – water fleas and aphids among the animals – but they take the sexual option when there is food shortage, crowding and generally poor conditions. At first sight requiring two parents instead of one is highly wasteful of resources and a risky procedure – you may not meet a suitable partner.

Possibly sex helps remove damaged DNA from offspring, by providing a fitter copy of a gene. Still, there are other methods of limiting such damage, favoured in particular by plants. Most hybrid wheat has six copies of each gene, rather than two. This is known as polyploidy.

Sex produces variety in offspring. This may be a useful survival strategy, though if a plant is already highly successful in its habitat, the mixing of genes can reduce the fitness of offspring.

It is now thought that one of the main reasons for the importance of sexual reproduction is the warfare between disease and host. We see this in action as microbes fight for their survival by evolving resistance to our medicines. In this 'arms race' theory, genetic variety is a far more successful strategy for the host than cloning, because genetically similar individuals are all susceptible to the disease. In an organically farmed wheat field, mildew is a common threat, but by growing mixtures of different varieties more wheat plants will survive. The traditional option is to assist the plants by using fungicides, and in this case a more productive but less resistant single variety can be grown. Here the plant has been selected to put more energy into growing grain than into fungal resistance, so the total grain yield per hectare is higher than in the organic case.

Times of famine

All life must cope with shortage of food. This is often dependent on climate. In temperate climates plants use complicated timing devices linked to shortening daylight as winter approaches. These internal clocks cause them to cut down growth and form tough protective scales around dormant winter buds. In hot, dry conditions shrubs are so closely attuned to climate that even after three years of drought, dead-looking sticks and twigs put out new leaves immediately the rains return.

How do plants 'remember' seasons without brains? This has been worked out down to the level of chemical changes. Many temperate plants need a cold spell of three to eight weeks at 4°–8°C to stimulate them into flower. One of the genes in their flowering system is locked into an 'off' state after exposure to cold, and this allows the plant to 'remember' it has been subjected to cold. The system then ensures the plants flower in the spring, not during the winter. Probably most living things have similar internal clocks.

To cope with seasonal cold or drought many plants die back to the ground, storing food energy in roots, bulbs and tubers (biennials and perennials). Some die completely and rely on their seeds to produce next year's plant (annuals). The common annual weed fat hen (*Chenopodium album*) has four types of seed. One is large and germinates immediately. The other three contain growth inhibiting chemicals which slowly decay or are leached out, so that the seeds germinate at different times.

Extreme conditions require special adaptations, and some plants can cope with the wind chill of high alpine mountains or iron- and copper-rich slagheaps. We use this trait to remove toxic wastes from contaminated ground by growing such plants and then harvesting them.

Storing information

Life is an explorer, using the information built into its genes. Information is a distinctive pattern of events that can be communicated and then interpreted by the receiver. It interacts with other events and flows around the system. In a computer the instructions are encoded in a binary form, 0s and 1s, and parcelled as 'bits'and 'bytes'. Information can also be a pattern of marks (alphabet or hieroglyph) or sound waves (bird warning songs, speech), though it is not merely the pattern. It has meaning.

DNA stores information concerned with the type, time, place and duration of protein production. In living things information flows in two directions – both from and to the genes. Feedback of information alters genetic sequences and in this way behavioural and environmental constraints are stored in the DNA. Continual changes in the DNA sequences prevent return to a simpler form. A multicellular organism can't become an independent group of cells again, because the route is no longer genetically available. Parthenogenesis, where the unfertilized egg develops directly into a new individual, is not available to mammals, though it was to our premammalian ancestors. Interestingly some creatures have lost information as they evolved. Tapeworms acquire digested food from the body of their host so their digestive system is very limited. They can spend more resources on reproducing neat little packets of eggs.

This hard-wired information contains highly useful data about the outside environment. It has been won through the lives and deaths of many other creatures, and exists to favour the breeding and prosperity of the organism. It is instinctive. But some creatures have evolved such complex information stores that they can select their actions from a data bank of possibilities. Humans are particularly adept at this, using speech and tools to spread information further and faster than genes can do.

Competition and cooperation

Self-survival is the name of the game, and this essential 'selfishness' is an ineradicable part of life's inheritance since food energy is a finite resource.

But the concept that nature is only competitive – red in tooth and claw – is outdated. Red-toothed carnivores are few, and highly dependent on the ratio of prey to predators. As prey (hare) increase, they provide more food for their predators (lynx), which also increase in numbers but more slowly. Lynx catch more hares, whose numbers then decline, followed by a decline in the lynx. These cycles are self-regulating and there are always fewer lynx than hares. If anything, nature is savagely green; plants have no mechanisms for affection, unlike lynx who care so tenderly for their cubs.

Want to get rid of your neighbours? Smothering and stealing sunlight are the techniques employed by plants. Some plants produce chemical weapons like the terpenes and phenols which they release into their surroundings to slow down their competitors' growth or kill them. In chaparral deserts there is marked zoning around sagebrush where they have poisoned the ground so nothing else can grow.

Cooperation is just as important as competition. Ganging together may be a good strategy if it makes you and your mates larger than your predators, but it also involves loss of independence. Long ago independent DNA replicators bound themselves into chromosomes so they all had access to more information, but when one replicated the others had to follow suit. Collections of similar cells like *Volvox* (a globular colony found in fresh water) must all swim together come what may. Individuals which live in a society must sacrifice autonomy.

Symbiosis, where different species live together for mutual benefit, is common at all levels of life from cells to societies. Even parasites, which take more from their hosts than they give, can develop a symbiotic relationship over time. Flowers are modified leaves that have developed with their pollinators since the time of the dinosaurs. The interaction is so close that some plants, like arums, can raise their flower temperature a few degrees above the ambient temperature. This encourages vaporization of their dung-mimicking scent so attracting dung beetles. Other flowers mimic the pollinator's mate and send out appropriate pheromones.

Plant roots are intimately in contact with certain fungal hyphae. Here the fungal threads supply salts and water to the root hairs and receive sugars in return. Lichens are another highly successful partnership.

Dynamic relationships

Unlike non-living things, life forms are not as discrete as they first appear. The boundary between individuals is sloppy – gene transfer occurs between bacteria, including those living inside us. Similarly there's no complete boundary between an individual and its environment. Food, gases and disease are taken in, pests and predators live off the external parts, internal organisms help break down food (occasionally turning aggressive), and evacuated wastes and death provide nutrients for other creatures. Certainly life is a matter of alliances and warfare!

Whole communities are dynamic. When farmland is put into set-aside, it is first dominated by ephemeral annual weeds and their animal partners. Then perennials take over, some growing into shrubs and trees. The balance shifts continually as different species explore, exploit and conserve. Resources are redistributed incessantly. Plants, fungi and animals change the environment in myriad ways through photosynthesis, decomposition, weathering rocks and turning over soil. Figure 1.7 explains the importance of death. Life depends on it for the recycling of resources, so we could not be here without it. Decay and decomposition replenish the soil that nourishes us.

At all levels development occurs through the ever-changing interdependencies between species, so complicated that it is impossible to trace back in time. Life is a web of dynamic interactions, and simple changes affect large systems, even the whole planet. The Gaia hypothesis is named after the Greek goddess of the earth. It supposes that life is capable of altering the planet to suit itself and that it can produce self-regulating mechanisms to keep the status quo. This is controversial and difficult to test. Gaia is not a person or agent as some rather loose writing indicates. However, our planet certainly forms a system with many interacting, developing and changing subsystems. It has strict boundaries and is far from equilibrium, and a small change in such situations can bring about massive alterations. We are right to be concerned that increase of atmospheric carbon dioxide from our use of fossil fuels may trigger a runaway greenhouse effect.

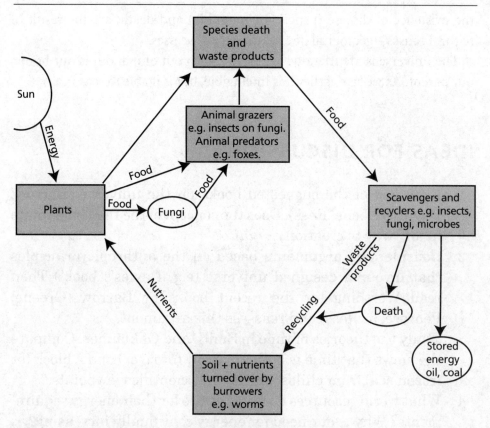

Figure 1.7 Recycling resources – life/death cycle.

Conclusions

The early universe contained this amazing potentiality for life to develop out of non-living materials. So what can this miracle tell us about ultimate Reality?

It develops variety of incredible kinds from simple resources. Living things are autonomous; the only constraints are those physical and chemical laws inherent in the Big Bang and the need to collect energy to grow and spread themselves where they will and just as they like. There is no design, for evolution is blind, and no life force or spirit needs to be added. There is no underlying purpose apparent other than producing variety freely and abundantly. Incidents are neutral. Earthquakes and tsunamis, plagues of locusts, the existence of disease (genetic or microbic) and death, are the result of natural causes – geological or evolutionary processes.

The universe is life friendly. We have grown out of it and it is our home, our parent. As we saw earlier it is intelligible, but is it able to reason?

IDEAS FOR DISCUSSION

1 Read one of the suggested books on the universe (Barrow, Davies, Greene, Rees). Does the concept of the Big Bang relate in any way to creation *ex nihilo*?

2 Consider the arguments based on the anthropic principles that favour a designed universe (e.g. Davies's book.) Then read Worthing (or the recent books by Barrow, Greene, Penrose, or Rees) and reassess this argument.

3 Study the theories of time in Smith and Oaklander. Compare the views that time is both an arrow (or river) and a block (or frozen sea) from philosophical and scientific viewpoints.

4 What world resources do humans use for their energy requirements? Why is our need for energy continually increasing?

5 Religion and science approach truth differently. On what do each base their beliefs? Is God mysterious as the universe is mysterious, or in some other special way?

6 Read Bartholomew and assess the importance of chance in the evolution of the universe.

7 Compare quantum and chaos theories with determinism. Can God know the future or alter the past? If so, does that prohibit human freedom?

8 Discuss the proposition that all the information about the construction of the universe and life is contained in a blade of grass.

9 Look up the life history of disease of cultivated plants, like take-all of wheat and barley, or potato blight. What effect do they have on food production? What measures can be taken

by farmers to reduce losses? What are your opinions of these measures?

10 Vitalism is the view that a life force is added to living things at some point in their history. Read Gould, Eldredge or Kauffman and compare vitalism with the current scientific view.

11 Read Dawkins and discuss his explanation of evolution by natural selection.

12 Read Ridley and consider the implications of his theories. Do they give you new insights? What difficulties do they raise for you?

13 Consider the importance of relationships in plant and animal communities (Wilson and Rayner). When a flower becomes extinct, what happens to the pollinator? How might such an extinction affect the food web in a particular habitat? How does this affect the way we view conservation?

REFERENCES AND FURTHER READING

Journal

New Scientist   Current developments useful for Chapters 1–4 and 8.

Websites

www.newscientist.com   *New Scientist* on line
www.the-ba.net   British Association for the Advancement of Science

Books

Super Bangs

John D Barrow, 2000, *The Universe That Discovered Itself*, Oxford: Oxford University Press

D J Bartholomew, 1984, *God of Chance*, London: SCM Press

David Bohm, 1980, *Wholeness and the Implicate Order*, Boston: Routledge and Kegan Paul – physics and Eastern religions

Paul Davies, 1982, *The Accidental Universe*, Cambridge: Cambridge University Press – also other books on cosmology and physics

Rebecca Elson, 2001, *A Responsibility to Awe*, Manchester: Oxford Poets, Carcanet Press

George Gamow and Russell Stannard, 1999, *The New World of Mr Tompkins*, Cambridge: Cambridge University Press

James Gleick, 1987, *Chaos*, Harmondsworth: Penguin

Brian Greene, 2000, *The Elegant Universe*, London: Vintage

Tony Hey and Patrick Walters, 1987, *The Quantum Universe*, Cambridge: Cambridge University Press

Roger Penrose, 1990, *The Emperor's New Mind*, Oxford: Oxford University Press

John Polkinghorne, 1990, *The Quantum World*, Harmondsworth: Penguin

Martin Rees, 2003, *Our Cosmic Habitat*, London: Phoenix

Q Smith and L N Oaklander, 1995, *Time, Change and Freedom*, London: Routledge

M W Worthing, 1996, *God, Creation and Contemporary Physics*, Minneapolis, MN: Fortress Press

Starter packs

Susan Aldridge, 1996, *The Thread of Life*, Cambridge: Cambridge University Press

David Attenborough, 1995, *The Private Life of Plants*, London: BBC Books

R J Berry, 1988, *God and Evolution*, London: Hodder and Stoughton

Richard Dawkins, 1986, *The Blind Watchmaker*, New York: Norton

Niles Eldredge, 1989, *Life Pulse*, Harmondsworth: Penguin

Stephen J Gould, 1989, *Wonderful Life*, New York: W W Norton

Anna Lewington, 2003, *Plants for People*, London: Transworld

Stuart Kauffman, 1995, *At Home in the Universe*, New York: Oxford University Press

John King, 1997, *Reach for the Sun*, Cambridge: Cambridge University Press

John Maynard Smith and Eörs Szathmáry, 1999, *The Origins of Life*, Oxford: Oxford University Press

John Postgate, 1992, *Microbes and Man*, 3rd edition, Cambridge: Cambridge University Press

Alan D M Rayner, 1997, *Degrees of Freedom*, London: Imperial College Press

Matt Ridley, 1993, *The Red Queen*, Harmondsworth: Penguin

Edward O Wilson, 1992, *The Diversity of Life*, London: Penguin Books

2

The Third Footprint – A Conscious Universe

You are sitting on planet earth with the ancient seas lapping at your toes. The rocks are covered with simple plants like mosses and lichens. You are in deep thought mode, only part-conscious of the passing centuries. The land masses drift, collide with one another, form mountains. The mountains wear away stone by stone, fall into the rivers and rebuild new land under shallow seas. Lung fish slither from pool to pool. Horsetails sprout between cracks in the rocks, wearing them away, and soil deepens. Forests of tree ferns appear. Insects dart through the clearings, pterodactyls swoop through the skies. Every living thing ignores you as it searches out food.

Climates change and grassy prairies take over from forests. You almost leap out of your skin when a harsh voice behind you says, 'Hi'. The voice comes from a rough looking female human, but she is different from these other creatures. She is aware of herself and of you and your reactions to her. She squats beside you and asks where you come from.

And this has all come out of the conditions created in that initial explosion billions of years ago. The universe has the potential to develop self-consciousness. How has such a great miracle come about?

Throughout recorded history humans have wondered about their consciousness and ability to reason. Many, perhaps most, have thought they are gifts from the gods, singling us out from the rest of creation. The standard Christian understanding for centuries has been that God gives reason to Man, and Man bestows God's rationality on the inferior creation.

It's sometimes said that without reason humans are mere animals. The Spanish artist Goya gave expression to the distress of the Spaniards under Napoleon's ferocious rule, entitling his picture of devouring brutes, *The sleep of reason brings forth monsters*. Like many other European intellectuals, he had originally welcomed the French Revolution which put reason before old superstitions. Yet that revolution spawned Napoleon. Reason slept; men became like animals.

Another idea, panpsychism, proposes that all particles of matter have a bit of consciousness, similar to that in humans. In this scenario humans are a conglomeration of conscious subatomic particles.

Consciousness is one of the most interesting problems in the scientific world today, raising a whole host of questions. Scientific knowledge spreads like some shrubs – snowberries (*Symphoricarpos* species) grow from a core plant whose roots send up suckers in all sorts of unlikely places. So while there is a general core of well-documented experimentally backed knowledge about the universe (gravity, evolution, development of cells and their chemical and physical properties, genetics, etc.), some fields are comparatively new and less well defined, like the study of consciousness. Scientists in varying fields look at the situation from different angles. The word consciousness itself is slippery, with different meanings according to context, so once we try to define it the edges blur. Are other animals conscious? If we hug a tree is it conscious of us? What is reason? What is mind? Is it a kind of field? A machine? Transcendent? How does it interconnect with brain?

We shall investigate the subject starting at the ground roots, by placing life forms in three categories of awareness. These groupings have fuzzy edges, but make discussion easier.

DEGREES OF AWARENESS

- **Interaction with the environment**
- **Recognition of others and response**
- **Self-consciousness and creativity – I'm only human**

Interaction with the environment

A pile of sand reorganizes itself as more sand is added to it. After a few small avalanches, a larger one causes the pile to settle into a new conformation. The sand acts according to particular physical rules and is unaware of its surroundings.

Life is different. Certainly there are mechanical and chemical constraints on a creature's actions, but living things act as coordinated wholes and respond actively to their environment. Plants, fungi, small animals and bacteria are aware of their environment in a more complex way than a pile of sand. They interact with gravity, light, air, water in diverse ways.

These creatures adapt to their environment without having to learn anything. Plants on a windowsill use energy to turn their leaves to the light, but their behaviour is governed by their genes, so they don't use up energy on learning by trial and error. This has the disadvantage that their range of responses to environmental change is small and inflexible. Woodlands along a receding shoreline die from salt exposure long before genetic change can halt decline – Birnam wood cannot march to Dunsinane. Such creatures spend successful lives, as have their ancestors for millions of years, but their level of awareness is low.

Recognition of others and response

As children we quickly learn to divide living things into plants (green, standing still, dull) and animals (running or flying around, interesting). Beetles' little legs have joints like ours. Slugs have intriguing eyes on horns. Stick insects mimic leaves and twigs and some even have growths like lichen on their bodies. They are also interesting because they learn. Ants search everywhere for food and will climb over little barricades that children set up in their paths. Their responses are fast and flexible and they can modify them to suit the changing environment, but they don't pass this knowledge genetically to their offspring. They pass on the ability to learn instead.

One of the reasons these animals are so different from plants and very simple animals is that they have neurosensory systems that give them far more information about their environment.

- Neurosensory systems – I spy with my little eye
- Neurosensory systems – I think, therefore I am?
- Hi there – the use of signals
- Special creation or special computer?

Neurosensory systems – I spy with my little eye

As multicellular animals became more elaborate, they had to develop ways of passing messages to all parts of their bodies – to muscles, digestive systems, sense organs. Tiny ones use hormones only – chemical signals that diffuse through their bodies. Larger ones also use nerve cells (neurons, neurones) that pass both chemical and electrical signals across *synapses* to and from the sense cells – the neurosensory system. Messages also pass to muscles and internal organs.

Sense cells are found all over our skin and grouped in complex organs like eyes, noses and ears. Several species of fish have electric organs which create a weak field around them, useful for navigation in muddy water, and bats have their own sonar equipment.

Our eyes are very intricate organs but simple eyes are still useful. The most elementary are found in *Chlamydomonas* and *Euglena*, both single-celled creatures living in ponds. Their orange eye spot shelters a light-sensitive receptor that detects intensity and direction of light – a very helpful develop-ment for free-moving creatures. Planarians, black flatworms between one and two centimetres long, are often fished up, while dyke-dipping. They have a definite head end with two rather more complex eyes. A bowl of black pigment shades sensory cells from light in all directions but one. The cells are connected to nerve cells that lead to the ganglion, a concentration of nervous tissue.

Squids have much more elaborate eyes, which look rather like ours. They are almost globular and work like a camera, allowing a small amount of light to enter. They have a lens and iris in the front, and a retina at the back for focusing images, which connects with their brains via an optic nerve. Squids are cephalopods – a delightful name meaning head-footed.

Sight, like flight, has evolved more than once. Eyes in mammals (phylum Chordata) and insects and lobsters (phylum Arthropoda) have a different developmental history. Lobsters have compound eyes on the end of a pair of jointed moveable stalks. There are hundreds of visual units in each eye, all with their own light-sensitive cells, shielding pigment, lens and nerve fibres that connect to the brain. Insect eyes are also compound as you can see if you look at the eye of a large fly. This arrangement is excellent for detecting movement, and for very small eyes is possibly more acute than the camera design.

Mammalian eyes have been studied for centuries. A large number of genes are involved in developing these, and some play a dual role. Key proteins used in the immune system are also involved in laying down connections between eye and brain during development. Deficiencies in one of these proteins result in disordered cell layers in the visual cortex. Such small flaws have disproportionately large effects on the individual's life.

Human sight is trichromatic – three types of cone cell in the retina respond to red, green and blue light respectively. We can in theory distinguish between more than two million colours. Our eyes are highly variable in their makeup. Blue cones are fairly uniform, but the genes that encode for the red and green are more variable. As these genes are carried on the X chromosome, and men only have one, then men are more likely to have impaired colour vision.

Eyes aren't just cameras. Like squid and beetles, we are selective in what we notice. We extract a few details from a scene and fill the rest in from imagination, so it's easy for a conjurer to trick us. Testimony from observers of a crime is notoriously subject to distortion, unless their attention was focused on the whole event. Recall may include added imagery from the memory, so that the observation is full of inaccuracies. Although they are amazingly accurate in reporting events, all sense organs are vulnerable to error during their embryonic development and in the way their messages are analysed by the brain.

Synapse	A tiny gap between the plasma membranes of a neuron and muscle cell, or neuron and glandular cell, or two neurons. Most mood-changing drugs exert their influence at the synapses.

Neurosensory systems – I think, therefore I am?

- Ganglia and brains
- Memory
- Pain and pleasure pathways
- A change of behaviour

Ganglia and brains

Small creatures have simple but useful nervous systems. Little hydras live in ponds, and they have a simple neuron network to coordinate their behaviour, so that if you touch one it will contract into a protective blob.

Ganglia (sing. ganglion) are collections of nervous tissue. Planarians have a two-lobed ganglion in their tiny heads connected to two strands of nerve cords with side extensions running the length of their bodies. This ganglion is not necessary for movement as planaria swim even without their little brain. But as the ganglion initiates behaviour, planarians are more coordinated than the hydras. It's unlikely that animals with one ganglion have anything corresponding to thoughts.

Many *invertebrates* have ganglia throughout their bodies connected by nerve cords and regulated by a larger brain in the head. This system is fast acting, and it coordinates body activities with sense cells and organs. Spiders' brains are connected to other ganglia in the body parts and so to organs such as the sensory hairs which cover their bodies. Fruit flies have a brain the size of a poppy seed. Scientists can, with great difficulty, insert an electrode and measure the brain waves. When something interests the fly, it pays attention and, strangely, the brain waves look like a very simple version of those in a human brain when it pays attention. How brains pay attention is important for the study of human brains. We are bombarded by stimuli but filter out most of it, only focusing on certain aspects. Humble fruit flies, experimental workhorses in many laboratories, may provide insight into the workings of our brains because, like us, they sleep. They also react in a similar fashion to anaesthetics. It seems that fruit flies may have memories, as they learn to avoid unpleasant experiences. If a fruitfly can dream, what would it dream about?

Invertebrates   Animals without backbones – sponges, jellyfish, worms, snails, starfish, insects and more. Vertebrates (with backbones) are fish, amphibians, reptiles, birds and mammals.

Memory

Our memories persist although the molecules in our brains are replaced many times in a lifetime. How are memories made? Memory storage requires alteration in biochemistry and structure in particular cells. When an animal meets a novel situation and changes its behaviour accordingly, then specific cells in its central nervous system alter their properties. This change can be measured, because it results in a cascade of biochemical processes. New proteins are synthesized, there are local changes to blood flow and oxygen uptake, and electrical properties of the neurons change as their outer membranes alter.

Sea slugs can retain memories for a few weeks. Studies of their brains recorded extra connections being built between their sensory and motor neurons. Animals with large brains like mammals have good long-term memories. A number of social mammals like elephants rely on the memory of the oldest member to guide them to waterholes in times of drought. Pigs remember for years any person who mistreats them, and chimpanzees recognize human friends after long absence.

Pain and pleasure pathways

Back in the 1950s researchers found that rats enjoyed a mild electrical shock to a particular part of the brain. They returned again and again to repeat the experience. The same addictive pleasure occurs in humans. The circuit diagram of this 'reward' centre was worked out by the 1980s, and it includes chemical transmitters like brain opioids (related to morphine, heroin and some analgesics) and dopamine (concerned with motivation).

There are similar pain pathways and both are connected to evolutionary ancient areas deep within the animal brain. These areas ensure survival and general care of the whole organism by warning of harm and giving an impetus to reproduction, eating and drinking. Pain and pleasure help learning and guide behaviour.

To feel pain a creature needs sense cells and a neural system, so this lets out plants, fungi and many simple organisms. For centuries people have assumed larger animals feel no pain. Or if they do, then it can't be compared with the way humans experience pain. Does a daddy longlegs feel pain when it loses a leg? Salamanders naturally regrow lost limbs, so how painful is the loss? We have also been told that a robin's song is merely an aggressive warning to keep off his patch. Does it experience joy as well? Then there is the fruitfly which learns to recognize a situation that causes pain, and so avoids it. Does it have moments of something akin to pleasure when it finds a ripe passion fruit?

We do not yet have a really good way of describing levels of pain or how animals experience it. Some researchers think that the prerequisite for experiencing pain is conscious self-awareness, and fish can't perceive pain as they lack that part of the brain that mammals use to process pain signals. However, some studies on trout recorded the animal's behavioural responses, such as breathing rate and the length of time to return to feeding after a painful episode, and the researchers concluded they do experience pain. Generally we now assume that many vertebrate animals perceive pain, but what about molluscs like squid and octopus whose brains have as many as thirty integrated brain lobes? They can learn extensively and make subtle visual distinctions, but pain levels are more difficult to gauge. Some scientists think that if an animal expresses the same chemicals as mammals do when they are distressed, then it must feel fear and pain, so our concern should extend to insects.

Another question relates to how much pain an individual feels. We know humans vary in their perceptions of pain, and this variation correlates directly with the amount of activity in the cerebral cortex during a painful episode.

Research on pain and pleasure raises important ethical questions for anyone working with animals whether in the lab or zoo, on the farm or keeping pets.

A change of behaviour

A number of animals seem to enjoy mood-altering drugs, as they go back for more. Vervet monkeys have human-like social drinking patterns. A small number are binge drinkers or heavy drinkers, most are moderate in their intake and a few are teetotal. Most cats go crazy for catnip (the plant *Nepeta cataria*), which contains a volatile chemical, though some don't react because they lack the appropriate receptor for the chemical in their nasal system.

Parasites can alter animal behaviour. Parasites generally have two host species. In Morice Lake, Canada, studies of bandied fish showed they became more reckless when parasitized by a trematode (fluke). They are then easy prey for the local kingfisher, who is the necessary host for completing the trematode's life cycle. There is some evidence for altered behaviour in humans infested with particular parasites such as the widespread *Toxoplasmic gondii*. Cats are the primary host. The parasite may form cysts in human brains and is implicated in psychoses.

Parasites have co-evolved with animals and can control ecosystems as effectively as top predators. As humans have such a wide range of food and habitats, we have more parasites than other species. Thirty-four live only on humans, and will surely miss us when we go extinct. These are all found in Africa, which was probably the early home of the human species. Are your parasites happily in control of you?

Neurosensory systems are essential for relating events and assessing their importance. They guide behaviour and ensure mobile creatures can live in harmony with their surroundings. Increase in awareness is closely correlated to brain size and complexity. It is becoming increasingly difficult to deny that animals with such abilities as these are conscious. But can they reason?

Hi there – using signals

To study reasoning ability in animals we can look at the way they signal their intentions and at some of their other skills.

- Warning
- Sexual selection and bonding
- Recognition and communal living
- Scents, sounds and vibrations
- Counting and tool-making

Warning

Insects signal *Danger*!, using startling patterns like the 'eyes' on peacock butterfly wings or the warning black and yellow stripes of hornets and other wasps. Harmless insects like hover flies mimic the same warning colours and copy similar flight patterns. Such signals are not under the control of the animal, so do not involve reasoning.

Other signals *are* controlled – the animal anticipates that their signal will be recognized and effective. Most work on such signalling has been done on vertebrates and insect societies. Bees perform intricate dances to announce the direction and place of a good supply of nectar. Vertebrate signalling is more sophisticated. Small birds have specialized alarm calls for different dangers. Individual birds may learn to give a false alarm call so that the other birds fly off and the caller has better access to food for a while. Then the other birds begin to ignore it. It loses its reputation. In fact, once a successful form or pattern of signals has been developed, there is endless opportunity for mimicry and deception, whether the signal is automatic or invented.

Sexual selection and bonding

Like warning signals, sexual selection is full of trickery. Female gulls eject sperm violently in favour of sperm from a more promising mate. Males in some species of dance flies offer silk-wrapped food gifts to females as these are unable to hunt. They copulate as she eats the food. As males prefer to give food to females whose swollen abdomens indicate their eggs are ready, the females trick the males by inflating their abdomens with air before approaching him. In other species the male tricks the female by giving her an empty silk parcel.

In sexual mating games, signals indicate fitness to be a good mate. High parasite infestation affects male sexual ornaments, so females prefer brightly coloured males because they have fewer parasites and may have genetic resistance. The young of brightly coloured three-spined stickleback grow more slowly than those of paler fish because bright coloration is energy expensive, but they also have more resistance to parasites. Courtship dances and pursuits help a pair of birds or butterflies to assess each other's fitness. Homosexual behaviour is not connected to mating, but it is widespread. It probably enhances social bonding and friendship and the same animals show heterosexual behaviour as well.

Recognition and communal living

Birds have different calls to meet particular situations, but they also have dialects as humans do, and females can recognize individual birds. Recordings of white crowned sparrows north of San Francisco found changes in dialect over roughly two miles. Many other animals can recognize individuals by their different scents, appearances, sounds and feel. Communal insects as well as vertebrates have such skills.

Some birds can imitate the noises round them. The mockingbird will copy songs from other species and the European starling can fool sheepdogs with its shepherd's whistle. Are these observant birds having a joke? Some can copy words and use them appropriately to label objects. Such bird abilities must have been honed in the wild, but we just do not know whether any birds can 'talk' to one another in any sense like humans. Those who study corvids (jackdaws, jays, rooks), with their large brains and social skills, find them as intelligent as many primates. They even claim such birds show self-awareness, an aptitude often thought to be confined to humans.

Signals help to define an animal's position in the pecking order. Often there is no fighting because animals don't want to risk injury, and here the signals help reduce the level of combat over mating and food items. There are negotiation games between animals and levels of aggression can be signalled by quite subtle clues – stance, movements of head, wings, legs, baring of teeth. Animals reveal their intentions by their body language – as do humans.

Scents, sounds and vibrations

Scent signals are as important as visual cues. Social insects use scents to recognize fellow nest members, and many animals produce pheromones to attract mates. Fish communicate by sound because it travels well in water where visibility can be low. They have a swim bladder, a gas-filled organ which helps control buoyancy, and they contract its muscles, so altering the length and pitch of their call. An evening chorus of fish calls along Australia's Great Barrier Reef can raise the noise level in the ocean by 35 decibels. Many fish have complicated social systems so sound communication is important. Female stink bugs, a widespread agricultural pest, attract males by drumming on their leaf in a special rhythm, guiding males to their precise position on the plant. Probably many insects use vibrations in this manner.

Counting and tool-making

A number of animals can estimate amounts. This is an important skill useful for judging fruit on a tree or the number of approaching predators. Salamanders choose between more and less when offered test tubes containing different numbers of fruit flies. The Einstein among birds, the grey parrot Alex, knows a large number of words. He understands hierarchies like colour and some abstract concepts like same/different. He counts the number of blue blocks in a mixture of red and blue and speaks both number and colour.

For a long time it was thought that tool-making distinguishes us from other animals. Not so. Even naive young ravens can solve the problems set them. They reason out that pulling a string attached to food outside their cage will bring it within reach, and they remember this skill in the correct sequence. Egyptian vultures open tough ostrich eggs by dropping stones on them. A crow named Betty bent wire into a hook to scoop food from a bucket. She had never experienced a pliant material like wire before, and she bent it in several ways before succeeding. Many primates use tools, and others in the troop learn to copy their skills.

It seems then that many animals can reason and this is linked to having a brain capable of storing memories. Increasing brain complexity and size correlate strongly with reasoning ability.

Special creation or special computer?

A number of experts in the field of artificial intelligence compare the mammalian brain to an information-processing system like a computer. Consider a pet animal like a rabbit or other mammal. Does it act like a robot functioning in a *Pavlovian fashion*, or is there something more at work inside that furry head?

It is true there are similarities with computers. The design of the fastest computers is based on the way human brains work. These computers carry out operations in parallel instead of sequentially like a PC, and use networks between many *computation nodes*.

The humanoid robot Cog has miniature motors instead of muscles and metal bars instead of bones and video cameras instead of eyes. Cog's brain is a collection of microprocessors designed as a neural net on a pattern similar to that in brains. Cog started ignorant and learnt from positive and negative feedback to adjust the strengths of the connections between 'neurons' accordingly. Gradually Cog has learnt to 'see' and grasp an object with the pincer at the end of its one arm. It has learnt to make eye contact and when people react to it, it can readjust some of its actions. Cog has been programmed to give recognizable and realistic responses like the contraction of facial features to show laughter.

How close then is the brain to a computer? There are numerous opinions.

Many neuroscientists consider brain/computer analogies trivial when they compare the two. Brains and their neurons are not closed systems like a computer or robot. Just as the boundary between humans and our environment is incomplete, so the brain as a whole is an open system. Its processing depends on its past history and on continual feedback between brain, body and the external world. It is continually altering its output, physiology and structure. Its neurons are surrounded by cell membranes that control the movements of varied molecules in and out of the cell and hold certain molecules in functional contact. Membranes are spanned by special proteins and these act as ion channels capable of speeding the transfer of small ions and molecules. The functions of the bodies inside the cell are equally complex.

Another criticism depends on quantum and chaos theories, which turn up in quite unexpected places (Chapter 1, under 'Strangely Charming' and 'Chaos, ruler of the Evil Empire'). Cells do not respond to information in a completely deterministic way because they have an in-built indeterminacy. The behaviour of the neuron is unpredictable however much one analyses its individual components.

The association of mind with brain is an example of the emergence of a radical new property, mind, which occurs when some systems become more complex. It is difficult to argue that computers or even the internet have this property.

So is that pet rabbit a computer-style robot?

Computation node	A point where some calculations are carried out on many inputs that produce a result passed on to other nodes.
Pavlovian fashion	Pavlov's dogs salivated when food arrived, a reflex reaction. He observed that when he rang a bell beforehand, they began to salivate as it rang but before food arrived. He theorized that a new nerve pathway had been established, and called it a conditioned reflex. This idea was extended to humans, giving rise last century

to the influential behaviourist theories of B F Skinner which are parodied in *Brave New World* by Aldous Huxley. Here, all behaviour becomes a process of stimuli and responses.

Self-consciousness and creativity – I'm only human

What is a human person? Christianity defines us with reference to God. We are specially created to have a personal relationship to him, and the more we become like him the more perfectly human we are. Many other religions, both past and present, don't necessarily take this line, but would in general agree that how we relate to god/gods/reality is vitally important.

The scientific definition looks at physical and intellectual components and behaviour. For historical reasons scientific disciplines have disparate views of consciousness. Science has always been organized on hierarchical lines, and scientists generally study their subject using reductionist methods.

- Hierarchical systems
- Reduction
- Emergence

Hierarchical systems

Matter is organized in a series of levels. There is the basic level of the atom, and above that a chemical level dealing with compounds of elements, including complex organic molecules. The next level is the behaviour of these molecules in cells. The sequence continues with multicellular organs and then the whole organism. Further hierarchies are populations of organisms, the ecosystems and then the complete biosphere.

A scientist specializes at a particular level. Science is divided broadly into physics, chemistry and biology, but each of these areas is subdivided into many other branches, some overlapping with the level above. Biochemistry studies the chemistry of biological reactions.

Reduction

It is often easiest to study a phenomenon by reducing it to its simplest components. Only when all these have been analysed can we produce a satisfactory law or theory (satisfactory in the sense that it covers all currently known facts about the original phenomenon). To understand sound you experiment with vibration, sound waves and their speed, sound in vacuums, echoes, resonance and so on. Then you're in a position to develop theories about it.

Reduction*ism* is the claim that the higher level is nothing but the lower one. All biology will eventually be explained in terms of physics and chemistry. You are only your genes, or your brain is merely a supercomputer. Here 'bottom-up' thinking explains the higher level as a collection of special cases of the more basic discipline.

Emergence

It is no longer accepted that all systems can be fully described by reference to the lower levels. In some systems the whole can be more than the sum of its parts, and quite new properties can emerge. Biochemistry became a major discipline in the last half of the previous century, but it didn't succeed in reducing biology to chemical reactions as many emergent properties were discovered during the study of DNA. You cannot understand biological systems from the theories of physics and chemistry alone, and need to develop new levels of description.

Emergence is widespread in nature. Think of a pair of termites interacting in a simple fashion. Then think of the much more complicated interactions between a whole colony of termites. The colony acts as a 'superorganism', producing a great mound with myriad tunnels, egg chambers and a ventilation system.

Subsystems certainly impose boundaries on higher levels (bottom-up causation). But the higher level system also influences lower levels (top-down causation). An animal can be seen as a restricted system consisting of chemicals that obey known physical laws. This bounded system can't change the physical laws, but it can vary their expression.

When we start to look at human consciousness, the principle of emergence becomes important. Minds may be an emergent property of a collection of brain cells. Scientists from many disciplines across the range of hierarchies have come together to discuss self-consciousness. Their combined insights provide us with new ideas about what it is to be human, and we shall consider some of them.

- Self-consciousness and brains
- Self-consciousness and creativity
- Are other animals self-conscious or creative?

Self-consciousness and brains

- Functions
- Damage
- Pleasure, fear and moods

Functions

From our own experience we may feel that there is an interaction between two dissimilar 'organs', the neural-based brain and our personality or mind. But how does the activity of brain cells give rise to the subjective experience of yourself walking across a field? Why does this experience of walking apparently relate to the actual physical world around you? Why are individual regions of the brain more active than others when you are reading? How do bodily 'memories' such as the use of limbs in cycling correlate with brain activity? Who am 'I' in the age of the internet where I connect to chat rooms using multiple identities?

If you are bewildered – be comforted. So are most people. This is where the multidisciplinary scientific approach is starting to offer some clues.

Very simply, brains are mainly a mass of neurons with known physical and chemical properties. A neuron has between one and ten thousand synapses, not all of which are passing information at the same time. A human brain consists of anatomically ancient regions at the top of the spinal cord collectively called the hindbrain. This coordinates reflex actions like breathing, coughing, heartbeat and balance. In the centre is a region also thought to be evolutionarily ancient which includes the hypothalamus. This regulates blood temperature and composition and hormone activity, and so affects basic drives like aggression, fear and sexuality. The forebrain dominates the rest of the brain, consisting chiefly of walnut-shaped cerebral hemispheres with a highly folded cortex. They evolved most recently. The cerebral hemispheres are responsible for many different brain functions including receipt of sensory information and memory. Brain regions act together and the limbic system, the brain's emotional system, connects several regions that all project eventually into the hypothalamus. The brain links with the nervous system running through the rest of our bodies, so it coordinates information derived from internal organs like lungs and liver, and the external stimuli which impact on our ears, eyes, skin and nose, together with memory and emotions. Experience gained is fed back into the system for future reference.

A sand-grain sized piece of human brain has about one hundred thousand neurons all acting in concert like a Mexican wave rippling through a football crowd. The waves have various rhythms, and probably help the brain to package information into coherent images and memories. Recent experiments studied variations in wave patterns using 'Mooney faces', black-and-white pictures which are difficult to recognize as faces. When people first looked at them gamma waves were recorded all over their visual cortex, but at the moment of recognition the gamma waves fell into step. Brain waves probably organize sensory information so that we are able to identify a particular object.

Brains provide us with a sense of position. Visual neurons in the brain portray the outside world and also place this image in a three-dimensional space relative to the body. Brains help us focus our attention by controlling our eye muscles so that our eyes move, depict and move again according to the information received.

The brain remembers images, say of a tree, so even when the external stimulus is no longer present there is a feedback loop between associated neurons. This reproduces the visual memory when someone says the word 'tree'. Neurons can also learn sequences. This, together with remembered images, enables us to plan and foresee the results of our actions based on past experiences. There is also a link with remembered bodily sensations such as how we felt during our first kiss. Imaginary plans are evaluated as exciting, wrong, good, fearsome and so on, so that our action is based on the feedback between neural firing patterns and emotions. Our memories also include the internalized rules of our upbringing and society, so that our thoughts are extremely elaborate.

'O memory, thou fond deceiver,' said the poet Oliver Goldsmith. He, like us, found that memories are pliable. Questioning can lead people into believing that events occurred in their past for which there is no evidence, and people will occasionally 'remember' and admit to crimes they did not commit. As false memories are rehearsed they become filled with more detail just like real memories, so there may be no reliable way of distinguishing between true and false.

Some neuroscientists question whether there is a controlling 'me' or 'you' at all. Most of the brain's information processing probably takes place at an unconscious level, like the preparation of a woman's body for pregnancy. Only certain events rise to the surface of our minds. So is the unconscious a part of 'me' or am 'I' just the conscious thinking self? And which part is in control? If you decide to move your arm, the brain processes necessary for this decision begin about half a second before you are aware you made it. Who or what made the decision?

Our individuality as humans rests on our genetic variability, differences in development of sense organs, brains and internal organs like liver and lungs, our upbringing and society and all we learn in life. So no two human beings can be exactly alike.

Damage

Damage caused by strokes or accidents helps medical researchers understand more about the functions of different parts of the brain and its relationship with other parts of the body.

Sometimes sensation persists from phantom limbs after amputation. Horatio Nelson, the English naval hero, lost his right arm in battle and afterwards felt pain in his right hand, which he construed as evidence for the existence of a soul. Today there are other explanations for this often distressing condition involving nerve pathways and the Penfield map – the representation of the body surface on the surface of a mammalian brain.

Brain damage that affects the emotional centres of the brain can cause a patient to believe those dearest to him or her are imposters – he or she recognizes their faces but no longer feels the emotional tie. Sometimes patients see themselves as two people, probably due to some dysfunction of the unifying areas of the brain.

There are a number of valuable spin-offs from research into artificial intelligence. Some paraplegics have learnt to use electrical brain impulses in coordination with a computer. Neural implant therapy is helping some sufferers with Parkinson's disease, and the tremors associated with cerebral palsy and multiple sclerosis.

Our understanding of the brain has led to an increase in drugs and techniques to reduce disorders and malfunctions. This introduces a number of ethical problems, especially where individual rights clash with those of society, and there are some examples in Chapter 8.

Pleasure, fear and moods

The reward circuit in humans, and probably other mammals, is associated with many pleasure centres in the cortex. Activity in these seems to correlate with many forms of pleasure – socializing, helping others, composing music, academic acclaim – and even achievements which may not appear at all pleasurable like crossing oceans in small rowing boats. Pleasure centres are encoded in our genes and so inherited, but pleasure in an actual event may well be reinforced by learning.

Recreational drugs are closely related to those pleasure-activating ones found naturally in the brain. Effects of the use of alcohol, tobacco, cannabis and opium and the problems of addiction are constantly being researched by studying the pleasure centres and craving pathways in the brain. Some drugs which block the craving route also block the craving, and these are being tested on cocaine addicts to help them recover.

Some researchers work on enhancing experiences. Brain-generated music is a brainwave biofeedback system where the user's head is attached by three leads to a computer, which calculates their unique alpha rhythm and generates music to match. This helps to increase the production of alpha waves by the user and brings the deep relaxation found in some forms of meditation. Sometimes it evokes feelings of transcendence.

Memory of pain produces fear and avoidance of painful situations in animals. Humans have such exceptionally good memories that our fears accumulate. Our social upbringing adds other people's fears to our memory store, so it's hardly surprising that we suffer from phobias. Fear of death and bereavement is particularly distressing for social animals like ourselves.

Moods are connected to the amygdala, part of the limbic system, and this is activated both when people experience a mood-related event and when they recall it. If our current mood is good we tend to remember other good moments from our past. We seem to learn neutral information more easily when in a good mood. That information will be stamped with the good mood so that both are recalled together. Places, smells and music also evoke memories linked to moods experienced at an earlier period. Moods can be altered socially. Laughter, jokes and wit are a social glue, helping us relax and bond.

Conversely, bad moods and depressions are also recalled by events, and reduce learning. Depressions are known to weaken the immune system, and a direct link has been discovered between brain activity and immune function. Therapists use techniques like music therapy to relax patients suffering from disorders like post-traumatic stress, where the patient continually relives a terrifying past.

Self-consciousness and creativity

Our personalities, as we have seen, are based on our highly sophisticated physical make-up and our experiences. They also include special skills exceeding those of other animals. Some people are exceptionally creative, and genius is often seen as a special gift – the word 'inspiration' means the breathing in of divine creativity. The ancient Greeks recognized nine Muses who gave their gifts to humans. They were daughters of Zeus and Mnemosyne, identified with arts and sciences. Euterpe was the inventor of the double flute, and the patroness of festivals associated with Dionysian or Baccanalian (Roman version) rites. She, like the other Muses, gave creativity to special individuals, who then used it to give pleasure to other humans. In the seventeenth century Descartes described intellectual freedom and creativity as proof that humans are made in God's image.

The poetic genius creates beauty and gives words to our deepest feelings. John Clare, a nineteenth-century farm labourer, wrote highly original nature poetry. He writes of Emmonsail Heath in winter, where 'the old heron from the lonely lake/starts slow and flaps his melancholy wing', a picture any modern heath walker recognizes. Edgar in Shakespeare's *King Lear* is afraid for his safety so he masquerades as Mad Tom. He tells himself that now his life has reached rock bottom, the future must be upwards. Then he sees his outcast, mutilated father and exclaims, 'The worst is not, so long as we can say, "This is the worst."' Those who are shocked into silence by personal tragedy or the horrors of war and natural devastation know exactly what he meant. There are geniuses in all walks of life – in music and art, the sciences, architecture, philosophy and religion.

So let us consider whether genius and creativity are gifts to special individuals or part of the inheritance of all humans.

* Perseverance, physical variability and the use of analogy
* Environment
* Goodbye, Muses. Hello, creative society

Perseverance, physical variability and the use of analogy

Creativity is affected by physical make-up. Those pleasure pathways in the brain are important here. If we use such pathways when we enjoy an activity, then the connections are strengthened. The feeling of pleasure is the reward that drives activities. This enjoyment is felt as much by the social dancer learning new steps as it is by creative artists. It helps us persevere, so that toil becomes pleasurable as we look to future benefits.

Studies of people who have some sort of mental anomaly compared with the norm have helped us rethink some ideas about talent. Savants are people with low general intelligence or very poor social skills who have areas of exceptional talent. Some can play any music by ear after hearing the tune once.

Synesthetes are people who can taste shapes or see colour in a sound. In this case there may be unusual linkages between the brain areas devoted to sight and sound which lie close together. It may well be that a genius has unusual brain connections which he or she can use in exceptional ways. Mozart could 'see' as well as hear his music unfold in his imagination. Did he have such a link? Ramanujan, the mathematical genius from an Indian village, had no formal mathematical teaching but discovered several new equations before he was twenty-two. He contributed original work at Cambridge for many years. He possibly had exceptional linkages in the brain area involved in computation but he himself explained his ability in terms of his village culture. The local goddess whispered the equations to him in his sleep.

Analogy is a skill highly developed in humans and closely related to creativity. Geniuses often connect things in a new way. In 1865 Kekulé reported that he worked out the circular shape of some carbon molecules while dozing. He dreamt of atoms twining and twisting like snakes until one of the snakes caught its tail in its mouth. This perception opened the way to a new branch of chemistry which underlies the production of modern medicines among a host of other manufactures. Charles Darwin made connections in many fields which led to his theory of evolution.

Perseverance, novel linkages and special skill in analogy all help create genius.

Environment

Society plays a large part by its recognition of special abilities. No doubt Handel would still have been highly musical had he been brought up in a farm labourer's family but his musical influence would have been much more local. Family support and the approval of literate society led to a much wider dissemination of his talents.

The greatest geniuses found their achievements on earlier ones. Without the pianoforte would Beethoven's music be so powerful? In Mozart's time a quite different keyboard instrument was in use, the harpsichord. This plucks strings, whereas the pianoforte strikes them with hammers. Its beginnings were probably in Italy at the end of the sixteenth century, but it was not until early in the eighteenth century that it was developed in its present form by Cristofori of Padua. The genius cannot exist alone.

Genius then does not appear to be a gift out of the blue, but a combination of individual traits, dependent on society's recognition and the achievements of others. There are many degrees of creativity and most of us have insightful moments, though rarely of world significance. Creativity is endemic among humans; a high incidence of creative breakthroughs is the prerogative of genius.

Goodbye, Muses. Hello, creative society

Creativity is often the function of a group. Together humans build great cities and monuments or achieve successes in sport and endurance. The combined creativity of the NASA teams enabled humans to stand on the moon. The importance of worldwide communications via the internet can hardly be exaggerated. Multitudes of new possibilities open up daily.

But while creativity can be used for mutual good it can also manipulate and destroy. Internet chat rooms and mobile phones raise questions about the flexibility of our identities. We can recreate ourselves and present a new persona. But so can those who communicate with us. How do we assess their reliability? Music, dance and art affect our deep emotions, but they are not always employed for the benefit of humanity. Inflammatory speeches and martial music easily awaken our aggression, and rabble-rousing despots harness this fury by playing on group fears. Since humans depend so heavily on the social group it is easy for us to be swayed by the crowd. The visual arts can present easily assimilated images of hated individuals or parties, leading to retaliation for supposed aggression. Political cartoons from the build-up to the two world wars last century are an obvious example.

Are other animals self-conscious or creative?

As we have seen, this is a much-debated area and there are no clear answers. Animals' lives are so varied and so little observed in the wild that it is difficult to come to conclusions about their abilities. Those with highly developed neurosensory systems are obvious candidates, especially vertebrates.

We don't think fish are self-aware, though many can remember an escape route from a net for at least eleven months. Their social intelligence is excellent as are their navigational skills. They build nests and burrows for their young and recognize other fish. They signal their intentions, so they must have some awareness of how other fish will react.

Some snakes use their combat position to perform novel tasks – is this creativity? A number of birds and mammals make and use tools, and some have simple language skills. Primates like chimpanzees can be taught many words. They can use them through sign language in a meaningful (i.e. syntactical) order. Like us, chimps live in complex social groups and are aware of the feelings of others to the extent that they know how to deceive another animal.

Those who study mammals and birds are inclined to think that as they have the same equipment as humans, it is possible that some, especially the highly socialized ones, are likely candidates for self-consciousness and creativity.

Conclusions

Recalling our initial proposition, that creativity, reason and self-consciousness are special gifts, it may be time to modify our ideas. Neither this belief nor the proposal that they are unique to humans are endorsed by all the facts. There appears to be a continuum of increasing awareness stemming from evolutionary principles embedded in the early universe. Nor is selfconsciousness more valuable to the living world than the simple awareness of other creatures. Some life forms – plants and bacteria – are neither self-aware, reasoning nor creative, yet without them we could not survive.

Panpsychism, which proposes that all particles of matter have a bit of consciousness, lacks evidence and seems an unnecessary complication. Increase in consciousness is so closely linked to the possession of a brain and increase in its size.

We know that the universe is friendly to life, and it looks as if it is friendly to self-consciousness too. What does this development tell us about the Reality supporting the universe? Since creatures capable of reasoning have developed within the universe system, reason and creativity are part of total Reality. But we have found nothing comparable to a neurosensory system outside planet earth. Can there be an encompassing Mind without such a system? This is as mysterious as universe intelligibility and its capacity to bear life. Humans are persons, so there must be something analogous to personhood within the supporting Reality. Pain and pleasure are necessary for consciousness to evolve. So is Reality indifferent to suffering among animals?

IDEAS FOR DISCUSSION

1   Blood flukes cause diseases like schistosomiasis in humans. Study the life cycle of this parasite and consider its effect worldwide.
2   Consider the ideas expressed in panpsychism. What support can you find for this theory?
3   Life is wonderful. How should we show our respect for other living things?
4   Read Rose. What sort of experiments should be allowed and on which animals? Look up current laws and permissions required. Do you find these adequate? Should we struggle to keep pets painfully alive just because we cannot bear to live

without them? How should domesticated animals be reared, housed, transported and killed? Check the regulations in the Department of Environment, Food and Rural Affairs (DEFRA) and the Farm Animal Welfare Council (FAWC). The latter has been assessing and advising on animal welfare since at least the early 1980s.

5   How accurately do our sense organs record an event? Consider the effect of developmental history on the organ, the way the brain analyses its input, the effect of memory and the distortions due to faulty perception.

6   There is a belief among the general public that we are able to identify psychiatric tendencies to criminality. Sould we imprison a person on the suspicion that they might commit a murder or other psychotic act in the future?

7   As we increasingly learn to understand memory and manipulate memory (see Rose; Carruthers and Chamberlain; Humphrey), could it ever be ethical to alter a depressed person's memories of an unhappy past in the hope of relieving present problems?

8   To what extent is the computer analogous to the human brain?

9   Humans have poor physical stamina and physique compared with many predators. Many of us live in hostile environments. What factors have made us so successful as a species? How much of our success is due to special gifts from a Creator?

10   'When I saw her with her child I felt quite sick because I knew she beat him up regularly.' The implication of such statements is that our internal organs are regulated by social norms. Consider the feedback of brain and body on your feeling of disgust or happiness.

11   Read Maynard Smith and Harper. What insights does it give you into insect behaviour? Discuss the different types of signals found in animal societies.

12   Read Carruthers and Chamberlain, or Humphrey, and discuss the psychology and evolution of human minds.

13   Read Ramachandran and Blakeslee. What effect does the brain have on our personality?

REFERENCES AND FURTHER READING

Websites

www.defra.gov.uk/animalh   Department of Environment, Food and Rural Affairs

www.fawc.org.uk   Farm Animal Welfare Council

www.legislation.hmso.gov.uk/si/si1998/19981974.htm   Legislation on welfare of animals in scientific experiments

www.ox.ac.uk   OXCSOM Oxford Centre for Science of the Mind.

Books

Margaret Boden, 1990, *The Creative Mind*, London: Sphere Books

Ralph Buchsbaum, M Buchsbaum, J Pearse and V Pearse, 1987, *Animals without Backbones*, 3rd edition, Chicago: University of Chicago Press

Peter Carruthers and Andrew Chamberlain, eds, 2000, *Evolution and the Human Mind*, Cambridge: Cambridge University Press

Gerald Edelman, 1992, *Bright Air, Brilliant Fire*, Harmondsworth: Penguin Books

Nicholas Humphrey, 2002, *The Mind Made Flesh*, Oxford: Oxford University Press

Richard Lewontin, 2000, *It Ain't Necessarily So*, London: Granta

John Maynard Smith and David Harper, 2003, *Animal Signals*, Oxford: Oxford University Press

Steven Pinker, 1994, *The Language Instinct*, Harmondsworth: Penguin

V S Ramachandran and Sandra Blakeslee, 1999, *Phantoms in the Brain*, London: Fourth Estate

Steven Rose, 1993, *Making of Memory*, London: Transworld

Christopher Wills, 1991, *The Wisdom of the Genes*, Oxford: Oxford University Press

3

The Fourth Footprint – Deal Justly, Love Mercy

The interminable Amazonian jungle is hot, sticky and uncomfortable. Food plants grow far apart; animals are alert and difficult to kill. It is the 1970s and you are an anthropologist living with an obscure tribe.

Their beliefs are totally different from your own. Their dead are dangerous non-beings, whose memories must be obliterated. This collective amnesia is extended to past generations, so time is non-accumulative. There is no history. There is no concept of divine transcendence, and no desire to contact gods. They have no national consciousness based on shared language, territory or religion, but social relationships between tribal groups are important, even if sometimes bloody.

And yet as the days pass you find similarities. Their code of behaviour is expressed in different ways from your own – the marriage system is different – but you find their sexual jokes funny. You recognize how women manage their menfolk while allowing them to think they are in charge. You compare the violence of men against their wives with that in your own culture. You observe the strength of friendships that have existed since childhood, and you remember your own friends and parents back home. They barter goods in ways familiar to you. Their songs and dances reveal a hidden subtlety to beliefs you first thought irrational. You listen to their love chants and their concepts seem familiar. You understand the limits of their trust in others as they barter goods with other tribes, just as you accept the ferocity of their murderous encounters. You share their belief that ethical rules govern society.

At night in your tent you wonder about this amazing miracle; ethical behaviour has arisen in the universe out of the blind physical and chemical laws obeyed by all living things. How did this come about?

- **First possibility – laws are given by the gods**
- **Second possibility – laws are developed by humans through experience**
- **Third possibility – laws are intrinsic to the universe**

FIRST POSSIBILITY – LAWS ARE GIVEN BY THE GODS

This is a very common religious theme. Society's rules have been handed down at some particular time by the gods themselves, to enable humans to live together in harmony. Events like famine, disease and untimely death are punishment for those who step out of line. Many past documents testify to the long history and strength of these ideas.

There is also the belief that at some point a soul or conscience is created in individual humans, forty days after conception according to the great medieval theologian Thomas Aquinas. This is the inner law of the heart. It's entrusted to us so that we may develop it and transcend our natural inclinations towards selfishness and greed. It guides us towards the good and the true, eventually bringing us in touch with spiritual realms – paradise or nirvana. This view of a spiritual realm of perfection and an inferior, imperfect natural world is widespread, ancient and has subtle variations. It is often referred to as the Platonic view, as it was promulgated by the influential Greek Plato in classical times.

The given rules themselves have a common basic theme, known as the Golden Rule. Religious writings include the following axioms. The Jewish Talmud tells us not to do to our fellows whatever is hateful to ourselves. 'One should never do to another that which one regards as injurious to oneself,' says the Hindu *Mahabharata*. The Taoist philosopher expects a good man to regard others' gains and losses as if they were his own. 'Do not do to others what you would not like yourself,' says Confucius. The Qur'an says we should desire for others those things we desire for ourselves. Jesus tells us to love one another. Some rules go further. The Jain's *Kritanga Sutra* tells us to treat all creatures in the world as we ourselves wish to be treated. The Buddhist *Sutta Nipata* recommends we love all living things as a mother cares for her son all her life. The Sioux Native Americans pray they may walk the earth remembering they are related to all living things.

SECOND POSSIBILITY – LAWS ARE DEVELOPED BY HUMANS THROUGH EXPERIENCE

This idea has become increasingly popular since the development of political science, sociology and psychology. Karl Marx's research into the causes of social and political change has been highly influential, even though many of his predictions didn't materialize. Examination of trends and beliefs within societies over historical time and sympathetic anthropology support the understanding that moral views are moulded by societies. Morality is relative and based on economics. A society needs rules to function, so its rules are defined by its social institutions and will be different from other societies. Some fundamental principles exist such as care of children, while a number of societies hold that all should have equality under the law.

Religions are to be respected for their role in providing social glue over the centuries. At their best they have encouraged just and merciful behaviour, qualities essential for a society's success and balance. But they have also supported sectarian war and the oppression of the poor, so a number of people believe they should be allowed to wither quietly away. Naturalism or scientism, the belief that scientific method can explain everything around us, should now be the basis for society's laws and ideologies.

THIRD POSSIBILITY – LAWS ARE INTRINSIC TO THE UNIVERSE

We have become accustomed to seeing ourselves as outside 'nature'. Other living things are 'natural'; humans are not. This leads to endless confusion. There is no way we can step outside the web of creation or the processes of evolution however much control we think we have. The inexorable requirement of energy for life, the limiting factors of disease, famine and competition, and the inevitability of death rule all lives, humans included.

Imagine a planet where the only living things are bacteria, fungi, plants and single-celled animals. Competition would be slow and without pain. An Eden of sorts. But our world has multicellular animals with neurosensory systems. They move fast, put their own interests first and have fierce attacking mechanisms. Why do some of them live in societies which inevitably impinge on their freedom of action?

Group living protects creatures from attack. If you can trust your neighbours to do the best for their own survival and if you can punish misconduct, then the talents of individuals can work together for the common good. There are many advantages in foraging and parenting together, and there is easier access to a variety of sexual partners. Any such society needs rules of behaviour to reduce individual aggression and greed and encourage teamwork. In some successful societies, such rules are probably encoded in the genes, but this still permits some individuality.

This chapter investigates some of these animal societies.

- **Insect societies – 'I will die to protect my colony'**
- **Vertebrate societies – 'We will share the common crust, the common danger'**
- **Primate world – chimpanzees – 'I know just how you feel, and I am going to use that knowledge'**
- **Primate world – humans – 'We will encode laws'**

Insect societies – 'I will die to protect my colony'

- Selfish genes
- Mathematical altruism
- Recognition

Selfish genes

Genes are the part of an individual that passes to their offspring, the units of selection. They are replicators, living inside us all. The evolutionary success of a gene depends on its ability to increase its frequency in the pool of all available genes. Genes within today's gene pool survive because the creatures carrying them in the past have survived long enough to pass them on. The view of some biologists is that we are blind robots programmed by our genes to exploit and deceive others so that the genes survive, come what may.

This is emotively described as selfishness, though obviously genes themselves cannot really be selfish, as this word is properly applicable to animals with moral codes. A number of scientists find the theory one-sided, though it does have useful applications.

Mathematical altruism

In the 1960s scientists debated why there is so much self-sacrifice among social insects. Warfare between ant colonies is massive and deadly but there is harmony within the colony, so the close relationship of all the colony through the queen was suggested as an answer. Sister wasps share three-quarters of their genes instead of half. If one considers the wasp to be the 'selfish' gene's way of reproducing itself, then altruism such as dying in defence of the colony is the best way to ensure genetic survival. Such colonies are successful and over time this behaviour can become genetically coded.

Computer simulations are used to demonstrate that intricate behaviour can evolve within a colony which will help the colony survive. Animals may not have to work out the strategy themselves if the general principles have been programmed into them during their evolution, but there is still room to apply such information in novel ways.

There are some concerns about the oddity of presenting biological altruism as selfishness. Also, we are assuming there are genes for a particular behaviour, but the actual causal links from genes to behaviour via neurons and brains have not yet been clearly defined.

Recognition

Social insects will attack strange insects, and some certainly recognize individual nest mates. Some have complicated relationships with other species. One of the first signs of aphid attack on a currant bush is the ants running up and down the stems. They 'milk' the aphids for their sweet secretions and protect them from danger. So they need to have memory, and we looked at current research into fruit fly memories in the last chapter.

Observation of colonies has revealed intricate behaviour. Bee dances are a complicated 'language'. Polistes queen wasps will punish lazy workers. Punishment requires an animal to have some concept of pain and also be aware that its use will alter the behaviour of another animal in the desired direction. Do social insects learn behaviour by watching others? How flexible is their genetically coded behaviour? These are interesting questions and currently we lack clear answers.

Vertebrate societies – 'We will share the common crust, the common danger'

Here we are discussing vertebrates other than primates. Vertebrates have large, well-developed brains. Mammals, birds and maybe some other vertebrates can reason out cause and effect and run at least two models of the world at the same time. They can make analogies. They have better skills of recognition and memory, and have developed a wide range of strategies for successful social living. Ability to read other minds possibly emerges as all these abilities increase in scale. Not many studies have been done in the wild, so our knowledge is rather limited.

- Altruism and games theories
- Sharing
- Empathy
- Animal schools

Altruism and games theories

Less closely related animals than the social insects still act altruistically. A ground squirrel sounds an alarm and so risks being noticed and killed by the predator. If it dies before mating, its genes will die with it. So why doesn't the group of genes responsible for the suicidal warning call die out too? Again this can be explained in part by the 'selfish gene' theory – if the warning saves more than two siblings who have the same gene grouping, then the gene will survive, and ultimately that is what is passed on from one generation to another. But in animals like vertebrates that can select from a wider repertoire of behaviours than insects, there may be other factors than kinship at work. Recently, unrelated male side-blotched lizards were recorded cooperating in certain mating behaviours. These lizards come in assorted colours, and colour-matching seemed to play the main part in their cooperation.

Games theories have been developed to explain cooperation. In any group of animals acting for the common good the cheat has a huge advantage, such as the lioness that holds back when her group attacks a large danger-ous animal. Eventually cheating behaviour should cause generosity and cooperation to be 'de-selected' and then groups would fall apart.

Mathematical models explain why this doesn't happen. The prisoner's dilemma is a classic game where two criminals are interrogated separately and must decide whether to confess and implicate their partners. The length of sentence depends on their mutual decisions. In this model, where both the prisoners trust each other and cooperate, then both are better off. Similar logic could take place between other animals.

Computer simulations demonstrate that tit-for-tat strategies will eventually dominate a population. In these, the animal (really a computer program) cooperates on its first encounter with the second animal, which will either cooperate in its turn or cheat. On the next encounter the first animal acts as the other had done. Such a strategy could become automatic, encoded in the genes. Tit-for-tat is only one variation of hundreds of possible strategies. Those based only on exploitation may be best for the short term, but they lose out over time. But these strategies do not always have a positive outcome. In situations where a mistake is made by one partner, both can be drawn into a war of attrition. Such situations arise during the mating season when a male animal makes a foolish challenge and the result is a battle harmful to both.

Memory is extremely important in these strategies. Often there's a time lag between giving and receiving and the giver expects reciprocal treatment. A new aptitude develops – the ability to trust and so form contracts. Not many animals other than vertebrates can remember past favours given and received.

These strategies have been observed in many wild communities, but not all. In the lioness example above, lions don't appear to play tit-for-tat. The leading lioness tends to take the same position at each hunt and observers haven't seen them punishing continual dawdlers by isolating them from the kill. Little vampire bats are different. They drink more blood than they need, and then regurgitate this to less fortunate bats. This favour is returned on a tit-for-tat basis, and the bats are good at remembering and punishing cheats. Stickleback fish make paired forays to inspect possible predators. They appear to remember those fish that are reliable partners in this risky undertaking.

Tit-for-tat can occur between different species. Reef cleaning stations are places where large fish come to be cleaned of parasites by smaller ones who gain food by this association. Yet the predators do not eat the small fish afterwards. The small fish are essential to their well-being and are individually recognized, possibly because they tend to live in the same section of reef for a long period. For tit-for-tat to work, animals must live socially and meet frequently.

A cheat may attempt to hide his dishonesty. An animal needs considerable subtlety to deceive, so this behaviour is probably not very widespread, but it has been recorded in primates and crows. In a carefully designed experiment where a number of penned crows was closely watched, a subordinate male was pushed away from food containers by a superior. The subordinate later removed several empty containers to a distance and pretended to look for food in them. When the superior male flew over to investigate and chase him away, he flew back to the food-filled containers and ate his fill in peace.

The first hint of the Golden Rule lies in tit-for-tat strategies. We do as the other did, but we also expect to receive the same in return.

Sharing

Animal societies share danger. Gazelles graze together nervously, their ears flicking to catch the soft hiss of moving grasses made by a stalking cheetah. Their widely spaced eyes are always searching for unusual movements in the shadows of scrub and rock and if one spots danger, its bobbing white tail alerts all the others.

Animals share in the hunt. Groups of swifts shriek noisily when they find a supply of insects, and they gather together to share the bonanza on warm summer evenings. Wolves devise complicated tactics to separate an animal from a herd.

Food-sharing is common. Cockerels call their hens to a patch of food. Prides of lions eat their kill together, under strict hierarchical rules where the senior animal (generally the male) retains the choicest part.

Many birds share nest-building and feeding of nestlings, and in a number of societies females share the task of watching their playful young. Care for young is thought to be the basis for some types of sexual bonding behaviour. Adult birds have been observed gaping at their partners like nestlings during mating play.

In these and many other ways the society bonds together and all animals benefit.

Empathy

Empathy is the ability to enter into the feelings of another and is connected to emotions. Emotions help manage actions. Primary emotions like the fight-or-flight response are innate and fast, and have been honed by natural selection. Sex in animals is controlled by hormones, pheromones and other chemicals, and in vertebrates is linked to the brain's limbic system. Such responses are inflexible, so secondary emotions involving brain centres in the cerebral cortex allow reflection. A number of vertebrate species have such systems, so perhaps they can empathize, though empathy was thought for a long time to be unique to primates. Recent studies seem to show it doesn't require a specialized brain area and has deep evolutionary roots. After a bird has learnt what a peck feels like possibly the brain becomes conditioned to trigger the same feeling when it sees others being pecked.

Empathy need not result in sympathetic action; often it's used to harm or punish. Punishment is necessary to control undesirable behaviour in a group. The animal which punishes must be able to appreciate that a cheating behaviour (snitching food) is inappropriate, coupled with some understanding of the sort of punishment that will solve the problem. It must also be prepared to risk damage to itself. Some species of fish discipline their mates and they also have procedures for reconciliation.

Most groups have a closely observed hierarchy or pecking order. This helps the group to cohere and act together quickly when necessary, such as in times of danger or during shared hunting. The order is enforced quite rigorously and in many cases punishment will act as warning to others in the group. We expect hens that act out of line will be pecked back into submission by a senior bird. So do the other hens. They watch the action closely, for a hen's life is full of interest – to the hen. They know that a peck is painful to them, and since they use it as a punishment they must be aware it is painful to another bird.

We observe that a number of animals feel fear. They also show rage and aggression. Quite docile cows will trample a trespassing dog to death if they have calves at foot. But what about affection? In one group of experiments a rat learnt that if it feeds it will trigger a small electric shock in a second rat. The first rat held back from food to prevent the shock. Observers at sea have watched pairs of whales play in ways that we would term loving in humans. Care for young is widespread, and some species extend care to others. Hunting dogs will lick and clean the orphaned piglet, lamb or chick, which is particularly hard on the chick.

Do animals feel grief? Elephants sometimes cover the last resting-place of a comrade with branches, returning to the simple grave later. Birds show real distress by searching and calling for their partner when it dies. We don't have a good biological explanation of how we humans experience our emotions, so it is not yet possible to relate animal appearances of grief to ours. It looks as though physiological processes like stomach upset and eyes sinking into their sockets are part of the mechanism that generates this emotion. If so, those animals showing such symptoms after loss of a friend may well be feeling grief.

Animal schools

- Care of the young
- Learning the rules
- Human teachers

Care of the young

Care of the young is a useful strategy for ensuring reproductive success but is costly for the parent. It is genetically supported but parents reinforce this by example. A number of fish build nests or burrows for their young. Pit vipers, a group that includes rattlesnakes, remain with their young for about ten days after the young hatch. Alligators carry their young very gently to safe places. More sophisticated care is found among birds and mammals who provide food, warmth and grooming.

Care continues as the young mature. A mother pheasant can distinguish between gulls and birds of prey far above her, and warn her chicks appropriately. This reinforces the chicks' innate response to a threatening shape. Ewes understand that their young are easily frightened. They patiently allow their large, grass-feeding lambs to suckle frantically when they are scared, even though the lamb knocks them about.

Caring behaviour may be very ancient. Female dinosaur fossils have been discovered still sitting on their eggs. Touchingly, they must have died while protecting their young.

Learning the rules

Parent and other senior animals teach society rules to the young by example and discipline. Dogs have a strong sense of social rules, inherited from their wolf-pack ancestry and instilled when they are puppies. The parent will punish misbehaviour, generally quite gently, unless the disciplined pup refuses to learn its lesson.

Fair play is learnt in youth by games and romps with peers. Play in young mammals rarely involves fighting. They use signals to indicate they're not being aggressive when they bite, and often allow a weaker player to win. This helps coordinate group behaviour but also teaches fairness – how to behave when sharing food, defending the group and grooming. Individual animals benefit because play has been shown to enlarge the brain and increase its connections. Some studies show that less social youngsters forge fewer bonds with their peers and tend to drift away from their social group. A high percentage of these drifters die young – over half in one study of wild dogs. A sense of fairness seems to benefit individual animals as well as the group.

Bonding can persist into adulthood. Dolphins, elephants and whales bond strongly to one another for life, assisting wounded mates. Related groups act together. They also exclude the outsider. Every dairy farmer is very watchful when he introduces a new cow to his existing herd. It takes some while for her to be accepted, and the herd display all kinds of restless excitement for a while.

All behavioural traits are complicated as environmental influences are strong, but fair play and nurturing of others may be partly genetic. If there is variation in levels of good behaviour and if this is rewarded by a greater likelihood of successful mating, then any genes connected to such behaviour could well accumulate over time.

Human teachers

Anyone who deals with mammals and birds knows that many remember kindness and punishment. No pony or dog could be trained otherwise. It is essential for the trainer to have understanding and educate the animal to be a willing partner, not a broken slave. The educator needs to develop the animal's latent qualities and guide faults and weaknesses in a positive direction. Schooling then becomes a game between trainer and animal.

Dog therapists often have to explain to the dog owner that they need to show the dog who is boss, as dogs are happiest with a clearly defined social position. Dogs are capable of internalizing house rules by obeying remembered commands even when their owner is absent, such as sitting on guard for long periods. They also cringe in anticipation of punishment when they have disobeyed, even before their owner has noticed the wrongdoing. They are upset when they compromise their relationship with their owner. So are they feeling anything approaching guilt or remorse?

Domesticated farm animals are not subject to such control, but they are trained. In the mountains of Wales sheep are taught to keep to particular grazing areas outside the farm boundary. Such training takes many years of herding and the cooperation of a number of shepherds. It adds considerable value to the flock when a farm is sold. Outbreaks of disease like foot-and-mouth where the whole flock is slaughtered destroy this delicate balance for good.

Sheep have special neural circuits in their brains used in recognition. These separate humans and dogs from sheep but their shepherd is categorized as a friendly sheep. Sheep identify their own sheepdog and flock together calmly when it approaches, but they scatter and panic before a strange dog. An impatient and noisy person makes a poor shepherd. So do the sheep train the shepherd and the dog?

Conclusions

A vertebrate has a greater variety of responses available to meet changing situations than do insects. This flexibility causes their societies to extend in novel directions. Affection has been added to selfishness. Animals give up their own comfort for the good of their young and they discipline them gently, aware of their weakness. Care of young expands into patterns of sexual bonding. Play and discipline become increasingly important as social rules increase in complexity. Reactions with other species are equally complex.

The primate world – chimpanzees – 'I know just how you feel and I am going to use that knowledge'

Intentionality is the term used for the ability to reflect on one's thoughts. First-order intentionality is shared by most mammals and birds. This is the ability to know one's own mind. Second-order is similar to that of a child of about five who can reflect on the beliefs of other minds. Chimpanzees but not monkeys reach this level in the appropriate tests. Adult humans can reach the fifth order which involves working out highly complex intentions and beliefs in both the self and the other. Such aptitudes require large brain capacity. See Figure 3.1.

Primate brains have large cortical regions with well-developed frontal lobes. Species' brains vary and are dissimilar both in size and functioning. For instance, certain patterns of gene expression act in the blood, liver and brains of humans, chimps and macaques. They work in the same way in the liver and blood of all three animals, but in human brains their action is unique. This means some operations of our brains will be different from the other primates. Some studies have looked at the specialized spindle cells found only in great apes, including humans. Their localities in the brain suggest they are connected to emotional responses, and we know the great apes have superior social skills and cognitive ability to all other animals, but the cells' functioning remains unclear.

Highly developed brains combined with social living result in more intricate social relationships. Primates are able to appreciate how an action can be misunderstood by another. They then use this knowledge to manipulate

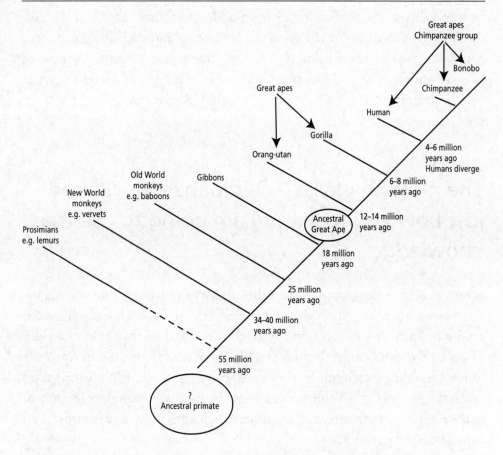

Figure 3.1   Evolutionary relationship between primate groups.

the behaviour of the other so that they benefit. This tactical deception is rare in other species, though we looked earlier at an example in crows.

This section considers some simple moral innovations in these complex primate societies, using chimpanzee society as our example, because they have been closely studied both in large enclosures and in the wild for many years.

- Follow my leader
- Mums and dads
- Mirror, mirror on the wall, who is the fairest?
- The sad variety of woe
- Internalized rules

Follow my leader

Many animal societies are hierarchical, a system that keeps communities strong against hostile neighbours and predators. Chimp society is no exception. The group is ranked according to seniority, strength and cleverness.

The group leader, the alpha male, has two roles. One is to ward off attacks by predators or other groups, and the other is to reduce conflict within the group. Chimps have different personalities and deal with situations in contrasting ways. The group recognize the character of an individual leader and his status depends on their view of him. Occasionally they combine in a group attack to overthrow him if he continually disrupts the group with power displays.

Some alpha males can stop a fight with a single step forward, while others make the problem worse. Some are very tolerant of weaker members, especially juveniles, who can be quite rough before he taps them away. Generally an alpha does not interfere on the side of his mates, but seems to consider how best to resolve the situation quickly. He has the ability to look at the situation from an objective view. Often he supports the weaker in a fight, even though the stronger is his friend. There can be a payoff to this generosity because rank is not wholly dependent on size and strength, and the group itself controls how its leader behaves. If he is heavy-handed or shows prejudice the weaker members will form alliances against him. So if the leader supports the weak he gains more general support and this may be of great advantage when young males seek to overthrow him. It is rare to find unbiased males in chimp society, so the group act together to keep a wise leader in power.

There are innumerable internal squabbles to be resolved, some with the potential to disrupt the whole group. When fights get serious between juveniles, the mothers will rush to protect their own. They will be joined by allies unless the situation is quickly resolved, and in these situations a respected and experienced alpha male can reduce tensions.

Other senior members of the society will take the controlling role when the alpha male is absent. Sometimes the highest ranking female will stop fights, but in general females have a very strong commitment to close relatives and friends and this reduces impartial dealing. Chimps have found ways of emphasizing leadership rather than dominance.

Mums and dads

There are differences between the sexes in their behaviour. Females are more peaceful, but if they quarrel violently there is less chance of repairing the relationship. Males are more aggressive but quicker to reconcile. Females tend to live dispersed through the forest, ceaselessly occupied with care for their highly dependent young. They avoid competition. Males are highly competitive over sex; their position in the hierarchy is extremely important to them for this purpose.

The alpha male has the first pick of females when they are on heat. He doesn't have it all his own way because low-rankers often hide with a cooperative female. Observers noted one occasion when the alpha male discovered a sneaky pairing with his favourite female. He chased the usurping male all round the enclosure until some watching females began to bark indignantly. They used the special sound that signals protest at intruders or aggressors. Gradually the whole group joined in until the alpha male stopped his attack.

There are important sex-for-food transactions during the hunt. If a group of animals includes females on heat, then an observer can predict they are about to go hunting. There are sexual differences in dealing with food. Males who don't join in till after the kill will get little or nothing, but females are allowed to eat whatever their role in the hunt. The alpha male may demand carcasses from other males, and distribute them himself, favouring females and mid-ranking males over males that are close to him in rank. Here the dominant retains his position by the use of gifts – possibly an early understanding of the usefulness of bribes.

Chimps mount another animal at play or when comforting or seeking reconciliation. Close male pairs play with genitals, and female pairs rub sexual areas together. Behaviour that we would term merely sexual has the wider significance of pleasure in friendship.

Mirror, mirror on the wall, who is the fairest?

Chimp young, just like the human variety, learn fair-sharing and sympathy for others early. They soon realize they can play more boisterously with the strong. They appear to be able to put themselves in the position of a crippled mate and treat it accordingly, a very rare ability among animals. They will hug distressed animals. They are guided by their mothers who will sort them out with determination when they play too roughly.

Young chimps love to tease others. When an adult is teased it will tickle or pretend to chase the youngster until it becomes tired of the game. At this point it signals it has had enough, and the youngsters learn to understand the signals and react accordingly. Play helps the chimps work out the rules of their society and as they grow up the teasing develops into displays of strength and provocation.

As well as kin preferences like mother and child there are many forms of alliances between peers, both shifting and stable. While young, chimps make strong bonds that can be life-long. Alliances are made in order to avenge past squabbles, for retaliation is as important as reconciliation. Unions for such purposes are rare in primates, other than humans.

Food-sharing is vitally important. A bonanza of food is welcomed by hooting, embracing, making up to dominants and generally celebrating as a group. This seems to alleviate any earlier group tensions, so that they can then share the food together. Mean behaviour is remembered and a chimp who rarely shares with others will be left to beg in vain on later occasions. Females will feed unrelated juveniles, and young females have been seen fetching food to share with a sick parent.

Chimps have recognized reconciliation procedures. For many years it was believed these were exclusively human, and that aggression is due to the character or frustration of an individual and nothing to do with group living. Observers of chimpanzee society have found that in fact the rage results when interests within the group collide. Senior animals may intervene to quell brutality. Afterwards the animals hug and kiss to the great excitement of onlooking chimps. The reconciled animals then groom each other to strengthen the bond of renewed friendship. Chimps depend so strongly on one another that fights mustn't be allowed to disrupt the group for long, and they show great ingenuity in finding solutions to forestall violence.

Chimps have enough flexibility to cope with more intensive living conditions in semi-natural zoos. Conflict resolution becomes increasingly important here so the society deals with troublemakers quickly. When there is a particularly serious disturbance which may endanger lives, the whole group may bark until the antagonists give way. This behaviour is the beginning of rule-making.

They are often very deceitful and are adept at fooling unwary human keepers. They seem to understand that conning others is only useful if it is a rare behaviour otherwise the deceiver will lose their trust. Deception can be used to gain sympathy like the pretence to have an injured limb.

Chimps show pleasure and happiness when grooming and playing, and make laughing noises. They become very emotional during reconciliation. Noisy events like rain storms cause them great excitement and they tear off tree branches and dance madly.

The sad variety of woe

When a chimp mother is absent from her child the infant calls desperately and searches for her. This is followed by despair, with loss of appetite and empty gaze. If her infant dies, the mother may carry the baby round with her for several days, screaming and wimpering. When older apes die the others may scream hysterically before an uncharacteristic silence falls on the group. They show signs of distress at sudden death, and remain uneasy for hours.

Chimps show kindness to the sick and dying, often caressing the sick animal. They lick away blood from the wounds of others, remove dirt and chase off flies. They also travel more slowly to give the wounded animal time to catch up.

They aren't always compassionate. Some wild chimpanzees walked unevenly because they were partially paralysed by polio and the human observers were upset to see how completely their community rejected them with fear and hostility. Chimps are adept at indirect revenge, attacking the weaker relative of their opponent. Warfare between chimpanzee groups is often extremely brutal. Groups can show considerable tactical skill, lying in wait and systematically murdering the males of another group before taking over their females and territory. Generally they don't show particular care for other species. They may tease them cruelly for their own amusement and will hunt and eat other primates.

Internalized rules

Chimpanzees behave quite differently when the boss is away and they seem to feel guilty afterwards. When the alpha male is removed from a group the subordinates take the opportunity to mate with the females, but they are constantly alert for the alpha's return. And when he does return they act with extreme submission, as if afraid he knows they have been misbehaving. They have internalized the rules of their society, a preliminary stage to the development of a conscience.

It is difficult to know whether they feel anything akin to remorse, that is, shame and self-punishment for an offence unobserved by the rest of the group. They certainly feel embarrassment. When they fall clumsily they look round to check whether anyone noticed before carrying on their way.

An observer of wild chimps watched one sit and stare at a waterfall for a long period. Was it experiencing wonder? If only they could tell us!

Conclusions

For morality to develop it seems essential to have group-living with the potential for conflict. There need to be society rules regulating behaviour and an animal must have the capacity to distinguish between what is acceptable and unacceptable. It needs to feel with and for others and to internalize the society rules before conscience can evolve. Ethical behaviour implies conscious understanding of right and wrong, and it is debatable whether chimpanzees have developed this.

Primate world – humans – 'We will encode laws'

One of the greatest differences between all other primates and ourselves is our development of speech. We pass information across generations and societies in this highly flexible way, and the invention of writing has magnified the availability of knowledge. We also benefit from our upright stance which frees our hands, and our opposable thumbs which increase dexterity. It seems that our genome is more flexible than that of other apes, so that we are quick to evolve new attributes and adapt to changing environments. Unfortunately such fluidity allows more failures, and several forms of mental retardation are due to these genetic mishaps.

In this section we will look at our inheritance a little more closely

- Positive – 'Can I see another's woe, and not be in sorrow too?'
- Negative – 'Love seeketh only self to please . . .'
- Making choices – free will?

Positive – 'Can I see another's woe, and not be in sorrow too?'

These words come from one of William Blake's deceptively simple *Songs of Innocence*. They remind us of our inheritance of sympathy and care for others, stretching back in time at least as far as that mother dinosaur protecting her eggs, and widespread in the animal community today. Resting on that foundation are prodigious human achievements.

We are born with the capacity to interpret the behaviour of others and to express the appropriate behaviour in return. Babies smile at smiling faces – but even blind babies smile. Very young children show sympathy for people in distress, hugging and patting them, and our ability to care is probably innate. As social knowledge develops, we learn from our observations and interactions about fair play, self-defence and generally how to deal with intricate social conditions.

In the adult world we use these early lessons to care for others. Human care of the sick and dying involves a vast range of personnel working cooperatively in many fields. It includes care for those suffering mentally from disease or the ordinary upheavals of life such as bereavement or loss of job. We care for our young just like many other animals, but our bonds are the stronger because human children need care for so much longer. Children need to learn a great deal to function well in our complicated societies, so we spend much energy in educating them in the history of our race, in philosophy, the arts and sciences.

Like chimpanzees we make long-term friendships and short-term alliances based on mutual trust and fair dealing, but we extend the possibilities far beyond anything other primates could appreciate. We trade and barter, improving our lives from the skills of strangers. Trade is one of our greatest successes. We are highly innovative in our development of technology because we can work together in groups which are not related by kinship.

We have learnt to live in close association with vast numbers of strangers without society falling apart completely. Without respect for moral qualities – which we share with chimpanzees – we could never maintain such a complicated society. Our skills of reconciliation are prodigious and we hone them every day throughout life. We attempt to regulate ourselves by enacting laws founded on justice and mercy. We try to resolve conflicts amicably for the good of all parties. In childhood we internalize the rules of our society so thoroughly that guilt at breaking them can cause severe damage to our lives. Our conscience is highly developed.

Many animals have a sense of beauty or the peacock's tail would never appeal to the peahen and the bower bird would build its bower in vain. But human creation of beauty is exceptional in all walks of life.

We are for ever sharing stories and anecdotes that help us deal with life. Love, stupidity and rejection are so common that many tales are concerned with them. There are dramas like that between Carmen and Don José and the mockery of stupid Malvolio in love in *Twelfth Night*. Over the centuries emotions remain recognizable. Nearly three thousand years ago the musician and poet Sappho sang of bittersweet love between women, and Jonathan was remembered by David:

I grieve for you, Jonathan my brother;
    dear and delightful you were to me;
your love for me was wonderful,
    to surpassing love of women.

We gain courage in distress from the bravery of other sufferers. Tennyson wrote of both grief and hope on the death of his friend Arthur Hallam in *In Memoriam*.

He is not here; but far away
    the noise of life begins again,
    and ghastly thro' the drizzling rain
On the bald street breaks the blank day . . .
I hold it true whate'er befall;
    I feel it, when I sorrow most;
    'Tis better to have loved and lost
Than never to have loved at all.

Our skills are such that those of other animals seem insignificant, so that we often treat them with contempt.

Negative – 'Love seeketh only self to please. . .'

Joys in another's loss of ease,' Blake continues in his *Songs of Experience*. The downside is based on our inheritance as well. Our knowledge about the world around us is extensive, but our use of knowledge is not neutral. We are selfish organisms, equipped with strong motivation to reproduce and control. Our self-assertion easily slips into aggression, and our group bonding ensures that aggression is directed to outsider groups. We enjoy destruction and easily turn to thuggery and violence, and we have far more vicious weapons to hand than any other animal due to our skill at manufacturing.

Sadism, the use of empathy to destroy another, is a well observed feature of many relationships. We use our knowledge of pain to torment others physically. The more we learn about psychological weaknesses the more we can increase such torture. We use natural fears like that of death and bereavement to control others.

Our desire for power leads to many abuses. Trade and industry provide many examples of the selfish use of power to acquire even more wealth and prestige. We are adept at cheating in spectacularly complicated ways so that we are rarely found out.

The list of our vices is as long as our virtues and their application is far more damaging than the vices of other animals.

Making choices – free will?

Ethics imply freedom of choice. But are we the slave of selfish genes and our upbringing?

Free-will problems have exercised human minds for centuries. The problem was acute for Christians in the years following Jesus' death, because they strongly believed in a controlling, all-knowing Creator God. Paul tackled it in the following way in his letter to the church in Rome (chapters 9, 10, 11). God ordains everything that happens. He shows mercy and pity when he wants to, 'but also makes men stubborn as he chooses. You will say, "Then why does God blame a man?"' Paul retorts, How dare you, a mere man, question God? The potter can make what vessels he likes with the clay and the clay must remain silent. 'What if God, desiring to exhibit his retribution at work and to make his power known, tolerated very patiently those vessels of retribution due for destruction, and did so in order to make known the full wealth of his splendour upon vessels which were objects of mercy?' From this and similar passages Augustine developed theories about *predestination* which were enlarged in European Christianity, especially by the Reformer John Calvin. This doctrine caused much distress to the insecure and fearful.

More common now is the use of free-will theories to support arguments for the existence of a loving God. The argument runs as follows. Why did an all-loving, all-powerful God make a less than perfect world with suffering and evil? The answer given is that we are in this world to learn how to become responsible, compassionate creatures. If we are to choose good freely, there must be the opportunity to choose evil. Free will is essential to moral life now and in heaven. This does not really explain why other animals must suffer.

The problem also surfaces in the determinism of the clockwork or block universe. Everything is known, so even though we may feel free at the point of choice, we are deluding ourselves. Basic uncertainty (quantum theory) and the impossibility of knowing the future (chaos theories) have changed perceptions of this solid determinism.

A number of popular scientific works emphasize our total dependence on our genes, human evolutionary history and upbringing (nature/nurture debates). How can we be blamed for wrongful behaviour if we are so strongly programmed? Rather illogically we still expect to be praised for our generosity.

However, we can never fully predict a person's behaviour, and even if we understood all the variables it would be impossible to calculate the interactions and come up with a certainty. We don't even know all the reasons for our own actions, but we still feel we are able to choose; we are responsible beings able to use discernment. Responsibility is very important to us, as it implies status, adulthood, acceptance in society. It is a badge of freedom. We believe we can evaluate a situation with some accuracy and then freely decide our course of action.

Our universe seems to include freedom to develop new possibilities. The living world provides more freedom not less as life becomes more elaborate. The possibilities available to a DNA molecule are far fewer and of a different order from those available to a beetle. A mammal can choose from an even wider repertoire of possibilities. A human has the greatest freedom of all. We are presented with different choices and can envisage unique possibilities, so we can't escape responsibility by claiming, 'It's my genes made me do it, m'lud.'

In fact to make a choice at all we need predictability – life would be insupportable if choice was perfectly open and free. It's difficult enough when faced with limitless food choices in the hypermarket, where you dither in an agony of indecision in front of the brilliantly coloured packages. There is enough freedom within the limits of our human nature for us to choose how we will play the cards life has dealt us. In our legal system we accept this dichotomy. We assume adults are responsible for their actions. Judgement is tempered by considering the effects of nature and nurture in any particular case.

Predestination	The doctrine that whatever will happen in the future has been fixed by God. He has already decided who will be saved and who damned for all eternity.

Conclusions

In the past we've often tried to separate ourselves completely from other animals, as if it's humiliating to compare ourselves with them. We have convinced ourselves we are special and superior, so we don't always treat the living world with proper respect. Perhaps it's time to reassess our roots.

In our search for the attributes of underlying Reality in the universe we've uncovered a number of distinctive qualities. Some scientists present the universe as cold and unfeeling, and life as selfish, but this seems to exclude many facts. Certainly there is no moral implication behind dynamic cosmic events so in that sense the universe is blind. There is no evidence that the Indian Ocean tsunami of December 2004 was due to human sin or even specifically aimed at humans, nor that the events of our lives, good or ill, are planned for us individually. Nor is personal probity rewarded by health and happiness any more than selfishness is punished. We cannot find an external Being who continually alters the laws of the universe just for *Homo sapiens* (more in Chapters 5 and 7). Instead we find mind-boggling potentialities continually being drawn out of the initial physical and chemical constraints, from galaxies to love and justice. Mercy is as fundamental to the universe as quarks and selfish genes, and we learn of love through self-awareness, pain, joy and loss. Death is the grim teacher. It's our privilege as humans to act with considerable freedom in response to life's events, expressing the underlying love and mercy if we wish.

There is one final question to ask. Does this Reality try to get in touch with us, and if so, what is its message?

IDEAS FOR DISCUSSION

1   If a particular gene assists replicas of itself in other bodies to succeed, then the altruism of the gene carrier is the result of gene 'selfishness'. Does this make the ant's behaviour less sacrificial? Does the theory affect the quality of human altruism? Compare Dawkins' and Midgley's approaches. What issues do they raise for you?

2   Compare the different approaches of the Roses and Wright to the influence of our genetic inheritance.

3   Read De Waal (or one of Jane Goodall's books – please search Google for these) and compare human society with that of other primates.

4   Is human nature devalued by the suggestion that it has evolved from our animal inheritance?

5   While it appears there can be reciprocity without morality, could morality exist without reciprocity?

6   Does society's changing perception of a person as they pass through the various stages of life change their personality? Often old people say they still feel young at heart, as if they are 'trapped' in an old body. What does this tell us about our perceptions of ourselves?

7   Domestic animals extend our human personalities as we interact with them. Consider this in relationship to a farm animal and a pet. Do farm animals have more space to 'be themselves' than pets?

8   Discuss the three ways human codes of conduct might have developed. Which one appears more likely to you?

9   If we could remove or reduce a particular trait such as desire for power over others, would we also affect other positive traits?

10 We introduce laws in order to regulate behaviour. How far can a law influence something like racism or sexism?

11 Read Dennett. Can a whole be more than the sum of its parts? Look into theories of free will from both the religious and

scientific points of view. How important is the concept of free will in society?

12   Games theories. How useful are they in explaining behaviour? See Diamond, Pinker, Ridley, Wright.

REFERENCES AND FURTHER READING

Jerome Barkow, Leda Cosmides and John Tooby, eds, 1992, *The Adapted Mind: Evolutionary Psychology and the Generation of Culture*, Oxford: Oxford University Press

Richard Dawkins, 1989, *The Selfish Gene*, 2nd edition, Oxford: Oxford University Press

Frans De Waal, 1996, *Goodnatured*, Cambridge, MA: Harvard University Press

Daniel C Dennett, 2003, *Freedom Evolves*, Harmondsworth: Penguin

Philippe Descola, 1997, *The Spears of Twilight*, London: HarperCollins

Jared Diamond, 1991, *The Rise and Fall of the Third Chimpanzee*, London: Vintage

William H Durham, 1991, *Coevolution: Genes, Culture and Human Diversity*, Stanford: Stanford University Press

Melvin Konner, 1982, *The Tangled Wing*, Harmondsworth: Penguin

Kevin Laland and Gillian Brown, 2001, *Sense and Nonsense*, Oxford: Oxford University Press

Mary Midgley, 1994, *The Ethical Primate*, London: Routledge

Steven Pinker, 2002, *The Blank Slate*, Harmondsworth: Penguin

Matt Ridley, 1996, *The Origins of Virtue*, Harmondsworth: Penguin

Hilary Rose and Steven Rose, eds, 2001, *Alas Poor Darwin*, London: Vintage

Michael Ruse, 1986, *Taking Darwin Seriously*, Oxford: Basil Blackwell

Edward O Wilson, 1975, *Sociobiology: The New Synthesis*, Cambridge, MA: Harvard University Press

Robert Wright, 1996, *The Moral Animal*, new edition, London: Abacus

4

The Fifth Footprint –
I Heard the Voice of God

There is a widespread idea that Reality is in touch with humans in a unique way. We have been singled out; we are special, even specially created for this purpose. The universe was designed to produce intelligent beings able to enter into a meaningful relationship with Reality. This is either supreme egoism or a miracle of breathtaking proportions, well worth investigating in either case.

In practice people expect to come closer to Reality through group worship and individual prayer and meditation. What sort of experiences can they expect?

You move to another city and as part of your drive to make new friends you join the congregation of the local cathedral. They are exceptionally friendly, making you feel welcome and giving you all sorts of practical tips about your new community – the excellent school, the reliable garage, the best butcher. They praise the bishop, dean and priests for their pastoral care and concern for the poor. Your respect for them increases. It is only gradually that you learn that the bishop is about to desert his family for his mistress, and that the cathedral vergers have worse conditions than employees of the secular state. When you raise these issues with your new friends you get the cold shoulder. You, a newcomer, have no right to criticize.

While mulling this over, you hear the story of Dan on the radio. Dan is a highly religious man who prays constantly to God. He goes to his sister-in-law Brenda's home and asks to use her phone, but she refuses. He mentally asks God, 'What do I do now?' God assures him it is right to push Brenda. He knocks her down and sits on her, asking God what he should do next. Just then his elder brother Ron, Brenda's husband, rushes in. Dan says to him, 'God commands you to fetch me a knife.' Once Dan has the knife God tells him he must slit the throats of Brenda and her baby daughter. He and Ron insist they have not committed a crime because they were acting under heavenly orders. Dan is a Mormon now in Utah State Prison.

After an accumulation of similar experiences many people give up on all religions. If these are examples of a loving and merciful God in action, then keep him. They go away and work out their own answers to life's questions.

This chapter takes a different course. It looks at the importance of religions and why they exert such a hold on us, and then it investigates individual religious experiences.

- **Religious tradition and practices**
- **Religious experiences**

RELIGIOUS TRADITION AND PRACTICES

- **Comparisons**
- **Sociology of religion**
- **Beauty and mystery**
- **Suffering, death and miracles of healing**

Comparisons

To understand the hold that religions exert it is constructive to look at how music influences us. It too affects us more deeply than words, and is widely seen as one of humanity's most spiritual activities. Schubert wrote one of his loveliest songs in praise of its ability to soothe and strengthen.

Music is basic to human life. Researchers watching mothers and babies find that babies respond more to singing than speaking. We consciously use music to alter our own mood. After a day of hard work, we slip a soothing CD into our player, or we use something more exciting to keep us alert on a long journey. People suffering traumas or handicaps all seem to benefit by using music as a form of communication. Autistic children sometimes start to respond to other people through music, while patients who lose speech and movement after a stroke often react to melodies they loved. When singers and musicians perform in sheltered housing for the elderly the audience becomes progressively more alert. Even if they suffer old age memory loss, they remember old songs and join in.

Music is pattern in sound. Specific rhythmic patterns reflect the natural rhythms of heartbeats and breathing. They also echo human vocalizations. Our voices sink and move more slowly when we are sad, so music with a falling cadence sounds sorrowful to us and we remember sad moments in our lives. Speech which indicates fear, joy or anger also has specific patterns, and music can mirror these and arouse such emotions. Pop songs change their rhythms according to the flavour of the day – since the 1980s they have speeded up from an average 120 beats per minute to 136 beats, reflecting the use of ecstasy in clubs.

Our emotions are delicately tuned to detect change, originally a survival mechanism. Composers insert sudden changes into a predictable pattern of tonality, harmony and rhythm, and this alerts our emotions. One such change is the appoggiatura, where a note suddenly sounds out of harmony with the melody and later resolves down to the key note. Syncopation is a displaced accent, and this too raises tension.

There is a strong social component to our love of music. Football choruses and religious hymns or chants all rely on human associations. During the thrills of a shared event like a football match our excited brain records surrounding events, so the music we hear is associated with emotional highs. People remember the excitement whenever they hear the songs again. In the same way people hum religious choruses to themselves after they have experienced spiritual ecstasy at a revival meeting. Those who share the excitement become friends.

Music has such a strong effect on most of us that it is used by others to affect our moods. Muzak is tailored by music stores to encourage sales. The worship of music's pop idols is a crowd phenomenon closely allied to worship of gods and their priests and priestesses. The group hysteria that may occur is likely to increase sales of recordings. Dance and music combine with political protest in South African crowds. Songs and repetitive choruses are used in many cultures to taunt and build up communal hatred of the enemy. Religious chants have been similarly used. 'Cry, God for Harry, England and St George!'

Religions too tap in to basic rhythms of life – birth and death, seedtime and harvest. They are tied to emotions in subtle ways, enhancing our sense of self-worth. The social element is very important, increasing bonding through shared ritual and myth. Religions are used to affect behaviour, order priorities and promote those in power, but they can also support opposition and nonconformity.

Sociology of religion

The history of morality and religion and how they affect and are affected by genes, minds and cultures is so very involved that any attempt at explanation must be inadequate and reductive. Sociological analyses have to be simplified because there is so much variety in practice and belief within a religion. Religions are so different that it's difficult to discover any underlying unity. There is an identifiable God in Islam, Christianity and Judaism. In Buddhism there is not, and for this reason William James excluded Buddhism from his foundational book, *The Varieties of Religious Experience*. Not all people have a desire to tap into a spirit world. At the beginning of the last chapter there is a story about life in an Amazonian tribe. The anthropologist who recorded the details found they had a deep mistrust of any other world. They didn't dare mention their dead for fear any allusion would open the gate to spiritual malice against the living, so they had no observable religious ceremonies.

It is not for sociology to question any beliefs or theologies, but their effects on a society can be analysed. The different ideas are deeply embedded in a particular culture, and they are full of historical nuances. They guide behaviour. They are the unquestioned assumptions that bind people into a unified tribe. Any within the tribe who query them may be treated as heretics or sinners. People who enter the tribe from another culture are expected to conform to the tribe's understanding of itself as well as its laws.

Christianity is the world's largest religion numerically, so many analyses are based on this one religion. The following review includes five features typical of religions and takes most of its examples from Christianity.

- Tradition and sacred knowledge
- Access to spiritual power through special techniques
- Believers who carry on the traditions
- Fellowship
- The downside

Tradition and sacred knowledge

Religions generally have a parallel world containing unseen deities, either male, female or both, and spirits. In Christianity there is one God, often but not always expressed in male Trinitarian terms, Father, Son and Holy Spirit. There are saints in heaven. Sometimes this term includes all living and dead adherents (the fellowship of saints), at other times it refers only to the specially honoured dead (like St David). Spirits are numerous (angels and devils), though some people query their existence. Ideas vary about God's requirements. Some people believe he prefers chastity to marriage, others reverse this order. There are differences in explaining his preferences on matters like alcohol, fasting and the confession of sins. The perspective of particular groups varies from the Roman Catholic emphasis on Mary to that of Pentecostalists on the Holy Spirit.

The sacred knowledge has been revealed to humans by the spiritual world, not discovered by observations of the material world. It explains the historical events in a nation's development and answers existential questions about the meaning of life and death and injustice in the world.

This wisdom is passed on to adherents and their children, often in the form of myth. Myths are widespread among all religions. Meaningful stories explain the origin of the world, helping people live in harmony with cosmic reality. The human fear of bereavement and pain is soothed by stories of heroes and heroines, telling how they coped nobly with suffering. They tell of great battles where gods side with humans to defeat the mutual enemy of darkness and obliteration. These stories are often a mixture of many cultures. The Welsh Mabinogi stories are medieval and include many references to much earlier Celtic myths. The name itself may relate to the ancient British God Maponos. Here the Christian medieval tradition is grafted onto the Celtic along with some classical allusions, and, in the song of Taliesin the bard, the cauldron of Ceridwen is mentioned alongside Moses, the Crucifixion and the survivors of Troy.

Access to spiritual power through special techniques

Prayer, sacraments and blessings or cursings pass on spiritual power. Through blessings simple material objects like water, bread and wine become direct links to the spiritual world. Exorcisms counteract the power of evil spirits. Celebrations honour the granting of power and grace to humans to live their lives according to God's requirements. In some cases this power to heal and strengthen is channelled through priests, in others through the whole community.

Ritual, the following of prescribed procedures, is important in everyday life. There are many social rituals that help stabilize communities, and religious ceremonies are often nationally important. Repeated ceremonies help to make sense of the world and bestow meaning on life's major events. They provide a vehicle for thanksgiving and worship. They give people a feeling of control as tribal history is recollected with emphasis on the saving actions of God and the courage of their great forebears. This gives reassurance of help especially during times of sickness, starvation or war. Attendance at worship proves commitment and absolves guilt.

Ceremonies, like myths, develop and change, and may include earlier religious traditions. Midwinter festivals were incorporated into Christianity. Christian rituals developed within a rural culture where famine, plague and early death were constant threats. In modern urban settings they no longer have such resonance, so they are adapted and updated.

Believers who carry on the traditions

During the last century there has been a general perception in Britain that Christianity is in decline. While nearly three-quarters of the population believe in God, church numbers are falling and many prefer a pick-and-mix approach to religion. Yet in America, the most scientific and technologically advanced country in the world, church attendance has increased from about a third at the end of the nineteenth century to half its population today. Evangelism is successful in many other countries worldwide too.

There is a huge range of traditions, varying between countries and sects, though altogether they show a large degree of *coherence*. A number of people suggest that the religious descriptions of reality are like scientific ones in that there is agreement about data on community experiences in worship and prayer.

Believers stress the importance to them of parental involvement. Like age, sex and occupation religion provides them with definition as a person. Women are generally far more involved in all forms of social worship than men and are responsible for introducing little children to the traditions. They are much less likely than men to hold influential positions.

Religion is widely believed to give answers to questions about life. Reasoned arguments about the faith are vitally important and books explaining Christian foundational beliefs are very popular. Some recent questionnaires asking people about their commitment to the Ten Commandments indicated that those referring to social questions were more important than those referring to God.

Spirituality is also important through popularized techniques of meditation. These bring believers closer to God and enable them to gain powerful guidance on important issues.

Coherence	A theory shows coherence when it includes all known relevant data, is as concise as possible and contains no discrepancies.

Fellowship

Group cohesion is important for strengthening faith, and doctrine and practice are directed towards promoting solidarity. Group members give support to one another through prayer and practical help in dealing with many of life's perplexities. Fellow believers are considered more reliable than outsiders and are expected to give a fair and honest assessment of a situation. Concern for others is emphasized. Those adherents who spend their lives in the welfare of others are praised on earth and expect high honour in heaven.

Fellowship is extended to the all-powerful transcendental world of God and the saints. The City of God is a sure stronghold against all the forces of darkness and doubt that lie in wait. The Church is the body of Christ, with all that that entails of eternal salvation and the support of both living and dead. Such fellowship gives believers such a feeling of security in an uncertain world that they are unlikely to step too far beyond recognized religious boundaries.

The downside

Like all human endeavours, there is always a downside. William James was concerned that scientific study of religion worldwide would reveal so much superstition and downright nastiness that the whole concept would suffer.

Humans have historically used religion as an important tool in deterring deviants. In Christianity this has taken the form of physical punishment, exclusion from ceremonies, ostracism and relegation to lowly social positions, all severe disciplines for social animals. Excommunication extends such punishment to eternity. 'Outside the Church,' said the Reformers, 'there is no salvation', and John Calvin is associated with the judicial murder of heretics. At the same time the Roman Catholic Inquisition tortured heretics before killing them, claiming that forced conversion mercifully saved them from everlasting torment. In some periods clergy have been prominent in rousing mobs to attack dissidents.

Other religions are no kinder. Honour killings are associated with religious beliefs. Reincarnation threatens punishment after death by a return to lowlier and unhappier life.

Outsider groups fare no better than internal ones. Moral rules of kindness are not in general extended to other groups, and all human societies tend to have these double standards. We are not alone. Having external enemies improves group solidarity among social animals like termites and chimpanzees. Yet not all animals have such murderous feelings towards other groups – flocks of birds don't set about exterminating one another.

Many of the internecine wars disfiguring our planet over the centuries have a religious element, and the Bible gives us clear details of the standards some two and a half thousand years ago. In Deuteronomy, chapter 7, the Israelites are warned by Moses not to intermarry with the Canaanites once they have defeated them. Israelite men are singled out for their particular vulnerability to the wiles of heathen women. Mass slaughter and destruction of all religious artefacts are the only reliable remedy against apostasy. In Joshua, chapter 6, Joshua's soldiers 'destroyed everything in the city (Jericho); they put everyone to the sword, men and women, young and old, and also cattle, sheep and asses'. Any silver, gold, copper and iron became part of the priests' treasury. The commandment against murder is inapplicable to the inhabitants of Canaan. This commitment to ethnic cleansing is shunned by most Christians today, but it remains linked to the tradition through emphasis on the holiness of scripture.

Beauty and mystery

Mystery is important to religions. The ancient Greek Eleusinian mysteries were full of secret rites known only to initiates, and the medieval mystery plays acted out the arcane beliefs of their time.

Religious ceremonies may incorporate the use of incense and expensive, holy and ancient artefacts (patens and chalices). Priests may wear highly ornamented vestments. Rich and poor alike are encouraged to add to the religion's splendour, and the poor are taught to expect blessings far exceeding the monetary value of their gifts. The intention is to proclaim not just earthly power and wealth, but also the beauty of the spiritual world that far exceeds its material counterpart. The holy is often enclosed in a building set aside for prayer and worship, and beautified with flowers as well as gold and silver. Beauty and mystery in religion deepen our understanding of life and our place in the universe. They give us greater significance and support us with the promise of spiritual help during times of trial.

In Keats's poem 'Lamia', the wealthy and handsome hero, Lycius, is seduced by the eponymous maiden into loving and marrying her. In reality the temptress is a snake, and she personifies the lure of the mysterious world of beauty and legend. At their wedding feast the philosopher Apollonius recognizes her for what she is, so he challenges her. She reverts to form. But Lycius, instead of being grateful, dies of sorrow at his bereavement. Apollonius represents the science of Keats's day, the reality that destroys the old myths. Keats trained as a doctor and he accepts it must be so, yet regrets the passing of earlier dreams and visions.

Some people still endorse Keats's parable. For them science is soulless and has no values. It reveals a cold reality, a meaningless universe indifferent to pain and lacking love or pity or joy. The selfish gene rules all. Only a God can inject the mystery of love into such an amoral and depraved cosmos. Only a religious faith can nurture beauty and compassion.

Suffering, death and miracles of healing

- Suffering and death
- Miracles of healing

Suffering and death

Suffering is compounded for humans. Our good memory and ability to appreciate the pain of others combine with our knowledge that all love and joy ends in death. Pain causes us to feel we are out of kilter with the universe, for no other creature has such a burden of grief to bear. Nor have any other animals developed such sophisticated systems to deal with the reality of pain.

Some say religion is an immature way of dealing with life's sorrows, because we are trying to win protection from non-existent beings by fulfilling man-made ritualistic and ethical obligations.

Religions are far more subtle than this. They recognize that both good and wicked suffer. They vary in their approach to the problem of how to cope with pain and grief but their success in bringing relief to the afflicted is well documented. The brief overview of a few religions that follows does not do justice to their sophistication.

Judaism developed the view that God controls history and reveals himself through it. Why then should he send suffering on the innocent? Job concludes that it is a test of faith which becomes redemptive as soon as he accepts it and prays for his friends. The prophets believe that even when the nation appears to be destroyed, God still has control. Suffering will liberate the nation though not the individual. This theme is taken up by the suffering servant in the second part of Isaiah. There is a refusal to demand divine retribution even for the sorrows of the Holocaust. Instead the faithful Jew reminds him- or herself of hope of redemption through pain.

Christianity's founder also accepts reality and is not defeated by it. Jesus alleviates suffering and acts positively. For him and his followers disaster is the place where God is found. Crucifixion is followed by resurrection. Death is the beginning of new life for those who follow Jesus.

Islam differs slightly in its emphasis. Suffering is contained within the omnipotence of God. He is in control of the universe he has created and therefore there is a good purpose hidden within the reality of pain. Sometimes it is punishment for sin, at other times a necessary test of faith which cannot grow without it. We must alleviate the sufferings of others and bear our own patiently. So we shall find peace of conscience and deeper understanding, and open the door of Paradise to ourselves and all who suffer.

In Hinduism there is a plurality of views, all valid in their own right. In general there is seen to be a moral law within the universe and our karma (the accumulation of our actions) affects our samsara (rebirth). Suffering belongs to the world of samsara and maya (translated simplistically as illusion). Detachment does not mean indifference to the suffering of others, but includes a compassionate response to pain in other life forms. It is the awareness that the essential self does not die because it is a manifestation of Brahman which is Being-itself. Bhakti is devotion to Being who is beyond personality.

Buddhism is equally realistic in its acceptance of suffering. The Four Noble Truths teach awareness that all suffer. Suffering (dukkha), both physical and mental, originates in the craving for sense pleasure, and renouncing this desire ends suffering. Once we accept that the Self is only the transitory form taken by the flow of energy and matter at a certain moment, we can escape the endless cycle of rebirth. Nirvana is attained through a deep acceptance of these realities, embodied in the Noble Eightfold Path, which includes ethical conduct and self-discipline. The bodhisattva follows the path to nirvana and then postpones their own final attainment to help others. The importance of compassion for all is vital to an understanding of coping with suffering within Buddhism. Monks who burn themselves are not motivated by suicide or protest, but with the hope of opening the hearts of the oppressors. It is a means of identification with sufferers, so that they look up from their misery and turn to the Path that leads through pain.

Miracles of healing

Many religions accept the possibility of intervention by their gods. This is an ancient belief. The Israelites at the time of Moses believed most, if not all, natural events were brought about by God. Priests who were close to God knew which events to interpret as miraculous – i.e. meaningful signs of his special intervention. Their understanding of cause and effect in the natural world was very limited.

For centuries there have been moral doubts – why does God cure my sickness but not that of my equally religious neighbour? By the eighteenth century scientists knew enough about natural causes and their effects for the philosopher David Hume to define a miracle as something which violates a natural event. Such miracles became more and more unlikely as science progressively explained the links between events, until they were classed as old superstitions. The second definition of miracle as an amazing event that opens our eyes to some new possibility was relegated to technical marvels. A building can be a miracle of engineering.

Many intervention miracles include events which were not well understood in pre-scientific eras or are garbled memories, but some, like the resurrection of Jesus, are essential for faith. Christianity supports a belief in special intervention as proofs of God's existence and power, though many modern miracles such as moving or weeping statues can be given natural explanations. Miracles of healing are more important to believers because they demonstrate God has lovingly heard and answered prayers.

One of the difficulties of detecting miracles is the different perceptions people have of events. What is a natural occurrence for some is for others a miraculous sign of God's care. A carefully planned experiment was recently conducted at Duke University Medical Centre to look into this issue. An extensive three-year investigation involved prayer groups from different religions and appraised their effect on recovery rates from heart operations. The results were issued in 2003 and showed no significant difference in recovery or health of patients whether or not they were prayed for. A number of Christians disapproved of testing God in this way.

Serious attempts are being made to discover how God might act within the universe as it is currently understood by science, and these are discussed further in Chapter 7.

RELIGIOUS EXPERIENCES

Words like spirit and soul are easy to use but difficult to define. Spirit/life force, soul/consciousness, soul/reason, soul/conscience and spirit/soul are often used synonymously. This leads to great confusion from which none of us is immune.

'What has soul in it differs from what has not in that the former displays life,' said Aristotle. In one popular hymn Jesus' love demands our souls *and* our lives. For Plato a human soul would take 'the form of an ass, a wolf or a kite' after death if it had been polluted by bodily appetites. For Ben Jonson Shakespeare was the Soul of the Age. Charles Dickens talked about a man being in good spirits, God is a spirit, and Tennyson's Ulysses had a gray and yearning spirit.

The word *spirit* itself developed from a Latin root meaning breath and is a portmanteau word, used in a number of contexts. We will look at the two main interpretations and then at experiences of the spiritual world.

- **Spirit as bias**
- **Emerging spirit**
- **Religious experiences**

Spirit as bias

A person or a group of people can have a spiritual or emotional bias. They may be friendly or insulting, happy or miserable. A group can show loyalty; it has team spirit. A person may be in an emotional state of high or low spirits; they can be joyful and spirited or possess a broken spirit. Used in this way spirit is the disposition of a person or community. A similar use is the assertion that the spirit of the law is more important than the letter of the law.

Our spirits can be enlarged by music and words as we recognize the universality of human feeling. From revolutionary Russia, Anna Akhmatova reminds us of the universal pain of parting as she stands by a Moscow rosebush remembering her last meeting there with her lover. Abiding love triumphs over her sorrow ('In Dream'). Ben Okri writes with terrible clarity of his African friend's sickness, alerting us to the reality behind the photographer's impersonal pictures of broken young men ('To One Dying of Leukaemia'). Five hundred years ago Thomas Malory valued faithful friendship as highly as we do. Sir Ector praises Launcelot as 'truest friend . . . truest lover . . . thou was the meekest man and the gentlest that ever ate in hall among ladies'.

In our triumphs over sorrow, our love and our friendship the universe expresses its bias through us. It is a dancing joy, it suffers, it celebrates, it is desolate with grief, it is at peace, it holds out its hands in welcome.

Emerging spirit

- Concepts of spirit
- Avaunt! And quit my sight!
- Into the Ganzfeld

Concepts of spirit

A spirit can be an actual thing inhabiting a body. The poet John Donne was Dean of St Paul's, London, in the 1620s. He described himself as 'a little world made cunningly/of Elements, and an Angelic sprite' (*Holy Sonnets*, V), and this view has been common for centuries.

Some suggest spirit is an emergent property of the human brain and body, others that it is breathed into us at some point, probably before birth. It is said we are put on earth to develop our spirit and when we die we will be judged accordingly. This kind of spirit can become an unhappy ghost after death, haunting the next generation. Or it may be benevolent, advising its descendants on the best line of action.

Some religions worship the spirits of springs and woods. These are mysterious and sometimes mischievous, not necessarily benign. Evil spirits are thought to inhabit eerie places or even suburban homes, requiring exorcism. Just as people can get in touch with good spirits, so they can succumb to devils and witchcraft.

Some people believe animals possess a spirit. In 1990 Pope John Paul II announced that animals do have souls and merit respect as they are as near to God as men are. It is unclear what 'soul' means here. If soul means 'life force' then single-celled animals and insects have them. If it means 'having emotions' then it could include a number of vertebrates. Possibly it means that some animals survive death.

In some religions our spirit is able to have a conscious relationship with a personal God, who will adjust the universe for our human benefit if we ask in faith. In others there is no concept of such a person but there is a spiritual realm, quite different from this world and possibly parallel to it. Some humans become conduits of spiritual power which gives them extra-sensory perception or the ability to heal sickness psychically.

Beliefs in another spiritual world are deeply embedded in many cultures, and some very ancient ideas are still available to us through the media. In the first century BCE the Roman poet Virgil wrote about Hades, the deadland swarming with nebulous souls. Here the unburied dead wander without rest for a hundred years, the wraiths of little children sob with loneliness, the suicides moan for their lost lives. Only blood sacrifice allows a living person to speak with them, and Aeneas, the founder of Rome, braves the dreadful journey to the dark halls of the dead and makes the necessary sacrifice. He sees the pale ghost of his lover Dido who killed herself when he betrayed her. Famous warriors covered in bloody but ghostly wounds jostle to speak to him. This view of the deadlands passed into Christianity in different forms. In medieval Christian stories Christ harrows Hades or Hell and brings the captive souls triumphantly to heaven.

Avaunt! And quit my sight!

Many of us would love to say Avaunt to a ghost. But unfortunately they faded away in the glare of better lighting systems.

Ghosts and other phenomena like table-rapping and poltergeists were first studied seriously by the Society for Psychical Research (SPR). This was founded in 1882 at Cambridge University and included a number of eminent scientists and philosophers. Investigations have continued ever since and there is a sister organization in the USA.

One very famous case is that of the nun, coach and headless coachman that haunted world-famed Borley Rectory in Essex, early last century. Harry Price, a famous psychic journalist of the time and associated with the American SPR, was heavily involved in the original investigations from 1929 until his death in 1948. As well as ghostly sightings there were poltergeist interruptions, and

Price set up numerous experiments, giving the case extensive publicity. He received widespread acclaim. The Rectory became the best-documented case of its type and the most visited haunted house in the country. Though the building itself burnt down in 1939, people continued to hold séances in the grounds until 1953. There had always been accusations of fraud, and the SPR re-investigated the whole matter, publishing a lengthy report in Volume 1 of the Proceedings of the Society in 1956. They checked the acoustics of the courtyard, made detailed plans of the house, questioned previous owners and visitors and reviewed Price's experimental procedures. They concluded that Price's enquiries and experimental design were extremely poor and that the case for paranormal phenomena of any kind was exceptionally weak. They found evidence that Price had hyped up original reports. Borley Rectory is no longer included in lists of must-visit spooky places.

This case is mentioned in some detail because it illustrates a number of the problems encountered by all researchers in this field. Believers in psi (psychic) phenomena report strange events which a non-believer can explain rationally. The erie sense of presences or apparitions in traditionally haunted spots owes much to cold draughts, low-frequency sound and variable magnetic fields. Real feelings of nausea and oppression result more from psychological make-up, our wired-in fear of dangerous situations, and the natural faults inherent in human recording devices – eyes, nose and ears. Combine all these with unexpected air movements, and all kind of spooks emerge. Then there is the exaggeration of the events themselves, for experiencing a ghost gives a person instant fame. Over a long period faulty memory can amplify the experience out of all recognition and the promised verification by others melts away. And of course there are downright lies, fraud and jokes. To date there is no reliable proof that any spirit haunts places after death, though ghost trains are still good for a laugh.

Into the Ganzfeld

In 1969 the American Parapsychological Association became respectable when it was granted affiliation with the American Association for the Advancement of Science. It had been a long haul to attain this standing.

Today research in this area is carried on in a number of universities. Yet it is still the poor relation, in spite of many well-publicized successes and support for *extra-sensory perception* (ESP) by some eminent psychologists. Why is this?

Belief in all kinds of psychic phenomena is widespread among members of the public, but most physicists are completely sceptical, because they are dealing with energy fields and forces between objects all the time. They adopt the attitude that psychic phenomena are so unlikely there is no point bothering about them. All the same, some reputable scientists have always been interested in *parapsychology*, and since the founding of the SPR there have been numerous investigations of ESP using established scientific procedures. Many scientists eventually quit the field, but there have always been claims that there is enough positive evidence to require further study.

First, researchers found that most phenomena faded away when subject to proper controls. Fraud was rife in the early years and was very publicly exposed, which had the unfortunate side-effect of increasing public scepticism for science in general. Psi experiments are rarely capable of being replicated – a *sine qua non* of science – and there have been considerable weaknesses in their design.

The field covered is wide. Psychic healing of physical complaints has been found to be highly dubious, though it may have mental benefits. Researchers have studied astrology by testing time twins – people born at the same moment – with negative results. They have tested astrologers for accuracy in blind readings of birth charts and in how well their predictions agree. Astrologers do not perform better than chance.

Reincarnation and alien abductions have been studied with similar results. Simpler explanations are more likely. Past life memories are apparently recalled by regression techniques during hypnosis. Where detailed study is possible, researchers have found that the subject has recovered lost memories of historical books they once read. This in itself is highly interesting for studies in consciousness, but is not evidence for reincarnation. Alien abduction at night is more likely to be due to *hypnagogic imagery*, sleep paralysis and bizarre dreams, combined with guided questioning by believers. Particular personalities are richly imaginative but fantasy-prone, and such personalities predominate among abductees.

Today's research areas involve *psychokinesis* (PK) and ESP. Psychokinesis originally studied the movement of small physical objects like pieces of metal. Today micro-PK tests much smaller events like diffraction patterns of beams of electrons. Subjects try to alter the stream of events issued by a random event generator. Researchers report some tests produce significant results that are unlikely to be due to chance alone.

ESP is tested by *Ganzfeld* methods which block sensory input to the subject's eyes and ears. An ESP sender in another room views a randomly chosen video sequence. The subject then studies several clips, aiming to choose the correct one. Meta-analyses are made of the results of many experiments. Some of these show a significant result while others do not.

Both believers and sceptics are involved in research, and the curious phenomena of the sheep-and-goats effect has been recorded where sceptics' results are less positive than believers'. Believers claim that sceptics obstruct results in any test by their very doubts. Currently a psychologist sceptic and parapsychologist believer are studying this experimenter effect.

Over the years vitriolic criticisms and counter-criticisms have been hurled with more anger than in most scientific debates. Many researchers in the psi field define an event as paranormal *only* if it flouts current scientific understanding, and there is much heady talk of future paradigm shifts in mainline science. Meanwhile the sceptics counterclaim that extraordinary claims require extraordinary proof. PK and ESP would overturn the discoveries of physics, biology and neuroscience, many of them consolidated by thousands of years of technical application. When did minds ever move mountains?

There are a number of other reasons for being cautious when exciting results are headlined in the media. Serious doubts about reliability of data are raised by the difficulties inherent in the particular experimental procedures. One is the problem of producing consistent random events, and this puzzle thwarts code makers and breakers as well as psi researchers. Even random numbers generated by computers are 'pseudorandom'.

Reliance on statistical decision-making is also problematical. Originally statistics were developed to help researchers evaluate whether their results could have occurred by chance. Statistical analyses are now used to search for otherwise undetectable patterns, and in a large sample a very small difference may become statistically significant. In mainstream science there are well-defined variables, but as there are none in parapsychology there is no method of evaluating the presence or absence of psi phenomena, or even whether they exist. Thus any statistical anomaly is assumed by psi researchers to be support for their hypothesis.

Current theories of psi state that its influences do not vary with distance and can operate backwards and forwards in time, which challenges fundamental physics. You may think that our old friends, quantum non-locality and entanglement, come into play here, but no. There are sound scientific reasons that this is most unlikely, though one must always leave open the possibility of new interpretations arising from future data.

Neuroscientists have found that perception, emotion and memory are the result of integration of millions of neurons and their internal mechanisms. Believers in psi must explain *how* extrasensory signals (that is, signals that are not sensed by biological means) influence the brain neurons in the correct sequence and along the known pathways, before they can claim to overturn current neuroscientific research. Some attempts have been made to theorize how this could occur. So far there is no substantive experimental data of the quality that scientists require to back up mainstream theories.

Scientific fields in mainstream science possess a common core of knowledge. Controversies lie at the periphery. Meanwhile parapsychology lacks core constructs, methodologies and demonstrable phenomena that are acceptable even to all parapsychologists. We are left with a range of statistical evidence based on a small number of successful experiments that cannot be replicated. The larger scientific community asks, Is there even enough evidence to prove there is a genuine subject out there?

Laboratory experiments seem a far cry from conditions in which telepathy is said to occur. We may suddenly intuit that harm has come to a loved one and later find this is true. In contrast, we have many such fears that turn out to be false. Meaningful coincidences are very common.

| Extrasensory perception (ESP, telepathy) | The passage of information from one mind to another through an unknown channel. No mechanisms known to physics (such as sound or light waves), chemistry or neuroscience are involved in this or psychokinesis. |

Ganzfeld	German for whole field.
Hypnagogic imagery	A very vivid experience on the border of sleep.
Parapsychology	The study of unusual (anomalous) human experiences.
Psychokinesis (PK, telekinesis)	The ability of minds to affect matter by non-physical means.

Religious experiences

When Sir Alistair Hardy set up the Religious Experience Research Unit (RERU) in Oxford in 1969 anyone who said they heard voices or saw lights or visions was well on the way to the funny farm. One symptom of schizophrenia is the hearing of disembodied voices.

The positive response of the RERU to such experiences made them more respectable. Recently epidemiological studies in the USA and the Netherlands have shown that one in ten people admit to hearing voices. As the incidence of schizophrenia in the population is far lower, doubt is being cast on the reliability of using this phenomenon as a symptom of mental disorder. All of us have inner speech, so perhaps some people experience it as coming from an external source without being mentally ill.

The RERU is now the Religious Experience Research Centre (RERC), and its data store is held at Lampeter, the University of Wales. Testimonies collected since 1969 provide a valuable research base. Early research classified the experiences as visual (visions, illumination, feeling of unity, out-of-body experiences), auditory, tactile, inward sensations and sense of a Presence. Since the RERU was set up, a large number of experiences has been catalogued worldwide. It is not easy to be certain of the numbers, but a rough estimate is that a third of all people have such experiences to a lesser or greater degree. Most of those reported are positive and may be life-changing, but a few are negative. Be aware that self-reporting is notoriously unreliable in the latter area for obvious reasons.

Scientists have been searching for the seat of the soul for centuries in the strangest of places, and brains are the top favourite today. There are some interesting discoveries. The limbic system is important, because early Alzheimer's disease often cripples this region and some sufferers report a loss in religious interest. Temporal lobe stimulation, both artificial and during epilepsy, can cause intense spiritual experiences. The left frontal lobe in particular seems to produce a natural high under certain conditions. We also know that some chemicals, whether artificial or produced by the body, bring about religious feelings. Some people never have such experiences, but this may merely be due to the genetic variability among humans.

A godspot in the brain raises interesting possibilities. Do other animals have such a site? Is it an end to the idea that a God puts an immortal soul into us at a particular moment? Do atheists have a godspot? If there is a God out there has he, or perhaps she, designed some of us specially to reveal heavenly information? And, very importantly, are these experiences trustworthy or ethical? Remember the story of Dan at the beginning of this chapter. He is not the only one to murder at the request of his God.

With this in mind we move on to a recent study. Unusual near-death experiences (NDEs) are frequently reported by the media. Recently the archives of the RERC were reassessed for NDEs along with later testimonies. NDEs are fairly consistently described in terms of entering a dark tunnel, meeting a being of light identified as a deceased relative or a religious figure, receiving comfort and strength and being ordered back to life. The identity of the religious figure depends on the culture of the experiencer. Non-Western accounts often report on a period of darkness rather than a tunnel. Some testimonies describe a negative experience of a place of fear and punishment. A number of people claim they actually leave their body (out-of-body experience or OBE). They perceive doctors and nurses tending them, but from a different vantage point such as the ceiling.

What is the evidence that people do actually leave their body? Unfortunately much of the evidence is found to be anecdotal. The experiencer often claims other people will support them, but they fail to do so. One particular story concerned a blind person who 'saw' significant details of her operating team's clothing while under anaesthetic. This whole story, including the person herself, were later found to be invented, and to date there is no clear-cut evidence of accurate perception during either an NDE or an OBE.

Meanwhile the neuroscientific model explains the experience of tunnels as a common feature of epilepsy, migraine, meditation and the influence of hal-lucinogenic drugs. Appearances of tunnels, spirals and lattices could well lie in the structure of the visual cortex, especially when disruption due to drugs or lack of oxygen causes random firing of neurons. Computer simulations of a dying brain replicate a dark tunnel with a growing light at the end. There are also explanations for the feeling of speeding through the tunnel. Psycho-logically it's likely that these occurences are self-interpreted and put into a life narrative which reflects the subject's upbringing and social influences, and this adds to the difficulties of analysis. As evidence for a soul that departs this life at death for another realm, NDEs leave much to be desired.

It is not at all certain that religious experiences provide reliable information about a spirit world. Their ethical content is highly variable, a phenomenon well understood by religious leaders who have always analysed the content of visions before approving them. Lady Julian of Norwich was cautious in explaining her rather heretical visions in terms of the Christian understand-ing of the fourteenth and early fifteenth century (*Revelations of Divine Love*).

Scientific discoveries don't necessarily deny the possibility that God or other spiritual beings are in touch with us through these natural means. Neither neuroscientific nor psychological models include the well-attested fact that sometimes such experiences change the whole orientation of the recipient's life. Certain people interpret the NDE as a call to service before they really die. Those who touch eternity say they lose all fear of death. Good, caring and honest men and women, those we consider spiritual leaders, often begin their career with an experience of God.

CONCLUSIONS

We haven't found the underlying Reality, we have only seen its footprints across the cosmos. The universe is too vast, explosive and dynamic for even our excellent brains to encompass, yet it constantly reminds us it is our home; we live under the shelter of Reality's wing. By tracing these five footprints we have unearthed amazing qualities – intelligibility, creativity, intelligence, personality, free will, justice and compassion – all intrinsic to our universe and based on those initial physical, chemical and evolutionary constraints.

Creatures have evolved which can make a conscious decision whether or not to comply with requirements of justice and love.

Religious leaders have emphasized the importance of our choice. They highlight the need for compassion and respect for all life, and advocate self-sacrifice for the good of others. Non-believers take a somewhat different stance, stressing the need for self-care as well as a commitment to the welfare of others. This recognition of responsibility is very precious – as far as we know it is unique to humans in the universe.

Meanwhile Reality continually bombards our senses with its reminders. The dance of a leaf falling to earth in autumn to feed the next generation of minute lives is Reality's 'Here am I' to us. We see Reality in the concern of ants for their larvae when their nest is disturbed or the anxiety of a ewe for her lost lamb. We hear Reality in birdsong and jazz, in the laughter of friends and parents' babytalk to their infant. We experience its deep compassion in the concern of strangers. Reality is known in every human, especially in those with an open heart. That openness can be found in anyone, whatever their status or beliefs. Occasionally people have even found fuller meaning to life in pain and grief, for here too love sometimes works its magic of peace and hope.

IDEAS FOR DISCUSSION

1 Read Fox's book and look into other evidence for near-death experiences. What is your opinion of them?
2 Read Bowker's book and consider how religions have tackled the problem of suffering.
3 Compare the letters from prison written by the Christian Bonhoeffer and the Muslim Jamali. Comment on their differences and similarities.
4 How would you reconcile the following:
   The Christian belief that souls are embodied and both will be resurrected together.
   The general belief that there is a bodiless entity (spirit/soul) that survives death.

The lack of any evidence for such an entity in our current understanding of consciousness.

5   Religious experiences include the impulse to harm others or oneself. Are the experiences due to an outside entity (god, devil or other spirit) or psychological make-up?

6   Can religious experiences be used as data to support a philosophy of revelation from God?

7   Read an anthropologist's description of spiritual beliefs in another culture (e.g. Descola, Chapter 3). Compare their beliefs with your own.

8   Look into the use of exorcism to remove the influence of evil spirits.

9   Read Alcock et al. and debate the views of pro- and anti-para-psychologists. Read Blackmore. Why did she leave the field of parapsychology?

10   Read Ward's book. Is the possession of a soul essential for morality?

11   Consider the hypothesis of Drees, and of Dawkins (*The Selfish Gene*), that only the material world exists, and examine their explanation of the evolution of human religious traditions. These views are quite widespread. What is your own opinion and what do you base it on?

12   Check out the websites and their links and enjoy the opposing views.

REFERENCES AND FURTHER READING

Websites

www.aspr.com   American Society for Psychical Research
www.gold.ac.uk/apru   Anomalistic Psychology Research Unit, Goldsmith's College, University of London
www.csicop.org   Committee for the Scientific Investigation of Claims of the Paranormal (CSICOP)

moebius.psy.ed.ac.uk   Koestler Parapsychology Unit, University of Edinburgh

www.spr.ac.uk   Society of Psychical Research (UK)

www.randi.org   James Randi site locates fraud and inaccuracies in the psi world

www.lamp.ac.uk   Religious Experience Research Centre (RERC) at Lampeter College, University of Wales

www.rhine.org   Rhine Research Centre investigates telepathy, precognition, healing, etc.

www.skeptics.org.uk   *Skeptic*. UK-based magazine exposing pseudo-science

Books

James Alcock, J Burns and A Freeman, eds, 2003, *Psi Wars* (*Journal of Consciousness Studies*, 10 no. 6–7), Exeter: Imprint Academic. A collection of papers by pro- and anti-psi researchers.

Susan Blackmore, 1986, *The Adventures of a Parapsychologist*, New York: Prometheus Books

Dietrich Bonhoeffer, 1992, *Letters and Papers from Prison*, trans. Reginald Fuller, Frank Clarke et al., London: SCM Press

John Bowker, 1970, *Problems of Suffering in Religions of the World*, Cambridge: Cambridge University Press

Laurence Brown, 1988, *The Psychology of Religion*, London: SPCK

W Drees, 1996, *Religion, Science and Naturalism*, Cambridge: Cambridge University Press

Mark Fox, 2003, *Religion, Spirituality and the Near-Death Experience*, London: Routledge

Sir Alister C. Hardy, 1979, *The Spiritual Nature of Man*, Oxford: Clarendon Press

John Hick, 1999, *The Fifth Dimension*, Oxford: One World

M F Jamali, 1965, *Letters on Islam*, London: Oxford Univesity Press

William James, 1902, *The Varieties of Religious Experience*, London: Collins

Keith Ward, 1992, *In Defence of the Soul*, Oxford: One World

Part 2

Science and Religion

We turn from our brief survey of some current scientific discoveries to look at the historical development of science/technology and religion and their changing relationship in Chapters 5 and 6. Currently scientific discoveries are challenging the ways in which religions express their ideas, and Chapter 7 looks at the Christian response. Chapter 8 considers some of the problems facing our world today, and the part that world religions and science can play in tackling them sensitively.

5

Remember the Ancestors

We have seen in Part 1 how living creatures deal with the problem of gathering enough energy for growth and movement, repair and reproduction. We have noted that all of us live on a planet with limited resources, so population growth in any species will be restricted by competition, disease and famine. We humans (scientifically the genus *Homo*) have secured large quantities of these resources due to our natural endowments. We have exceptional powers of dexterity, excel at cooperation and have first-class intelligence and memory. Our technical skills are based on experiences covering thousands of years.

This chapter explains how we came to be so successful, but also how the solutions we devised have themselves resulted in the original difficulty returning in a new form. Our ingenuity found further solutions, and so technology has developed piecemeal. Originally there was no body of scientific knowledge based on experiment and observation. Instead there was ad hoc know-how, much of it based on quite erroneous principles, and it was not until *1500 CE* that Europeans began to develop the *scientific method* on which modern science is so successfully based (see Chapter 6). From earliest times technology and religion developed together, but manual work was gradually relegated to an inferior position, although technological skill continued to support religious and social structures.

First we shall look at some worldwide achievements of the *Homo* species in general. Then we home in to a particular area, the Near East, to look at the development of some early civilizations. The three monotheistic religions of Judaism, Christianity and Islam originate here. We then follow the fortunes of Christianity as it becomes the major religion of the Roman Empire, and continues to develop as that empire declines with the loss of much of its technological expertise. Returning to the Near East we look at Islamic development of its technological inheritance from Egypt, Greece, Rome, Persia, India and the Far East, and how this knowledge began to filter into western Europe during the late Middle Ages.

- **Hunting, fishing and gathering**
- **Farmers**
- **Wandering tribes and ziggurats**
- **Sea People and Assyrian hordes**
- **Greeks and Romans**
- **Decaying Empire**
- **Islam and Muhammad**
- **The European Middle Ages**

1500 CE	In the following chapters BP, before present, is used to indicate approximate dates for very ancient remains. CE, current era, and BCE, before current era, refer to the dating system based on Jesus' birth, synonymous with AD and BC.
Scientific method	The change from philosophical discussion about the world to a reliance on observation, theory and experiments.

HUNTING, FISHING AND GATHERING

- **Fire**
- **Wise men**

Fire

The scattered fossils of ancient members of the genus *Homo* make classification into species unreliable. *Homo habilis*, *H. erectus* and *H. sapiens* (us) are the three species generally (but not universally) recognized. They developed speech, so now information could be conveyed in a new, faster way than genetically. Only *Homo sapiens*, modern man, exists today.

Homo habilis left stone tools at Olduvai Gorge in Tanzania about 2.2 to 1.6 million years ago. *Homo erectus* (1.6 to 0.5 million years ago) was probably the first to leave Africa for Eurasia. Their tools were more sophisticated than those of *H. habilis*. The invention of cooking and altering the state of clay and stones by heating may date to this period, but early remains of controlled fire are controversial. Many proposed hearths may be fires left by lightning strikes, and there is a big difference between using a natural fire and being able to light and control one yourself. The control of fire is one of the oldest and most important achievements of humans. The success of *H. habilis* may be due to cooking high-protein meat, so killing harmful organisms and improving digestibility.

The possible religion of these early humans can only be the subject of speculation. No doubt they wondered about their universe as much as we do. Probably they had stories to explain life and death, terrifying storms, savannah fires, volcanoes, friendly plants yielding food, and the wanderings of deer and elephant. Much later stories celebrate the capture of fire from the gods (Prometheus), but we cannot know whether our earliest ancestors had such beliefs.

Wise men

Archaic *Homo sapiens* appears on the scene about 500,000 BP. They used similar stone tools to *H. habilis*. The Lion Cavern in Swaziland, Africa, has been mined for ochre for millennia, possibly since 120,000 BP. Ochre is iron ore, red, yellow and brown. Our ancestors used it in burials and cave paintings but possibly in other ways as well. Some modern human societies mix the powder with grease to protect their bodies from insects and sun, others use it as a medicine or salve for sores when mixed with spit or water. It is used both magically and practically for covering newborn babies. Ochre may have served all these functions for our ancestors too.

Our ancestors followed their prey animals in the search for food and water. They probably made comparisons between the changing seasons and movements of sun, stars and planets across the sky. On their journey they collected small game, tubers, fruits, nuts and grass grains, noting where, when and how the plants grew. They would have used plants as medicines and poisons. As they moved through the bush they would pick up salmonellosis and scrub typhus from insect vectors, and diseases like bubonic plague, anthrax and tetanus from the animals they hunted and ate. Their skeletons are robust, so their general diet was good. Some severe wounds show healing, so there was excellent community care.

Neanderthals are related to modern humans, and their remains date from 230,000 to 36,000 BP. A number of their burials include remains of flowers, showing respect and concern for their dead. The flowers they left have medicinal properties like yarrow, hollyhock, groundsel and ragwort. Neanderthals had certainly mastered fire. They have left artefacts in deep caves in southern France, so they must have used lamps and *torches* during exploration. Genetic checks suggest Neanderthals did not contribute to the DNA of modern humans, and their extinction is still a mystery. But by 33,000 BP, modern *Homo sapiens* were the only survivors of the *Homo* lines.

From this time on artefacts show rapid advances in technology, art, social organization and trade. Quarrying dates back some fifty thousand years, but mines appear now, the earliest in Egypt. First signs of ceramic technology are found in the Czech Republic, dated 26,000 years ago, long before even the earliest Japanese pottery (12,500 BP). At Dolni Vestonice there are numerous fragments of fired clay figurines, both human and animal. The fracturing shows that the firing technique caused explosive breakage. Modern experimenters were surprised to find they needed considerable expertise to shatter their copies, so possibly the making and then controlled destruction had some sort of ritualistic meaning. Possible lunar markings are found on a carved stone dating from this period, and there are artefacts from central Siberia which appear to predict both lunar and solar eclipses 24,000 years ago.

There are very few remains that give clues to religious beliefs. The oldest known figurine to be accepted by professional archaeologists is at least a quarter of a million years old. The Berekhat Ram figurine was found at the site of that name in the Golan Heights, Israel, lying between two ancient and datable basalt flows. It is a small female-shaped pebble with artificially added grooves. From Halle, Germany, come four notched bones, possibly pre-*Homo sapiens*. Close analysis showed that the markings on one bone were made by the same tool. It is possible they are symbols used for communication.

The Red Lady of Gower, Wales, is a skeleton dated 22,000 years old. She is actually a he. The original discoverers thought that as he had been buried with seashell necklaces he must be a female, which tells us more about the archaeologists' preconceptions than the corpse. He had been a healthy young man. His friends had scattered red ochre on his body and buried him with a mammoth's skull, carved bones, antlers and those necklaces, all highly valuable commodities.

We are unable to access the religious understanding of these people as we cannot decipher the meaning behind their cave art or burial practices. We can only infer that religion was important to them and that it used practices we would call sympathetic magic connected with the mystery of birth, summoning beasts to be killed, injuring enemies at a distance or celebrating a journey into death with grave goods.

> Torches   Wood or other inflammable material dipped in animal fat or oil and then lit.

FARMERS

The term Neolithic or New Stone Age is used when an economy's mainstay is tending crops and domesticated livestock, prior to the use of bronze. The date of this gradual change varies throughout the world, and each continent has its individual history. In the Near East the Neolithic period began as the last Ice Age ended, about 10,000 years ago, and ended in 3500 BCE when bronze became widely used. The Fertile Crescent of the Near East is the bow-shaped region stretching from the Persian Gulf along the Tigris-Euphrates river system through greater Syria along the eastern Mediterranean and then south into the Nile valley in Africa.

Why did people first settle here? One of the main problems of farming is that soil fertility decreases as the nutrients are removed in successive crops. 'Slash, burn and then move to the next "field"' systems allow fallow time for natural replenishment, but such a system can only support small villages. Adding dung is another method of returning nutrients, but it also encourages infestations like worms in livestock and humans. So early civilizations grew along large rivers, where the yearly floods renewed soil minerals by dumping disease-free silt.

Other advantages include a warmer year-round climate than that of Europe or northern Asia, so crops could be grown continuously. Also there was a wide variety of plants and animals available for domestication. There are at least 200,000 species of flowering and fruiting plants in the world, but only a few thousand are edible. Of these a few hundred are eaten regularly. The grasses emmer wheat, einkorn wheat and barley, the pulses pea, chickpea and lentil, and bitter vetch and flax for rope and linen grew (and still grow) wild in the Fertile Crescent. They were domesticated by continual breeding and selection over thousands of years, and modern varieties are very different from their wild counterparts. Today 80% of the world's annual crop production consists of plants domesticated thousands of years ago.

Many animals cannot be bred successfully in captivity, and some continents like the Americas and Australia are less fortunate in the range of animals available for domestication. Western Asia and North Africa are the home of dogs, goats, sheep, cattle and pigs. These amenable species were bred to improve those qualities most useful to humans, like steadiness in haulage or increased milk, wool, hide and meat production. Farmers rejected flighty or aggressive stock from breeding lines. In return the animals gained protection from predators, easy access to food and water and good care when sick or wounded. There was probably a mixed type of economy, with some villagers moving back into a more nomadic life when food was scarce locally.

It sounds idyllic. But agriculture brought its own problems. Extensive crop growing provides easy food for other animals and plant diseases and, just as they do today, insect plagues of locusts, aphids, weevils, caterpillars and midges devoured the crops. Eelworms, slugs and cutworms munched through them. Fungi, bacteria and viruses flourished, known picturesquely as blights, rots, rusts, smuts, yellows, mildews and wilts. Safe storage from insects and larger animals like rats has always been a major problem.

Increased carbohydrate intake at the expense of meat protein was not a sufficient diet for the general population. Some years river flooding was inadequate and dreaded famine stalked the villages. Where could settled communities turn for food when everyone was hungry? Raiding parties become more common.

Human diseases increased as well. Studies of ancient human remains from different parts of the world show a decline in health as people begin to adopt plant-growing and animal domestication. Out of thirteen regional studies, ten showed a reduction in average life expectancy once the community was fully sedentary. Close contact with domesticated animals brought rabies, leprosy, tuberculosis and diphtheria. Milk can transmit at least thirty diseases. Slash, burn, dig agriculture around the villages disrupted the environment, so that diseases carried by insect vectors increased. Malaria, *schistosomiasis* and tuberculosis are still three of humanity's worst diseases. Poisonous fungal spores in wheat and barley also brought sickness. Coprolites, fossil dung, show an increasing worm burden. There were occupational hazards like malformed wrists among grinders of corn.

As societies spread, technology advanced even without the use of bronze and iron. Probable pre-writing symbols in cave paintings date back to 10,000 BP. People needed to count their herds and weigh their grain so mathematics developed, and by 8,000 BP early accounting used clay tokens. Different shapes represented lambs, he-goats and ewes in lamb. Ancient bones dating from the beginning of this period have groupings of marks, probably aids to calculation.

Religion was closely bound up with farming practices. Many religious sites appear to be aligned to movement of heavenly bodies since astronomy was vital for the calculation of times and seasons, the expected time of river flooding and the appropriate time for harvesting. Religious ceremonies were well developed around the Mediterranean. We see the gradual growth of elaborate hierarchies, with priests or priestesses and village leaders receiving support from the farmers and craftsmen. There are tantalizing glimpses of early female-based religions. Huge numbers of female figurines and feminized clay models of temples have been unearthed in the ruins of circular stone temples. Some ancient paintings of the goddess show her giving birth to rams and bulls.

One of the oldest towns is Jericho in southern *Palestine*, founded near a spring. The earliest settlers, about 10,000 BCE, were possibly semi-nomadic. They left only post-hole patterns of insubstantial dwellings. By 7000 BCE Jericho was a permanent settlement with a stone tower and massive walls. There are no remains of domestic animals and animal bones are chiefly gazelle. Barley and emmer wheat had been domesticated. Later house floors were made of lime plaster and stained and polished in red, orange or pink. Often the skulls of the dead were removed and then remodelled with plaster to rebuild the features in a sophisticated and highly technical manner. There are also painted lime plaster statues modelled over reeds and twine. Figurines of people and animals show an understanding of scale, dimensions and perspective. There was a 500-year gap in site occupation around the sixth millenium, probably due to climate change. When settlement occurs again, pottery appears.

Palestine	The Graeco–Roman name for the southern part of the greater Syrian region on the Fertile Crescent. Canaan in ancient documents is somewhat smaller than the territory defined by Joshua in Numbers, but the two names are often used synonymously.
Schistosomiasis	Lung, liver and bladder infection by tiny parasites.

WANDERING TRIBES AND ZIGGURATS

- **Building cities**
- **Nomads in Palestine**

Building cities

The Bronze Age in the Near East covers the period from 3500 to 1200 BCE. In areas best suited for agriculture, settlements grew from villages to the status of small cities. Throughout Palestine archaeologists have unearthed prosperous towns with stone administrative buildings and temples.

One of the most fruitful inventions was the wheel and axle. Cattle could now pull carts with solid wooden wheels and by the second millenium horses were being used in chariots with spoked wheels. Potters used wheels for making graceful jugs, plates and bowls, often highly decorated.

Metal technology advanced as metalworkers began to understand the principles of alloying. Beautiful gold jewellery has been recovered from burials. Small inventions raised the standard of living, like post-and-sockets for hanging doors and spindles for making wool thread.

Trade in surplus produce opened routes between Palestine and Egypt first, later expanding to Turkey, Syria and Mesopotamia. Donkeys were the most popular animals for land transport but dromedaries also carried goods after 1200 BCE. As boat design and building improved more commodities were carried by sea and river. Trade required more sophisticated writing and cumbersome cuneiform was replaced with an alphabetic system during the second millennium. It was essentially similar to the one we use today.

Farming became more specialized. Instead of hand-digging tools, oxen were trained to draw simple wood ploughs strengthened by stone points. They broke up the soil more thoroughly, improving it for plant roots. Farmers built reservoirs for irrigation. They added broad bean, garlic, onion and fenugreek to their crops, and cultivated fruit – olives, dates, pomegranates, figs and grapes. As well as these settled farming communities there were groups practising *transhumance* in hill areas. There were also semi-nomadic groups with sheep and goats who cultivated a small number of plants, and true nomads who moved continuously with their herds, but were linked with the settled zones for water and pasture access. In drought periods some would turn to a more nomadic system, but when the early and late rains were plentiful more would engage in crop-growing.

Judging the time of crop-sowing led to a boom in mathematics. In the third millennium Nile valley priests worked out the year's length to just over 365 days. In Mesopotamia they developed the sexagesimal system of 360° in a circle and 60 minutes in an hour. Architects could calculate right angles by the time the great pyramids near Cairo (c.2600 BCE) and the ziggurat of Ur (2100 BCE) were built. A triangle with sides of units in the ratio 3, 4, 5 will always form a right angle between the sides of three and four units.

Sheep, goats and cattle increased in numbers and farmers tried rather strange methods to improve their stock. In Genesis 30.25–43, Jacob breeds animals with striped or spotted coats by showing peeled branches to goats and sheep on heat. This improbable technique was apparently highly successful.

It can't have been a peaceful period, for defensive walls were continually rebuilt. Nor was life easy for the majority – slavery or serfdom was the lot of most people. By this time some cities were so large they were above the critical threshold required to support herd diseases. Measles, a severe disease of the period, requires a population of several thousand to spread successfully. Such diseases travelled swiftly through crowded, filthy cities, carried by air, water, direct contact and insects.

Transhumance	Seasonal migration of livestock (cattle, sheep and goats). Still practised between valley and high pastures in mountainous areas of Europe.

Nomads in Palestine

The Palestinian system of small city states included well-established laws guaranteeing the position of the local ruler and his family. The rest of the kingdom was employed by him as literate public administrators, artisans, merchants and soldiers. Armies were a mixture of professionals and peasants conscripted as 'cannon fodder'. Peasants also supplied unpaid and untrained labour to the state. Most of their farm produce was paid as tax to the administration, from which they received a minimal return – stored grain in times of famine and some protection from robbers and armies. Some turned to banditry when they lost everything.

During the Bronze Age the stability and economic wealth of Palestine depended on that of its far larger neighbour, Egypt, which prized the Palestinian specialities of wine, olive oil, cattle, wheat and cedar. The Pharaohs of the New Kingdom conquered the area as far as the Euphrates, so Palestine commanded a lucrative position at the junction of several trade routes. Administration and political conditions are detailed in many clay documents and include international trade relations, taxation, price structures and treaties.

The Hebrew scriptures place Israel's early nomadic history in this period – the patriarchs, the move to Egypt and the Exodus four hundred years later (possibly 2200 to 1700 BCE). To date there is no evidence for the Hebrew stories outside the Old Testament and many archaeologists consider they are folktales. Nor is there evidence for Joshua's conquest of highland Palestine, and many cities mentioned were not in existence or had been destroyed far earlier. This does not mean there are no interesting links between Egypt and Palestine, mostly post-dating the Exodus story. In an Egyptian noble's tomb of about 1900 there are wall paintings of Palestinians at the Egyptian court, and the Hyksos rulers of Egypt from 1750 to 1550 were almost certainly from the north. The Amarna letters on stone tablets describe a period of turmoil in Palestine during the fourteenth century when bandits called Hapiru menaced the city states. This is a general term for bandits, and does not specify Hebrews directly. Israel is first mentioned by Pharaoh Merneptah in 1207 BCE as a strong tribal confederacy which he promoted to oversee tribal interests on the border zone between Egypt and the rival Hittite Empire to the north.

SEA PEOPLE AND ASSYRIAN HORDES

- **Iron Age**
- **Writing the Old Testament**

Iron Age

Though iron-smelting was developed in the fourteenth century, it is not found in common use until 1200 BCE, the start of the Iron Age. Even then it supplemented bronze rather than displacing it. Its later development is due to very different techniques of smelting and working and the higher temperatures required.

By now priestly hierarchies or king-priests guided much of everyday life. They pronounced days for sowing, harvesting and going into battle. They presided over ceremonies concerned with kingly death and diseases like leprosy, and were keepers of religious mysteries and recorders of tribal history and laws.

External sources and local archaeological discoveries corroborate many of the events recorded in the Bible at this time. Egypt and Palestine were both invaded by the Sea People from Greece and Anatolia (in modern Turkey). They were a civilized people, settling along the coast of southern Palestine, where they were named Philistines. Biblical contempt has turned this name into a term of abuse, but they had more expertise in iron-working, building and pottery than the Israelite tribes. They controlled the sea trading routes and began to expand their territory inland around 1000 BCE.

The Israelites lived in the barren hill country east of the coast, and they elected Saul to defend them against encroaching Philistines. David was probably a guerilla leader. As king he expanded the state of Israel to cover most of Palestine. After the death of Solomon in 928 BCE, the kingdom split into northern Israel and southern Judah. As the Assyrians became more powerful and extended their empire westwards, Israel ceased to exist as an independent state. In 625 Babylon took power from Assyria. Jerusalem was destroyed in 587 by Nebuchadnezzar and its people taken to Babylon as slaves. Archaeological remains show extensive burning of Judaean cities. Lachish and Azekah were the last two to fall. The Judaean commander of a military post between the two cities sent an *ostracon* to Lachish. He said he could no longer see the signal fires of Azekah and was waiting, probably in vain, to see those from Lachish.

2 Chronicles 36.16–21 reads like an eye-witness account of the fall of Judah. 'The anger of the Lord burst out against his people and could not be appeased.' The army of Nebuchadnezzer 'spared neither young man nor maiden, neither the old nor the weak; God gave them all into his power . . . And they burnt down the house of God, razed the city wall of Jerusalem . . . until everything was destroyed. Those who escaped the sword . . . became slaves.' Psalm 137 encapsulates their grief and desire for revenge. 'Happy is he who shall seize *your* (Babylon's) children and dash them against the rock!' It summarizes the impotent rage of humans down the ages who have suffered cruelty at the hands of the more powerful.

Most of the deported were skilled artisans and administrators, and some 80% of Jews remained in Judah in drastically impoverished circumstances. In 538 BCE there was little for the exiles to return to and many preferred to settle permanently in Mesopotamia. It was difficult to persuade enough people to return to rebuild Jerusalem.

> Ostracon   A letter written in black ink on potsherd, in this case in alphabetic Hebrew.

Writing the Old Testament

In this period and for many following centuries, natural events were explained as the chaotic activity of various gods. Non-biblical documents record anguished prayers to various deities of wind and storm beseeching them to be calm. The gods brought victory or defeat in war. Homer (ninth century, if he existed) describes the gods discussing the outcome of the Trojan wars in the *Iliad* and *Odyssey*. They judged humans and punished them with plague and famine. In Sophocles' *Oedipus Rex*, written about 420 BCE, the

Thebans are distraught. Blight, plague and abortion ravage the land, sent by the gods as punishment for King Oedipus' sins. The Old Testament continually explains famine, drought, war, plagues and exile as God's punishment for Israel's sins.

The Old Testament is a collection of historical documents, prophetical books and wisdom literature. Very little appears to have been written down until the time of the kings. Some fragments, like Deborah's song, possibly predate David, but the earliest events occurred well over a thousand years before they were drafted. Most of the material that became the Old Testament was probably collected shortly before and during the Exile in Babylon, when it was extensively edited and expounded. Different scrolls contain contradictions, priestly concerns with temple worship loom large and the laws do not cover quite important problems. Compared with other writings of this period, there is no evidence that Israel had a different religion or even special insight into the divine. Creation myths and laws have some marked similarities with those of Mesopotamia.

All the same there are many fascinating details. A huge bronze bowl called the Sea of the Temple required casting. Its circumference was thirty *cubits* and its diameter ten. (1 Kings 7.23–6). This rule of thumb measurement (circumference = 3 × diameter) is close to the accurate one of Archimedes in the third century. Medical and hygienic knowledge of the day is found in Leviticus.

What was the aim of the editors of this collection?

When leading Jews were exiled in Babylonia, they could not accept the taunts of local people comparing their feeble Yahweh with triumphant Babylonian gods. Nor could they accept that their God had punished them unjustly. What was the reason for his destruction of their nation? They searched their documents and concluded that Yahweh, God above all gods, had enrolled them in the great task of bringing enlightenment and peace to the world, and they had failed him. He had reminded them time after time of their covenant by sending famine, drought and plague, but they hadn't listened. The exiled editors raised the hope that Yahweh had not cast them away for ever. Hadn't he led them out of slavery in Egypt with his powerful hand? They listed God's requirements for his reinstated people in minute detail, including sacrifices and an annual national atonement. Loving obedience to these and commitment to justice and mercy would ensure that wars, famine, floods and plagues would never destroy them again. They could still become God's light to the nations.

Other explanations were not available to them. Today we appreciate that their position as a small trading state on the crossroads between much larger nations always rendered them liable to annexation. They were often in hock to their neighbours, and while they craved independence as a sign of God's pleasure, the likelihood of achieving it for long was almost zero. The land was liable to drought because it lacked a large river system like the Nile or Tigris-Euphrates to provide irrigation. Soil was not replenished annually, so it quickly lost fertility while its disease burden increased. Israel was further vulnerable to new diseases spread by traders and armies following the major routes. Internal economic problems were largely due to her own hierarchical system. Rulers, priests and associated administrators expropriated much of the country's wealth. High taxes brought slavery to the poor and sick. There was no safety net of a welfare state and the only help the sick or failing peasant and artisan families could expect was occasional charity. This situation raised the wrath of the prophets, but it was centuries before a comprehensive solution would be envisaged.

Cubit   The cubit is a measurement of length that was based on the length of the forearm. Cubits were variable throughout the region and only slowly became standardized.

GREEKS AND ROMANS

- **Philosophy and technology**
- **Riots in Palestine**

Philosophy and technology

Present-day Western civilization owes much to those of classical Greece and Rome. The period stretches from about 460 BCE when Athenians developed ideas of democratic government to 476 CE when the last emperor of Rome was deposed.

Both Greeks and Romans developed and cherished parks and gardens. The Romans in particular had a great love of the land and many documents give advice on farming methods. They developed green manuring, the ploughing-in of lupins. *Grafting* preserved valued fruit trees. But buying and selling was concentrated in the hands of the wealthy, and farmers and artisans lost any power they had over real wealth. The poor and sick lived in a chronic state of debt with slavery a constant hazard. Some turned to brigandage, and tyrant rulers were always concerned about uprisings once iron weapons became increasingly available. Crucifixion was a popular punishment meted out by both Greeks and Romans.

The Greeks introduced concepts important for modern science and philosophy and throughout the period there were great advances in geometry and in technical understanding. In the fourth century BCE Aristotle, tutor to Alexander the Great, proposed rigorous scientific procedures and the use of dialectic in reasoning. These ideas became the foundation for the scientific approach of the Renaissance. Work on conic sections at his research school, the Lyceum, provided the basis for Kepler and Newton's work on planetary orbits (see Chapter 6). Archimedes in the third century developed an early form of the calculus nearly two thousand years before Newton, and worked out the different densities of materials by immersion in water.

Mathematical and technical skills were combined with religious philosophies. Pythagorean physics included a mystical bias towards a type of contemplation enabling the practitioner to reach a state like nirvana.

Purification of metals suggested purification of human souls by detachment. When the Greeks invented an arrow-shooting machine, Zeno proved logically that an arrow can't move at all. Fortunately it wasn't considered necessary at that time for him to subject himself to a practical test. For Plato change was synonymous with degeneration, and the world of matter inferior to that of ideas.

The city of Alexandria in Egypt was particularly renowned for its learning and extensive library. Philo, a Jewish philosopher and theologian born there about 13 BCE, studied the Greek classics and attempted to synthesize faith and reason. Hebrew was a foreign language to him; he wrote in Greek. He conceived of a God perfect in form and spirit, and wondered why he should create lowly matter. So he resurrected a Presocratic idea of a mediator, the Logos, who was the idea of ideas, the first-begotten son of the uncreated father, a second god who held together the great chain of being. These concepts entered Christianity by way of John's Gospel.

Technological discoveries were many, and chemistry developed by trial and – mainly – error. At least nine metals could be prepared from ores, including mercury, for by now the basic principles of oxidation and reduction were understood. Alkalis, acids and alcohol were in use and beautiful glass articles were blown and decorated. Proficiency in glass-blowing provided the skills necessary for the later Arabian invention of distillation. The Romans worked out the formula for cement (lime and volcanic ash). With this strong material they constructed domes, arches and arched vaults in aqueducts, amphitheatres and basilicas, but the recipe was lost as the Empire decayed.

Compound pulley systems, the windlass and even a water-driven organ with stops and keys were invented. In the second century CE a rudimentary steam engine was constructed. Enough information was available by then for a transition to an industrial revolution, but as the economy relied on slavery there was no market for the large-scale manufacture of goods.

By the beginning of the period trade routes extended around the Mediterranean and across Asia. To facilitate trade the Lydians (part of modern Turkey) first used stamped bullion as money about 650 BCE. 'As rich as Croesus' remembers one of its kings. The Greek historian Heraclitus recorded the silk route from China across the Eurasian Steppe in the sixth century BCE. Trade and war rely on map-making, and the size and circumference of the earth was first calculated 200 years before Jesus' birth. Better surveying was possible using mirrors.

The ancient Egyptians had developed latrines and other useful ideas on hygiene. Greeks and Romans continued this tradition and Hippocrates of Cos (c.400 BCE) based his treatises on clinical observations. One idea that persisted for centuries was that of the four humours in the body, blood, bile, phlegm and black bile, all influenced by stars and planets. In the second century CE, Galen's theories became the foundation of Islamic and later medieval European medicine. So little was known about the body and diseases that most medical theories were of small practical value and plagues continued to disrupt society, some so seriously that they assisted in the collapse of Roman rule.

As the Roman Empire weakened it was split into an eastern section ruled from Constantinople (modern Istanbul) and a western one ruled by Rome. Much classical knowledge was lost to Europe as the western Empire disintegrated due to the inroads of Germanic tribes, but it was carried eastwards by displaced people.

> Grafting   A twig from the chosen tree is bound firmly into a cut section of the rootstock until they unite. Most modern cultivated roses and fruit trees are grafted.

Riots in Palestine

In the fourth century BCE, Alexander the Great took control of Palestine when he conquered the Persians. After his death infighting between the Seleucids (Syria) and the descendants of Ptolemy (Egypt) brought unrest to Palestine because it lay between the rivals. Under the influence of the Seleucids Greek technology filtered into Palestine.

Greek gods and goddesses were anathema to orthodox Jews and they rebelled when the Temple in Jerusalem was rededicated to Zeus. Under the leadership of the Maccabees the Jews became independent, and over the following 79 years they even expanded their territory. Then the Hasmonaean monarchy attempted complete control by combining the offices of high-priest and king, which led to internal power struggles and further uprisings. When the Pharisees called on the help of their neighbouring Seleucid monarch he settled the matter with mass crucifixions. Rome drove the Seleucids out of Syria between 67 and 63 BCE, and the Hasmonaean kingdom was reduced to Judaea and Idumaea. Pompey entered the Holy of Holies in the Temple in 63 BCE and the high priest just managed to avert another mass revolt.

Roman rule caused great civil unrest. Religious leaders like the Pharisees were looking for a Maccabean-style saviour to bring independence and lead the nation into their covenanted inheritance as the Chosen People. Israel would then execute God's judgement on the heathen prior to the promised reign of peace and joy for all nations. The leaders expected such a saviour to come from their own ranks, so they didn't welcome the many popular messiahs of this time, one of whom was Jesus. Jesus was doubly threatening because he said the Messiah was king of peace, in opposition to the Pharisees' expectations. He prophesied that their insistence on a violent ejection of the Romans would bring destruction (Matthew 24.15–22). So it turned out, some thirty years later. Jesus also taught people to break some of the holy laws (Matthew 12.1–14). In the Pharisees' eyes this was tantamount to disobeying God, and would lead to a punishment at least as severe as the exile in Babylon. It was better, they said, that one man should die rather than the whole nation be destroyed.

The Jews revolted in 66 CE and Jerusalem was destroyed. The *Qumran* site was also demolished then. Jews holed up in Herod's fortress-palace at Masada in 73/4 CE committed suicide rather than surrender. In 132 CE the Jews rebelled again and were defeated. Jerusalem was renamed Aelia Capitolina and occupied by gentiles. Jews were only permitted to enter once yearly on the anniversary of its destruction to lament at the site of Herod's Temple.

Qumran   The monastery of a strict religious group of Jews, the Essenes, who moved to Qumran about 150 BCE because of their disagreement with the Hasmonaean assumption of high-priestly power. Scrolls found there in 1947 are the earliest versions of many biblical books, and an important resource for scholarship.

DECAYING EMPIRE

Early Christians expected Jesus' imminent return, but as the years passed they began to collect material about him for future generations. Christianity spread first among the Jewish communities scattered throughout the Roman Empire. Gradually it became a distinctive religion in its own right, though there were many local variations. In 313 the Emperor Constantine gave Christianity equal status with other cults, but there was bitter infighting over beliefs. In 325 the Emperor ordered a grand council at Nicaea and the Nicene Creed was agreed. This was strictly Trinitarian and bishops who refused to sign were excommunicated. Some years later the canon of the New Testament was decided and most alternative writings destroyed. Many heretics fled east to friendlier countries, some as far as China. Others settled in Syria, Persia and India, carrying classical learning that was eventually incorporated into Islamic science.

Once the Christians were free of earlier policies of persecution, they used their power to mob pagans. Hypatia, a Greek mathematician, was stoned to death by a Christian rabble and laws were passed during Constantine's reign abominating Jews as murderers of God's Son.

Christians now built grand churches and developed an elaborate organization which held European society together during the decay of the Roman Empire and for centuries afterwards. There was a professional priesthood, with patriarchs ruling over the largest communities in Constantinople, Antioch, Alexandria and Rome. The Roman papacy claimed supremacy through St Peter, which was not acceptable in Constantinople. As the old Empire divided into east and west, so their Christian communities developed different views on major topics like the status of human beings. In the fourth century Augustine developed the doctrine that humans are born morally warped. The western Church welcomed this approach, which was continued by Thomas Aquinas in the Middle Ages and passed into Protestantism at the Reformation. The eastern Church preferred Irenaeus' approach – humans are born ignorant rather than flawed.

The early Church Fathers threshed out philosophical problems, extolling virginity and the ascetic life over marriage. Sexuality was a product of the Fall in Eden and required strict control. Mysticism was important and Tertullian could say, 'I believe because it is absurd'. Inspiration and revelation became a higher source of truth than reason or the senses. The whole duty of humans was to live a life worthy of God in this vale of suffering. Technology was of much less importance, since it could never assist in humanity's eternal salvation.

ISLAM AND MUHAMMAD

Islam was the driving force behind the development of Arabic civilization. At its widest extent in the eighth century it spread from Spain and along the North African coast to the river Indus. After the eleventh century the economic system gradually decayed. Islam's attraction lies in its appeal for universal brotherhood. It requires simple but strict personal rituals, and offers a sure hope of Paradise. Both rich and poor were, and are, devoted to Muhammad's memory and the Qur'an.

Islam was popular but militant, and it took over the old eastern Roman Empire and its classical learning. Many new capital cities grew up and their cultivated middle classes discussed scientific and religious theories enthusiastically. Travellers along the trade routes carried ancient wisdom and new discoveries from Spain in the west to the furthest reaches of China and Korea. They left accurate accounts of their journeys through Asia and North and Central Africa at a time when Europeans were being deluged with mere legends of fabulous lands.

Islamic scientists drew upon available sources from Greece and Rome, Egypt, Persia, India and China, and made major advances in many fields. They introduced the concept of zero in mathematics, and replaced clumsy Roman numerals with flexible Arabic ones developed from Hindu origins. Indian mathematicians invented early algebra, so simplifying computation. This was used extensively by the Arabs. The Muslim Empire inherited the keen astronomical observations of earlier Babylon. Many calculations since have relied on this valuable resource. Islamic mathematicians used trigonometry to improve both surveying and astronomy.

Medicine was practical. Advice included cooking and diet as well as hygiene and the best way of coping with different climates in the extensive

Muslim Empire. The Islamic world improved on their inheritance of Egyptian skill in dealing with eye diseases. They studied eye structure and used crystal and glass lenses for magnification and reading. The scientist Alhazen (*c.*1038) wrote a thesis that was used as the basis for telescopes in the European Renaissance.

Scientific chemistry was founded by Islamic scientists and metallurgists. Localized chemical industries produced soda, alum, iron sulphate and nitre which were exported across the known world, and used particularly in textile manufacturing. They expanded theories which later fed into Western ideas, providing a good working basis for chemistry up till the eighteenth century.

Most Islamic scientific books followed the rational approach of modern science, but there were also mystical aspects incorporating Plato's magical numbers and Aristotle's theories on hierarchies. The Persian Sufi mystical poet of the thirteenth century Jalalu'l-Din Rumi describes evaporation as the powerful spirit of the wind sucking up water from a tank. He was not using poetic simile, but writing from within a particular world belief in *djinn*. Such ideas superseded scientific ones. Scholars now subscribed to the principle of two truths as Christianity did – spiritual truth obtained from revealed writing and tradition is superior to reasoned truth. Scientific theories could no longer be advanced and gradually scientists became wandering scholars attached to local dynasties.

In 1453 Constantinople, the capital of the Byzantine Empire, fell to the Ottoman Turks. Scholars now fled westwards taking their learning and fresh ideas in religion, scientific method and the arts.

| Djinn, plural of djinni | Supernatural spirits which can take human or animal form. |

THE EUROPEAN MIDDLE AGES

- **Feudalism**
- **Scholars**

Feudalism

European feudal society was based on obligations in both directions between ruler and ruled. Justice was grounded on the understanding that all, lord and king as well as peasant, will be judged by God. Trials included the judicial ordeal, first mentioned in Numbers 5.11–31, where women accused of adultery had to drink truth-water. In the Middle Ages defendants might have to walk across red-hot plough shares or hold hot iron. In the thirteenth century the practice was abandoned because results were often ambiguous and it was considered impious to force God to respond to a human test.

The Church liturgy included many agricultural themes. The fasting of Lent was fixed at the time of year when food supplies were running low after the long winter. Simple systems of annual crop rotations were devised which included manuring, but much of the old Roman expertise had been lost. Starvation was a constant threat for poor peasants. Maximum yield was merely five times the meagre sowing rate and the grains produced were thin and poor. Blight and rusts decimated the growing crop and weeds like thistles and ragwort obliterated it. Old wheat and barley varieties shed grain easily from the ear, so much was lost before harvest. More was eaten by the lord's pigeons. Storage was as difficult as ever. The paucity of animal food required older cattle and toothless sheep (crones) to be slaughtered in the autumn and salted for winter food.

The Church commended patience to the peasants. God sent these things to test faith. Meanwhile monasteries flourished. In England they turned to highly profitable sheep farming and exported long wool to Flemish weavers. They grew vines, making a wine so vinegary it had to be sweetened with honey and flavoured with spices. *Will Langland* wrote his 'dream' of Piers Ploughman, a type of Christ who reproaches the wealthy of church, monastery for their exploitation of the poor. He does not spare the beggar to be a cripple either. An impoverished farmer tells Piers how small strip. 'I will put on my working clothes, all darned and patched, my leggings and my old gloves to keep my fingers warm; and I'll hang my hopper around my neck . . . with a *bushel* of rye inside.'

Meanwhile urban life prospered wherever guilds protected workers from exploitation, but there was no defence against the old problems of poor sanitation and infections. The most severe was the Black Death, bubonic plague, which rapidly spread across the terrified countries of Europe in the 1340s, leaving about a quarter of the population dead.

It was a time of warfare when magnificent castles were built across Europe, so massive that they could be defended by a few bowmen. Religious antagonism was directed against the Islamic faith because Islam controlled access to the Holy Land. Popes advertised Crusades as a pilgrimage, with the full remission of penalties for sins. Fighting was bitter, and one observer said about the indiscriminate sack of Jerusalem in 1099, 'the pyres they made (of the corpses) were like pyramids'. The scholar and saint Anselm condemned this wanton slaughter.

Probably the only long-term military gain from the Crusades was control of the Mediterranean sea routes. The relationship between Islam and Christianity was soured for centuries, even till today. The Crusaders were not too troubled about sacking the cities of eastern Orthodox Christianity, and Constantinople was plundered during the Fourth Crusade. This is still a bitter memory.

While their menfolk were away on crusades elite women administered household and estates. Others became abbesses in charge of large convents. They were praised for their devotion to Christ and their heavenly visions, and sometimes idolized, as in Dante's short poems to his beloved Beatrice. At other times they played a more earthy role, like duplicitous Criseyde in Chaucer's *Troilus and Criseyde*. Townswomen sometimes ran businesses of brewing, leather dying and armour manufacture as well as traditional spinning and sewing. They also carried thatch, turves and tiles for house-building and helped load ships. During the ravages of the Black Death, their position was strengthened, only to wane again once the working population recovered its numbers.

Trade was hampered as the good Roman roads decayed. Who at this time could have prophesied the birth of scientific method and our modern world? Yet even in this inauspicious era, inventions seeped in from the east. Gunpowder, a Chinese invention, ended the supremacy of castles. The skills of war were also harnessed to more peaceful purposes like the use of explosives in mining and quarrying. Expertise acquired in precision boring of cannon and muskets was used later in steam engine production. A whole new branch of mathematics, dynamics, studied the movement of bodies in violent motion.

Mechanical power systems improved. There were already water mills, and by 1150 windmills reached Europe, probably another Chinese invention like the associated trip hammer and crank. Their power was used for *fulling* cloth, blowing bellows, forging iron and sawing wood. Dray horses had always been harnessed with a band across the chest, which restricted their windpipe. Horse collars, also Chinese in origin, increased their pulling power fivefold. Other imported inventions were clocks with cogwheels, and the mariner's compass and sternpost rudder. Ships could hold on course with sails set closer to the wind, and voyages could be made in rougher weather. Ocean navigation was safer so that, 'In fourteen hundred and ninety two, Columbus sailed the ocean blue.'

Another great achievement, home-grown this time, was in architecture. The old churches of Europe are some of the most beautiful buildings ever built, with their intricate carvings, graceful vaults and flying buttresses, soaring spires and massive towers with heavy bells.

By this time block-printing was in use, mainly for cards for divination. Movable metal type was first invented in the fourteenth century by the Koreans, and the technique spread rapidly through Europe, where linen waste was employed in the manufacture of quality paper. Demand for books was immense. At first the Bible and religious tracts were most popular, followed by literature from rediscovered classical writers translated from Arabic. This invention spread knowledge among the general population, reducing the control of priests and rulers. Dissent became more intellectual and better organized.

Feudalism began to fail when the plagues reduced the working population. Those left could bargain for improved income and conditions, but at

he human labour was being replaced by mechanical means. Wars
avier taxation and the angry peasantry lost patience. The Men of
ed on London in the Peasants' Revolt of 1381, chanting, 'When
Adam delved (dug) and Eve span, who was then the gentleman?' Why should
they be treated as inferior to king, lord, priest?

Bushels	Bushels are volumetric measurements, not directly translatable into weights.
Fulling	The shrinking and beating or pressing of cloth to make it heavier and more compact.
Will Langland	Will Langland is almost certainly a pseudonym. *Piers Ploughman* was written towards the end of the fourteenth century and there are three versions and probably several authors. It uses a deliberately rustic dialect.

Scholars

Church scholars battled to reconcile earlier religious traditions with the new
scholarship from the east, based on Arabic and classical works. Universities
sprang up throughout Europe to educate the clergy. Teaching was based on
classical learning and followed the Islamic model by including arithmetic,
geometry and music. There was little scientific investigation because it was
not necessary to salvation to know about this present world. Such materialism
was a positive handicap. Life was hard, death came early and, while suffering
should be ameliorated, everyone knew that the causes of disease and pain
were human sin. By bearing suffering patiently the soul grew in closeness
to God. The religious orders praised holy chastity. St Bernard likened the
monk's approach to God to a good wife before her husband, beseeching him
to grant her a kiss.

Anselm refined earlier explanations of Christ's sacrifice which had linked
it to the Passover sacrifice of the lamb, following Paul's first letter to the
Corinthians, 5.7. Anselm expressed this act of atonement in medieval terms.

Man owed allegiance to God like a knight to his king and Jesus stands in as champion for sinful Man. Peter Abelard in the twelfth century suggested that when people realized the cost to God of Jesus' crucifixion their hard hearts would soften, they would repent and be saved. In the thirteenth century Thomas Aquinas explained the natural universe and the plan of salvation with discussions of every point both for and against his position. Reason, he said, is the handmaid of faith and on its own cannot explain the universe story, yet faith and reason never conflict. His *Summa Theologica* forms the basis of the Roman Catholic Church's doctrine today.

Yet there were dissenters within the clergy. In England John Wyclif, a fourteenth-century Oxford don, instigated the first translation of the Bible into English, denied *transubstantiation*, and abhorred the greed of monasticism. He was condemned as a heretic and put on trial, but the London mob wrecked the proceedings. The Lollards supported his heresies, even declaring that war was contrary to the New Testament. The 1401 Act de Heretico Comburendo allowed burning for people who dared express such corrupt beliefs.

Into the well-ordered scheme of salvation came the infant of scientific method. At first it seemed far less threatening than the numerous heresies heralding the schism of the Protestant Reformation in the sixteenth century. But as careful experiments tested preconceptions, the common sense of the Middle Ages was found to be full of non-sense.

Throughout the period covered by this chapter humans gradually appropriated more of the world's resources. They devised means of controlling food supplies through farming, and some improved methods of dealing with disease and accidents. They improved physical comfort by controlling fire and inventing the plough, wheel, metallurgy, writing and trade. Religions acted as custodians of knowledge about many of these activities, so were vitally important to the whole economy. They provided explanations for national and personal circumstances, and ceremonies that tied their communities together.

It is only now that a divide starts to appear between technological discoveries and religious interpretations of the universe. Gradually doctrines founded on the old beliefs began to look less secure.

Transubstantiation   The turning of bread and wine into the
body and blood of Christ during the Mass.
Priestly power stemmed from this doctrine.

IDEAS FOR DISCUSSION

1   Compare the diseases mentioned in the Bible (e.g. in Leviticus) with a modern study of ancient disease (e.g. Filer).

2   Compare Lemche's interpretation of early Israelite society with that in Edwards et al., *The Cambridge Ancient History*.

3   Research the effect of plagues (e.g. the North African plague of 252 CE) on the early Christian community. Why did plagues sometimes speed the progress of Christianity? How did people at the time explain them? What is the modern theory of the development of epidemics?

4   Compare religious laws in the Old Testament with those of surrounding countries in the period 1000 to 500 BCE.

5   Research technological achievements at the time the Old Testament was written.

6   The Greeks and Romans were renowned for philosophical and technical achievements. How were their philosophies affected by their understanding of technology?

7   Research the achievements of Islamic scientists (Sadar)

8   Research early Christian heresies. Are there similar ideas among Christians today? If so, are they based on different interpretations of biblical texts?

9   Read Fiorenza on the invisibility of women in early Christian documents. Use Leyser and compare the life of elite and peasant women in England between 450 and 1500 CE

10   Research British peasant life and different farming systems in the Middle Ages. How did Church ceremonies and liturgies tie in with these practices?

11   The Crusades. How did they affect dealings between the

Eastern and Western Churches and between Christianity and Islam? Why were they so popular?

12 Sacred writings are received revelations from a god or gods, and for many Christians the Bible is sacrosanct. Doubts have been cast on its accuracy in a number of areas. What are these and what is your view on the reliability of the Bible as the Word of God?

REFERENCES AND FURTHER READING

Robert Bartlett, 1986, *Trial by Fire and Water*, Oxford: Oxford University Press

J D Bernal, 1969, *Science in History*, 4 volumes, Harmondsworth: Penguin

Jared Diamond, 1997, *Guns, Germs and Steel*, London: Vintage.

I E S Edwards, C J Gadd and N G L Hammond, 1970–5, *The Cambridge Ancient History*, 3rd edition, Cambridge: Cambridge University Press

Joyce Filer, 1995, *Disease*, London: British Museum

Elisabeth Schüssler Fiorenza, 1983, *In Memory of Her*, London: SCM Press

John, Lord of Joinville and Geoffroi de Villehardouin, thirteenth century, *Chronicles of the Crusades*, translated by M R B Shaw, 1963, Harmondsworth: Penguin.

Arno Karlen, 1995, *Plague's Progress*, London: Gollancz.

Robin Lane Fox, 1986, *Pagans and Christians*, Harmondsworth: Penguin

William Langland, *c.*1370, *Piers the Ploughman*, translated by J F Goodridge, 1959, Harmondsworth: Penguin

Niels Peter Lemche, 1988, *Ancient Israel*, Sheffield: Sheffield Academic Press

Henrietta Leyser, 1996, *Medieval Women*, London: Orion

Oliver Rackham, 1986, *The History of the Countryside*, London: J M Dent & Sons

Richard Rudgley, 1998, *Lost Civilisations of the Stone Age*, London: Random

Z Sadar, 1989, *Explorations in Islamic Science*, London: Mansell

Hershel Shanks, 1992, *Christianity and Rabbinic Judaism*, London: SPCK

Jonathon N Tubb and Rupert L Chapman, 1990, *Archaeology and the Bible*, London: British Museum

N T Wright, 1996, *Original Jesus*, London: Lion

6

First, Enquire Diligently

Modern science is based on the development of scientific method. This emerged in the European *Renaissance* and was supported by technological achievements originating from outside the continent, such as type-printing of books and better lenses for telescopes.

This chapter focuses on Europe with an emphasis on changes in British life and thought stemming from the new discoveries. Many medieval ideas were radically altered and new philosophies promoted. Practices and arguments that seemed common sense before the Renaissance need considerable reinterpretation before we can understand them today.

The chapter contains snapshots of changing ideas and how the establishment of the day welcomed or opposed them. It looks at the new developments over four periods, the *Renaissance* and *Reformation* (fifteenth to seventeenth centuries), the Enlightenment (eighteenth century), the Industrial Revolution of the nineteenth century and finally the twentieth century. At the beginning of the Renaissance science was a relatively unimportant branch of Christian learning, natural philosophy. By the end of the twentieth century it consisted of a wide number of independent disciplines and technological skills which were run by professionals. It had applications in all walks of life.

Reformation   Sixteenth-century movement that started out to reform the established Church but eventually developed into independent Protestant churches.

Renaissance	The period when Arabic learning (which included Greek, Egyptian, Babylonian, Indian and Chinese traditions) became available to Western scholars, from roughly 1450 CE.

- Renaissance and the Birth of Modern Science
- Eighteenth Century – Enlightenment
- Nineteenth Century – Industrial Revolution
- Twentieth Century – A Relative Era

RENAISSANCE AND THE BIRTH OF MODERN SCIENCE

- Books and broomsticks
- Vegetable lamb meets natural philosophers

Books and broomsticks

From the mid-1400s, printing by movable type led to the enthusiastic spread of new ideas. William Caxton was the first English printer and translated many French works. Radical ideas about the importance of the individual and the use of reason and experiment brought about a profound change in outlook. The Frenchman and philosopher René Descartes was interested in scientific method, and he put forward a world system that eventually superseded that of the medieval schoolmen.

The Catholic Church based at Rome had control over western and most of central Europe, and it didn't welcome many of the independent scholarly works, fearing the collapse of its carefully planned scheme of salvation and reduction in its political power. The hated Reformation of Luther and Calvin was supported by translations of the Bible into the vernacular. These were rushed to the new printing presses along with new and heretical commentaries. The *Inquisition* halted the printing of Coverdale's Bible in Paris, and William Tyndale, translator of the first printed English New Testament, was put to death for heresy.

Before long Europe was embroiled in a series of religious wars between the reformers (Protestants) and orthodox (Roman Catholics). These raged across France in the 1500s while in England the Tudor monarchy switched their loyalty from Rome to Reform and back with concomitant brutality. Fighting continued in Europe in the Thirty Years' War during the 1600s, ostensibly religious but actually based on international power struggles.

The Church in Rome was not only concerned with heresy. For centuries it had tried to subdue folk magic. Prayer to God was not always success-ful and so beliefs in the efficacy of holy springs and stones and the incan-tations, rituals and medicines of folk doctors were widespread. Instead of these popular superstitions, the Church offered incantations, rituals, relics, holy water, the Mass, along with anointing or cursing by priests. Humanists, like the Dutchman Erasmus in the early sixteenth century, considered many elements of Church ritual equally superstitious.

Throughout Christian Europe people had been taught to fear devils who could seduce them into selling their souls to heresy and depravity, so ending up in hell. Grim reminders of eternal torments were depicted in paintings, carvings and printed woodcuts. In the late Middle Ages belief in the power of witches erupted into a frenzy of terror and in 1484 the Pope ordered tor-ture to procure convictions. From this date until 1750 more than 100,000 people, mainly poor, old and illiterate women, were prosecuted for witch-craft. Mass hunts, trials and executions took place between 1580 and 1630. Torture was crude but effective, and the so-called witches were ordered to confess to sexual orgies with demons, flying to witches' sabbaths and other nonsense – in which many of them believed.

Most prosecutions took place in west-central Europe, a hotbed of heresy in the late Middle Ages and now the centre of Reformation upheavals. There were many small states and duchies in this area that continually changed their religious allegiances and were free to act as they wished.

A number of judges and clergymen discounted witchcraft, and the first country to end witch trials was the Netherlands, possibly influenced by Erasmus's views. America's last witchcraft trial was in Salem, Massachusetts, in 1692. In Britain three Acts of Parliament dated 1542, 1563 and 1604 had made witchcraft a statutory offence. The final one was repealed in 1736. The last legal execution in Europe was in Switzerland in 1782, though belief in witchcraft was reported in the nineteenth century around Orleans in France and Dorset in England. Even today there are a number of people who believe that spells are effectual.

During these upheavals new religious groups emerged. During the English Commonwealth (1649–59) England was governed as a republic with considerable religious tolerance. Quakers and Baptists flourished, though the more radical ideas of Levellers and Ranters were deplored. The Ranters scorned the view that the devil was real. He merely symbolized suppressed desires. The Levellers argued that the poorest Englishman's life should be respected equally with the greatest and he should have the right to choose who governed him. But Commonwealth leaders replied that only those owning permanent fixed property should have the right to vote and enter Parliament. The Levellers retorted they had put their lives at risk to support *Cromwell* during the *Civil War*. Had they merely fought for a change of masters and permanent slavery?

Civil War (1642–9)	Between Parliament and the Royalists. It ended with the beheading of Charles I.
Cromwell, Oliver (1599–1658)	Puritan leader on Parliamentarian side during the Civil War, and later Lord Protector of the Commonwealth.
Inquisition (1232–1820)	Judicial organization set up by the Roman Catholic Church to suppress heresy.

Vegetable lamb meets natural philosophers

This was the world of the early scientists or natural philosophers. In the eyes of the Church of Rome their discoveries were far less important than heresies and superstitions.

There were some very strange beliefs among the early scientists. You can find the Vegetable Lamb in the Natural History Museum in London. It has four legs (actually stalks) sticking out from a fern rhizome. Even as late as the seventeenth century it was considered proof that animals grow from the ground like plants.

The natural philosophers of the Renaissance relied on Ptolemy's second-century model of an earth central to the universe (see Figure 6.1). Wasn't Copernicus obviously wrong to publish the opposite in 1543? He may have relied on detailed Arabic observations, but anyone walking on the earth knows that we move and it doesn't. There would be a constant wind blowing if the earth moved, wouldn't there? The Reformer Martin Luther was not happy with this novelty either. Hadn't Joshua successfully commanded the sun to stand still? Giordano Bruno supported the Copernican model and was burnt to death in 1600 after a run-in with the Inquisition, though he died for promoting heresy as well as scientific innovation.

Arabic and European chemistry was a magical mix of astrology and alchemy. Everyone knew that the bubbling that occurred during smelting and other chemical experiments was caused by invisible spirits. It was many years before chemists shook themselves free of theories related to such notions.

New ideas were further hampered by the belief that past generations had had the greatest knowledge about the world. Humanity degenerated after Adam's fall from grace, so this knowledge became corrupted. Scientists were merely rediscovering old truths, and there were no new ones to be revealed. Slowly the idea began to spread that the ancestors were not as learned as had been supposed. Any son of Adam could manufacture a theory to fit his data.

The Italian Galileo Galilei (1564–1642) built his discoveries on Islamic observations. He experimented extensively and was skilled in making instruments, presenting his first telescope with a magnification of ×10 to the Doge of Venice. He was not always so politically astute, saying publicly that where biblical teaching contradicted observation then the latter should win the argument. Even his Church critics had to agree that the Milky Way is made up of stars and the moon's surface is not perfectly smooth, but they denied his interpretations. Galileo was forbidden to publicize his theories. He disobeyed and was brought before the Inquisition for a show trial. The memory of Bruno combined with fear of torture finally silenced him.

Yet Galileo's discoveries were not so easily suppressed. Careful calculations

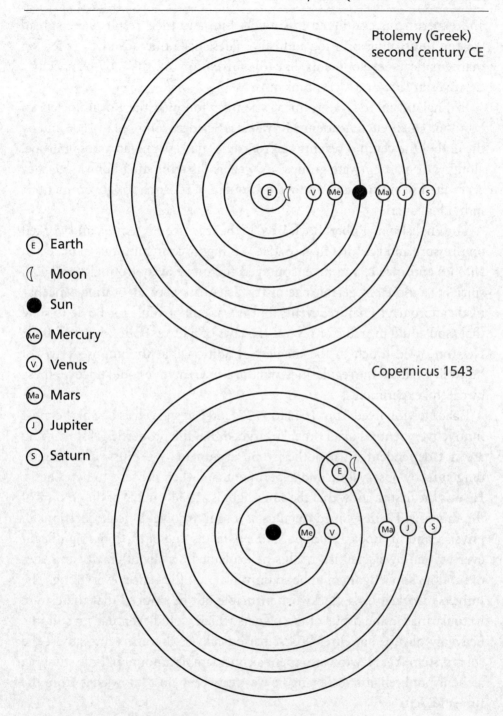

Ptolemy (Greek)
second century CE

E   Earth

☾   Moon

⬤   Sun

Me Mercury

V   Venus

Ma Mars

J   Jupiter

S   Saturn

Copernicus 1543

Figure 6.1   Early theories of the Solar System.

and experiments continued to support him and their results were spread via the flourishing printing industry. These scientific advances relied on mathematical developments like the invention of rules of perspective, decimals in 1585 and logarithms in 1614.

In England in 1662 a group of scientists founded the Royal Society of London. The French Académie Royale des Sciences followed in 1666 and by the end of the century seventy such societies had sprung up across Europe, along with many private groups. As well as disseminating knowledge they accredited scientific work and were a source of research for government or individual queries.

The Englishman Robert Boyle lived in the seventeenth century and worked on pressure and volumes in gases. He was highly contemptuous of beliefs in witches and magic, and he encouraged the move away from alchemy and spirits to a more respectable chemistry. Scientists were advocating a mechanistic approach to natural events, but it was still possible for Boyle to state that God could overrule or reverse the laws of nature. Both Boyle and Isaac Newton owed much to the medieval tradition that the imposed laws of Yahweh included the regularities of natural law. Anyone could uncover these by careful experiments.

Isaac Newton lived from 1642 to 1727, and is respected as one of the most innovative scientists of all time. He argued that the properties of something are not dependent on hypothesis and argument. We must 'first enquire diligently' by observation and experiment, and then proceed to hypothesis. He was the first to show that the sun's light is actually made of the colours of the rainbow. He developed calculus as a tool to solve difficult questions in physics, and his book *Principia Mathematica* is one of the most significant ever written by a scientist. In this he explained his law of gravity and laws of motion, showing them to be so universal that they affect everything. The universe worked on a clockwork principle but he noticed that there were irregularities in the orbits of the planets which would eventually result in a heavenly pileup. But eureka! God periodically sent comets to readjust the solar system. Yet Newton also spent a considerable amount of time studying alchemy and religion, believing he was recovering lost knowledge from the time of Eden.

The first complete anatomy of the human body had been published at the same time as Copernicus's model of the solar system. Good anatomical drawings provided the basis for William Harvey's discovery of the circulation of the blood (published 1628). This challenged the ancient Greek view that the heart was the seat of reason while the brain moderated its heat, and was a major advance in medical knowledge.

Technology advanced rapidly alongside the many scientific discoveries. In Germany Reformation pastors taught that work is as valuable as prayer in God's sight. They passed knowledge on to their illiterate flocks about developments in the fields of mining, metallurgy and chemistry. Blast furnaces and improved casting lowered the cost of manufacturing iron goods, but eventually shortage of wood reduced output. It was now that coal mining became important. The mines were small partnership ventures at first, but they grouped together in companies and divided their takings into shares in an early form of capitalism. The cost of gear encouraged the miners to set up a system of share purchasing by non-working partners. When the wars of religion upset mining across central Germany the miners emigrated to Spain and the New World. Many travelled to England and their expertise in metallurgy helped to found future wealth.

The new scientific method was becoming increasingly successful. At the same time God was becoming more distant. He was now out there somewhere beyond the stars, with very little to do in the way of ordering the universe once he had started it going. But he still provided the life force and designed animals and plants, didn't he? It was not until the nineteenth century that God lost these jobs too.

EIGHTEENTH CENTURY – ENLIGHTENMENT

- **The rights of Man – sometimes**
- **Ill fares the Land**
- **A furnace seal'd**
- **Friendly societies and religious societies**
- **A long shining fly**

The rights of man – sometimes

The Enlightenment is sometimes called the Age of Reason. In the previous century scholars represented reason as tradition, authority and stability, but the new free-thinking philosophers examined religion, politics, morality and social life from a practical point of view.

As usual, Europe was embroiled in conflicts. Wars of succession occupied the military of many countries. Britain was troubled by Jacobite rebellions in Scotland and colonial rebellions in North America.

In France Voltaire questioned the rule of these warring kings. He campaigned for religious tolerance and the rights of man and he mocked the old Roman concept of a 'just war'. Immanuel Kant inspired the ideals of the Romantic movement. He too supported the rights of man but criticized pure reason. There was a higher spiritual realm, he taught, which is more real and where the new scientific methods have no value. It was a time of new writing, musical and artistic exploration through the works of Goethe, the Bach family, Handel, Haydn and Mozart, the artists Velásquez and Goya and many others.

In 1776 the Americans declared independence and later welcomed Britain's *bête noire*, the exiled Thomas Paine who wrote *The Rights of Man*. In 1789 the French Revolution overthrew the idle and affluent monarchy and aristocracy, framing a new constitution based on the ideals of reason, along with liberty, equality and fraternity. This successful uprising and the ensuing reign of terror united the rulers of surrounding countries against the new Republic, but Napoleon Bonaparte's brilliant military tactics secured the safety of France. The nascent Republic died when he crowned himself Emperor in 1804.

It was during this period that early capitalism established the principles of competition in trade and production. Boom and bust alternated rapidly. Risky ventures like the South Sea and the Mississippi Companies burst their speculative bubbles, ruining investors. But more reliable enterprises were established by new entrepreneurs, laying the foundations for the coming Industrial Revolution. Trade expanded, bringing exotic materials like sugar and cotton with exciting new manufacturing possibilities.

Trade raised interesting questions about Christianity. It was increasingly clear that civilization was not just a prerogative of Christians, and other religions claimed an equal number of miracles to support their views. There were even doubts about Bishop Ussher's calculation that the earth was created in 4004 BCE. If there had been an Emperor of China in 3000 BCE how did this tie in with Adam and Eve?

The plantations and mines had a voracious need for unskilled workers and the notorious trade triangle exchanged European goods for African slaves, transported them to the Americas and sold them like cattle in exchange for plantation sugar and cotton for Europe. The Bible did not condemn slavery; rights of man did not extend to all humans. The philosopher Rousseau and the American Quakers are among those who protested, but slavery did not become illegal till the nineteenth century. Many fortunes were made by this iniquitous trade.

Ill fares the land

There had been no major advances in farming methods since the Romans, and starvation was common for the poor. In England the *open field system* had already disappeared from large areas, for since the thirteenth century peasant farmers had been exchanging strips and then hedging their enlarged fields. Now Enclosure Acts speeded the process to the advantage of larger farmers. Dispossessed peasants lost both livelihood and any voting rights they might have.

The poet Oliver Goldsmith regretted this step in 'The Deserted Village'. 'Ill fares the land, to hastening ills a prey/ Where wealth accumulates, and men decay. . . . A bold peasantry, their country's pride/ When once destroy'd can never be supplied.'

The truth was more complicated. Peasant cattle and sheep kept on the commons were lame, blind and scabby, too pinched to make a profit. No-one bothered to improve the commons pasture. The cornlands were worn out from continual removal of nutrients for human needs, and the expense of ploughing and manuring absorbed any profit. The quantity of corn at harvest was barely enough to provide seed corn for the following year, let alone feed family and livestock over the winter.

With enclosures it was possible to improve flocks and herds by selective breeding and better physical care. New crops like turnips increased the stocking ratio and kept the animals healthy through the winter, providing more manure for the land. 'A full bullock-yard and a full *fold* make a full granary' was the motto. The French wars kept the price of corn high from the 1760s until they ended at Waterloo in 1815, and the new money encouraged all kinds of improvements in field machinery, seed quality and land management. The British Board of Agriculture arranged a ten-year series of lectures on agricultural chemistry in the early nineteenth century. This first agricultural revolution improved food in quality and quantity and fed the industrial revolution of the following century. But starvation was still a strong possibility and the price of the staple food, bread, fluctuated wildly.

Fold	A moveable fencing system to control sheep grazing.
Open field system	The system where peasant farmers, both bondmen and free, lived in villages surrounded by unfenced arable fields cultivated in common. A typical three-course system grew one block of winter corn, one of spring corn, beans or peas and a third was left fallow (weeds) for grazing and manuring. This regime rotated annually. There were many other farming systems.

A furnace seal'd

Water power sources for the new factories were unable to cope with demand and in 1785 James Watt's steam engine was put into use. Improved machinery like the spinning jenny increased the output per employee but work was plentiful.

The landless peasants and their families trudged to the towns, hoping for indoor labour and better, more reliable pay, even if the streets didn't run with ale. Many skilled workers saved enough capital to found independent workshops. But for the majority pay was low, hours were long, and children often had to be employed to help feed the family. William Blake was a poet and artisan engraver. Knowing firsthand the difficulties faced by the poor, he used industrial imagery. He described the indifference shown by the manufacturers as: 'The Human Form, (is) a fiery Forge./ The Human Face, a Furnace seal'd.'

Thomas Jefferson was shocked when he visited England and saw the state of the working poor. Between 1700 and 1750 60 crimes were added to the capital list in England. Both Christians and free-thinkers saw the need to reform the criminal code and reduce punishments. Societies were set up to fund orphanages and refuges for beggars, debtors, young criminals and prostitutes.

> Thomas Jefferson   Third President of the USA (1801–9).
> (1743–1826)

Friendly societies and religious societies

In the expanding cities the old protective medieval guilds had fallen into disuse. In their place factory workers founded friendly societies, laying the traditions of later trade unions. The friendly societies were self-funded and included sick insurance. They emphasized self-discipline and community welfare. Society members were expected to behave decently and discuss important matters rather than chat idly over beer and baccy. They could be fined for taking God's name in vain. By the end of the eighteenth century these societies had about 648,000 members. Some prohibited disloyal discussion, though probably a number provided cover for political activity.

This was risky. Political societies were indeed set up by tradesmen, shopkeepers and mechanics in Sheffield, Derby, Manchester and London at the end of the century. The London Corresponding Society (1792) advocated the still revolutionary goal of universal *suffrage* for men. Senior members were imprisoned in 1794 and charged with high treason. Punishment could be partial hanging and disembowelling while still alive but the Grand Jury refused to convict. There was dancing in the streets at their release. The 'wild Mob' that had so terrorized kings and parliaments was becoming a political animal.

Religious societies flourished. Methodism was founded by the Wesleys, John and his younger brother Charles. They instructed hard-working and respectable artisans in personal piety and self-regulation. They also evangelized new mining and industrial communities. They based their message on the assurance of forgiveness of sins and love and care for neighbours, encouraging loyalty to employers, however obnoxious. Christians believed they were on the road to perfection and some claimed to have reached this happy state. The societies discussed this possibility and also the religious hysteria associated with mass conversions, like speaking in tongues.

Suffrage   The right to vote.

A long shining fly

Science was becoming an increasingly important vocation. Many scientists questioned the revelations of the past but it was still possible to describe an event as being both providential and natural. Certainly not all scientists were free-thinkers, and clerics actively supported the new sciences.

Joseph Priestley first studied in a nonconformist school and became a minister, eventually a *Unitarian*. He was also one of the founders of modern chemistry. This had lagged behind the other sciences because there was no reliable way of measuring the temperature of the reactions until Gabriel Fahrenheit invented the mercury thermometer in 1714. Priestley, Watt, and Josiah Wedgwood, one of the founders of the pottery industry, were members of an exemplary Birmingham scientific society, the Lunar Society. Priestly also supported the American colonies and the ideals of the French Revolution. In 1791 he attended a dinner in Birmingham to celebrate the second anniversary of the Revolution. His political opponents organized a mob that destroyed his library and equipment, and shortly after he emigrated to Pennsylvania, America. Some of his phrases on liberty were incorporated into the Declaration of Independence by Thomas Jefferson.

Antoine Laurent Lavoisier was another notable chemist, living in Paris. His wife Marie was his constant assistant, keeping notes and making expert drawings of his many experiments with gases. He invented the first table of the chemical elements and gave chemistry a logical language. As a liberal he tried unsuccessfully to reform the burdensome tax system. He was a minor member of the nobility, and paid the penalty of his position in 1794 when he was executed during the Jacobin terror.

Another French scientist, Pierre Laplace, solved Isaac Newton's problem with the irregularities in planetary orbits. He is reputed to have said to Napoleon concerning God's interventions, 'I have no need of that hypothesis.'

Another major advance was the classification of animals and plants. The Swedish Carl Linnaeus devised the *binomial* system of *taxonomy*. This is arranged hierarchically from the largest category, the Kingdom (e.g. the Plant Kingdom) down to the individual species (e.g. *Bellis perennis*, the daisy). He put humans and apes in the same group, though he was circumspect in his scientific naming of humans, knowing that theologians would not approve. He was a believer in God, but doubtful about the Flood and puzzled by fossils. By now these were widely accepted as remains of creatures no longer in existence.

Many country clergymen were greatly interested in natural history. Gilbert White of Selborne made many careful observations. He reported on the troublesome 'long shining fly' that laid eggs in the bacon haunches smoked and dried in the chimneys. Their maggots were called 'jumpers' and they ate the meat 'down to the bone'. He classified it according to Linnaeus's system. Such observant naturalists have been the backbone of natural history studies. Old records on arrival and departure dates for migrant birds and plant flowering times provide evidence for global warming today.

Binomial	Two names.
Taxonomy	Classification of living things based on similarities of origin and structure.
Unitarian	Christians who deny the doctrine of the Trinity. Reason and conscience form the basis of their belief and practice.

NINETEENTH CENTURY – INDUSTRIAL REVOLUTION

- **The old farmhouses are down**
- **'If I am out of work . . .'**
- **Bind up the broken-hearted**
- **Descent with modification**

The old farmhouses are down

Beneath the prosperity of the nineteenth century lay appalling conditions for those who toiled on the land. Digging, ploughing, weeding, harvesting and animal care are all arduous and dirty, and often dangerous to fitness and health. The hours were long and pay was inevitably less than in the cities.

On the land new machinery improved working conditions, but as it spread so did rural unemployment. When the wars with France ended, food poured in from Europe, America and the Empire in exchange for manufactured goods. *Tithing* was another ancient burden, not commuted into a money payment until 1836. English farming went into steep decline, and poor harvests and high rents led to the abandonment of many farms.

William Cobbett rode round the home shires championing the failing yeomen farmers. 'When the old farmhouses are down (and down they must be come in time) what a miserable thing the country will be!' In 1830, the same year that he published *Rural Rides*, there was a serious revolt by farm labourers against food prices. Prosperity returned slowly, but everything was in such poor condition that landlords and their tenant farmers were slow to reinvest. The 1850s were better years for most farmers until outbreaks of *rinderpest* and foot-and-mouth ruined many. The first Act making the slaughter of diseased animals compulsory was passed in 1866.

This boom-or-bust situation continued through the century. During prosperous times many farmers improved their land and in 1838 the Royal Agricultural Society of England was established. It allied practical farmers with men of capital and science. Research stations like Rothamsted studied soil chemistry, uncovering the important principle that soil fertility depends on continual replacement of nitrates, phosphates and potassium (NPK). Food production rose once this was understood.

One of the greatest farming tragedies was caused by potato blight, *Phytophthera infestans*. It was first recorded in America in 1843 and by 1845 was affecting every country in Europe. There was no cure until the invention of fungicides. Ireland was particularly badly hit. Its population had multiplied rapidly from 1.5 million in 1790 to 9 million in the 1840s. Harvests across Europe were particularly poor and the price of grain was high worldwide. Disaster struck when the potatoes rotted in field and storage clamp. There was no telegraph as yet between England and Ireland, but newspapers, especially *The Times*, daily recorded Irish starvation, cholera and typhus. European grain shortages and English inertia due to the philosophy of free trade and the theories of *Thomas Robert Malthus*, added to the Irish tragedy. Many who survived emigrated to America.

Thomas Robert Malthus	According to Malthus, populations increase by geometrical progression while food can only be increased arithmetically. Population will always outstrip food, therefore famine will limit population.
Rinderpest or cattle plague	A viral disease of cattle like foot-and-mouth, but more acute and contagious. Currently eradicated from Britain.
Tithing	Payment of a tenth part of all land produce, livestock and profits of tradesmen, artificers, millers and fishermen (see Numbers 18.21). It was a moral duty to give this amount to the Church in Europe from the fourth century onwards, and gradually became legally enforced with fines for non-payment. In England after the suppression of the monasteries (1530s) tithes were allocated to parishes and lay people, and became the endless cause of disputes and

litigation, adding to rural antagonism to the Church. Payment was in kind, discouraging improvements in farming practice.

'If I am out of work . . .'

. . . for weeks in the bad times, and the winter comes, with black frost and keen east wind, and there is no coal for the grate and no clothes for the bed, and the thin bones are seen through the ragged clothes, does the rich man share his plenty with me, as he ought to do, if his religion wasn't a humbug?

Elizabeth Gaskell, a deeply Christian writer, wrote this protest on behalf of the oppressed industrial workers in her novel *Mary Barton*, published in 1848. Their conditions were as iniquitous as those of land labourers.

Yet for many the nineteenth century was a time of increased prosperity. In 1844 the French Industrial Exposition gave a great boost to French industry. Not to be outdone, the British Great Exhibition followed in 1851. It showcased the products of Empire and new industrial inventions. The newly rich already had financial power over their workforce and now they gained political power as well as they took up seats in Parliament. They passed the important Limited Liabilities Act in 1855 which curtailed investors' risk, so increasing money available for innovations. Power engineering and electrical and chemical industrial processes made science indispensable to these entrepreneurs, but their decisions were dominated by fears of social unrest leading to an upheaval like the French Revolution.

As workers continued to leave the unpleasant conditions of the countryside, cities expanded into appalling slums. Increasing dirt, smoke and filth were major hazards for city dwellers. The stench of human excreta in the Thames prevented Parliament convening some years. Most of the population were wage labourers, and their position was precarious. When machines took over their jobs, *Luddite* uprisings ensured that the capitalist entrepreneurs installed more machines. Machines do not revolt.

A song popular among the Manchester weavers had the refrain, 'We have bigger tyrants in *Boneys* of our own.' In 1819, four years after Waterloo, a large and orderly political reform meeting in St Peter's Fields, Manchester, was firmly quashed. Charging cavalry killed 11, and 400 were injured. The rally speaker was imprisoned and the leaders dismissed as illiterate, half-starved and unemployed rabble-rousers. Illiterate they were not. But they certainly supported the hungry and unemployed. The magistrates involved were commended by the Home Secretary for quelling a riot and the event is remembered as the Peterloo massacre.

In spite of opposition, attempts continued at forming trade unions. In 1834 a small union of farmworkers from Dorchester (the Tolpuddle Martyrs) were sentenced to transportation for seven years, though this was remitted in 1836. The Chartists of 1839 to 1848 presented three large petitions to Parliament requesting universal male suffrage, secret ballots and an end to property qualifications for Members of Parliament. All petitions were roundly rejected. But gradually Reform Acts were passed that improved voting rights and the electoral basis of Parliament and overhauled town and city government. By the turn of the century the nascent Labour Party was supporting social reforms proposed by the Liberal Governments.

Gradually general health improved with the introduction of main drainage and the invention of flush toilets, regular refuse removal and cleaner water. Disease was still thought to be spread by 'miasmas' or vapours until 1878 when Louis Pasteur proposed the germ theory of infection. He recommended inoculation which had been developed in the previous century.

| Boney | Napoleon Bonaparte, recently defeated at Waterloo. |
| Luddite | A person named after the hypothetical Ned Ludd, an eighteenth-century workman who destroyed industrial machinery. |

Bind up the broken-hearted

In the early years of the century Europe was largely Christian and its leaders assumed that the French cult of Reason would gradually fade away. Across Europe the lesson of tolerance had been learned, and many countries gradually extended freedom of faith to all their citizens, even where that faith was a minority one.

Across Britain old churches were renovated and new ones built. Many mill and factory owners attended them and supported them financially, and it could be obligatory for their workers to be present as well. The theological emphasis was on an emotional and subjective view of God in contrast to the objectivity of science. Theological statements were seen as parallel to scientific ones, not similar.

Pilgrimage increased in popularity as trains and better roads made travelling safer, easier and faster. Religious tolerance allowed the reopening of the old Roman Catholic shrine of Walsingham in Norfolk, while Assisi in Italy was promoted for its association with St Francis, one of the most attractive of saints. New visions and miracles created shrines such as Knock in Ireland.

Enthusiasm for helping the less fortunate filled the burgeoning churches and chapels. Missions flourished in the Empire where education and medical aid were provided as well as evangelism. Missionaries were held in the highest esteem at home for their courage in penetrating unexplored parts of the globe. The dangers of diseases like yellow fever and malaria were very real in a century without prophylactics. The strength of Christianity today in southern Africa, South America and other countries is testimony to the respect felt by many of the resident populations for the missionaries.

All churches were involved in improving conditions at home as well. Wealthy Quaker families took steps to improve the welfare of their employees. The Tory MP Lord Shaftesbury opposed parliamentary reform but championed all bills that improved conditions in factories and mines. He was heavily involved in philanthropic work, as were many other Christians. Societies like the Salvation Army provided practical aid to the wretched and writers brought the plight of the poor to their readers. Christians also actively supported early plans to protect the environment.

But there were problems.

Scholars retranslated the Bible using ancient documents. Texts like Job 19.26, in the King James version, 'though after my skin worms destroy this body yet in my flesh shall I see God', had obviously been misunderstood by earlier translators. It could not possibly mean resurrection, but it was still being used at burial services to give comfort to the bereaved. Should it be removed or not? Archaeological evidence from the Near East was confusing. Archaeologists followed the biblical timescale, but the discoveries did not add up.

After 1860 the ideals of socialism came to the fore, formulated by Karl Marx. He aimed for the destruction of capitalism, which had brought so much misery in industrial England. The socialist parties often denounced churches for their part in capitalist oppression. In reply to such criticisms a Christian Socialist Party was founded, and the clergyman Charles Kingsley was a prominent member. His *Water Babies* was written for children, but is a serious exposé of the wrongs perpetrated on the poor.

The churches, both Anglican and nonconformist, lost their monopoly on education as it was felt the state could provide a more comprehensive system. State funding required that schools should be undenominational while still providing a Christian education. The Education Act of 1870 set up locally elected school boards which could compel attendance to the age of thirteen. The poor didn't pay, and by 1918 all fees were paid through general taxation.

By now the newly developed psychology of Sigmund Freud was representing religious belief as merely an infantile reliance on an internalized father figure.

Many people were interested in other religions. Spiritualism received a boost from the fraudulent claims of the Fox sisters in Hydesville, New York, in 1848. They kept their code secret until 1888. People flocked enthusiastically to displays of table-rappings and tiltings. General curiosity and tales of deception led to the founding of the Society for Psychical Research to examine the strange phenomena. Sir Oliver Lodge, who made major contributions to electromagnetic theory, was first president. In the 1870s Mary Baker Eddy founded Christian Science. She taught that pain, disease and death were 'errors' and that there was a harmful occult force which malicious people exuded to damage others. Witchcraft again?

All these new ideas raised more pressing problems than scientific ones and on the whole the relationships between scientists and theologians were positive. But by the end of the century disagreements developed into a more major conflict. Pope Pius IX declared that no Pope need submit to current ideas of progress or liberalism. Scientists responded with a series of popular books representing religions as old superstitions. Once they had played a valuable role but now they should be allowed to wither away in peace. This proclamation of conflict between noble scientists and ignorant clerics is quite an old concept if you substitute philosophers or workers for scientists.

Descent with modification

Science was the preserve of the academic but amateur gentleman at the beginning of the century. By the end it was the province of the professional man. Many of these were professing Christians, but the number of clerics in the Royal Society had fallen dramatically. Scientists became increasingly confident as they developed methods of examining the world in a rational and impersonal way, distancing religious and political views from their methods. All the same, hidden prejudice often prevailed. One was the use of reductionist theory as a philosophy, another was concealed racism.

The list of discoveries made in the nineteenth century is prodigious, and only a few can be mentioned. Napoleon introduced the metric system over much of Europe when he was Emperor. Weights and measures were also standardized, a most necessary introduction for the comparison of experiments. One of the greatest of mathematicians, Karl Friedrich Gauss, worked on *non-Euclidean geometry*,which was the foundation for Einstein's work. Collection of data led directly to statistical analysis, and the sociologist Emile Durkheim began the search for trends within human populations, in the hope of predicting the future more accurately. Railways, iron ships and roads with tarmac improved trade. Information was spread by telegraph and telephone, while manufactured gas and later electricity lit dark streets and provided power in the home. The vibrant colours of new chemical dyes were incorporated in artists' paints with stunning results. The lost formula for hydraulic cement was rediscovered in 1824 and revolutionized the building of church, factory and home. Michael Faraday, the great electrician, began his career as an assistant at the *Royal Institute* in 1813. He invented the dynamo and his work in electrochemistry has applications for many industrial processes today. He started Christmas lectures for children which still continue.

The introduction of historical ideas into the scientific programme proved to be one of the most important innovations of the century. Ideas about evolution had been around for a while, and the naturalist Charles Darwin combined them with Malthus's theories and his own observations. He published *The Origin of Species* in 1859. Together with Alfred Russell Wallace, another naturalist, he suggested that descent with modification (evolutionary change) was caused by natural selection of inherited characteristics. Neither of them understood the mechanism of inheritance, but improved microscopes showed that living things are made up of cells with nuclei and chromosomes. By the 1880s biologists had worked out that inheritance is connected with the latter.

One of Darwin's problems was whether there had been enough time in earth's history for evolution. The geologist Charles Lyall explained how natural events changed the earth's surface, giving a much greater age to the earth than had previously been supposed.

Charles Kingsley supported Darwin effusively. God the creator of self-developing creatures was as fine a concept as God the creator of individual species. Most Christians and non-believers were inclined to welcome these new ideas, though some were critical and satirical magazines had a field-day with monkey cartoons.

But the application of evolutionary theory was not wholly benign. While it received a hostile reception in South Carolina, because it highlighted the close connection between plantation owners and slaves, in New Zealand it was used to support racism towards Maoris. Scientists assiduously measured brains and concluded that intelligence and a disposition for civilization depended on brain size. At the same time data, such as notoriously skewed early IQ tests, showed conclusively that black-skinned people were the lowest grade while the white-skinned were superior. Few people questioned whether facts had been selected because they fitted the all-pervasive racism of the day while conflicting data had been ignored.

These results and Darwinism were extrapolated into a widely supported system of eugenics which called for measures to prevent the breeding of the insane, drunkards, the poor, sex offenders and criminals. Further development wreaked havoc in Nazi Europe in the twentieth century.

Non-Euclidean geometry	A form of geometry based on curved surfaces. Euclid (c.330–275 BCE) dealt with flat surfaces only.
Royal Institute, London	The Royal Institute was founded as a research establishment in 1799 by the American Count Rumford.

TWENTIETH CENTURY – A RELATIVE ERA

At the beginning of the century science was triumphant. It was now the province of highly trained specialists essential in industry and it figured ever more largely in society as a whole. Just as Christian missionaries in the nineteenth century had expected heathen religion to give way under the impact of Truth, so scientists now assumed Christianity would fade away in the light of Reason. By the end of the century the achievements of science were in doubt and Christianity was attracting a new and wider audience. How did this happen?

- **Green revolution**
- **Social revolution and suffragettes**
- **Spiralling DNA**
- **Worldwide Church**

Green revolution

The century that started so auspiciously for science and technology soon tumbled into vicious world wars with gross cruelties perpetrated by all sides. Research that resulted in the massacre of civilians by atomic bombs or efficient gas chambers came under question. God's behaviour was challenged too. His aid in maiming and killing had been invoked by all parties, an ambiguity not lost on the war poets. Was he in support of trench horror and fire-bombed cities? God died more thoroughly than he ever did on Calvary's hill.

People turned instead to rebuilding a better world for everyone, with enough success for this tragic century to be eventually named the Century of the Common Man. We will look first at the attempt to provide quality food sufficient for all.

During the early twentieth century food production declined in Britain. Those early photographs of happy labourers sporting in the hay fields are far from the truth. Conditions for labourers were so bad that some joined up for the Great War of 1914–18 to escape. During the world wars increased food production was financially rewarded, but between the wars agriculture suffered from the Great Depression.

As the industrial base developed in former colonies, there was a decline in the old trade of British manufactured goods for foreign food. The population continued to increase and Britain needed its farmers. So after the Second World War the subsidy system was retained as a useful method of controlling food production. It also provided a social function in supporting poorer hill farmers.

At the same time homes, light industry and roads regurgitated concrete and tarmac across the best farming land nationwide. Customers demanded food free from blemishes of pest and disease, so farmers increased pesticide use. More food had to be provided from ever decreasing acreages and poorer quality land which needed more fertilizers. Pastures once only adequate for grazing had to be ploughed for crops, though the total area under the plough increased less than 6% above the 1945 records. By the 1970s farmers produced three-quarters of our indigenous crops and had enough to export. They had doubled the output per hectare for the majority of food products.

At the same time livestock conditions were radically improved. Better diet, housing and veterinary care revolutionized welfare from mid-century onwards. The finished product was far cleaner and free from worms and diseases like tuberculosis. Pay and working conditions improved as new machinery relegated many mind-numbing, back-breaking jobs to the past. Bread riots and widespread starvation became a forgotten nightmare. The food choice of the whole population was magnified beyond the wildest dreams of earlier centuries.

It came at a cost. The necessity of producing more food in smaller space led to factory animal farming. Less than perfect food crops were turned into animal food or composted. In the 1960s farmers, agricultural scientists and wildlife organizations were becoming increasingly concerned about pollution, soil erosion, possible pesticide residues in food and damage to wildlife, so since the 1980s subsidies have gradually been shifted towards solving environmental problems. Novel disease in the human food chain is always a concern, and bovine spongiform encephalopathy (BSE) was no exception. There was also heightened anxiety about disease in eggs and new hygienic measures were quickly put in place. All these fears resulted in a lack of confidence in farming skill among the general public, even including conspiracy theories (for example Rowell).

Social revolution and suffragettes

Better diet was not the only improvement to lifestyle. Widespread availability of education was coupled with better working conditions, superior housing and comfortable homes. Universal suffrage at last and the use of statistics, market analyses and polls gave voice to opinions that had rarely been heard before. State welfare provided a much-needed safety net.

One important result of social change was the recognition of women's rights. For centuries women were under male legal protection which was biased towards the interests of men. Women's lives were circumscribed by marriage, and child-bearing and rearing. Elite women had a few choices open to them, but they could not move into the professions. Poor women had no careers. Many made their living from seasonal jobs or cottage industries like spinning. As the industrial revolution progressed jobs in the home were lost and they and their children had to work long hours in factories or mines. If sick, unmarried, deserted or barren they were especially vulnerable and might have to resort to begging and prostitution.

Most churches, including their women, supported these double standards. Didn't the Bible say that marriage and child-bearing were essential for women's salvation (Genesis 3.16 and 1 Timothy 2.11–15)? Scientists too, who were almost invariably male, approved of the prevailing system. Those skull measurements of the previous century verified women's inferior status from her smaller brain. White women were still assumed to be superior to black women. If the latter had sexist husbands they were kept firmly in their proper place at the very bottom of society.

In the twentieth century the balance started to be redressed. Reluctantly men allowed women into universities. Women gained the vote and their political voice was heard. And science in the form of contraception freed them from the burden of unwanted pregnancies and illegal abortion. As society's views altered so did scientific data. Readjustments showed that when body size was taken into account, women's brain size was equal to men's. But in full-time work there is still an 18% gap between the pay awarded to men and to women due to the employment of women in jobs with traditionally lower pay (e.g. packaging rather than loading).

Spiralling DNA

We looked at a few of the discoveries of the past century in Part 1. Others include better understanding of the atom and the chemical composition of the double helix of DNA. These have many practical applications today, and Chapter 8 discusses some of them.

In the second half of the twentieth century stunning pictures from space showed our planet earth as a small ship in a vast universe, carrying a beautiful but fragile load of living creatures. Evidence that the world acts as a self-contained system increased global and environmental concerns. Much research today is grounded on this realization of our close relationship with other life forms and our reliance on one another.

Although scientific method had been so successful, questions began to be raised. Science now had its own philosophers, notably Karl Popper, who introduced the idea of *falsification*, and Thomas Kuhn, who added *paradigm shifts*. Postmodern philosophers criticized scientific objectivity on the grounds that discoveries are not value-free. There is no true knowledge, only different ways of seeing the world (Paul Feyerabend). But scientists in general assume they are working with reality, as their findings do not vary with culture, place or time, and that relativity as a philosophy does not apply.

Our ability to fix things had never seemed more secure – but was it? Increasing doubts about the efficacy of new technologies are causing great concern among scientists and non-scientists alike as Chapter 8 explains.

Falsification	A theory will be discarded if experimental results do not confirm it and if the results fit better into an alternative theory. For a theory to be considered scientific, it must be possible for it to be falsified.
Paradigm shifts	Laws and theories (paradigms) are based on slow and cumulative evidence. A major shift occurred when Newtonian physics became a special case of Einstein's relativity.

Worldwide Church

Religious statistics are somewhat unreliable, but current estimates are that Christianity is the largest of the world religions. About half its members are actively committed. In 1900 half of all Christians were European, but the huge increase in Latin American, African and Asian churches over the century has resulted in this proportion dropping to one quarter. In general, theological matters are decided in Europe and the USA, but the rest of the world is beginning to show some muscle, especially on the current issue of homosexuality.

Throughout the century, church attendance declined in many denominations and many of the old questions were raised again, often by church members. In what way was the Bible the word of God, true and faultless? Its historical details had been considerably revised. The hatred of the Old Testament God for other religions had been questioned for years, and now other religious documents from the Old Testament period showed it to be one-sided in its judgement. Current world religions did not seem to be inferior ethically. More sympathetic anthropologists recorded minor religions in a way that often challenged Christian superiority.

From the time of *Piers Plowman* the hierarchical and paternal approach of many churches had been questioned, including their cosiness with the ruling elite. In the 1960s liberation theology emphasized God as the one who makes humans free. Latin American Catholic clergy held consciousness-raising rallies and were denounced for Marxism. Martin Luther King in the USA guided the civil rights movement for Afro-Americans along non-violent lines, following the example of the Indian Mahatma Gandhi. The feminist movement of the 1970s dared to claim that God should no longer be wholly described in masculine terms such as Father, Warrior King, Judge. The Bible should be feminized and God addressed equally as She.

In Britain disgust with the religious squabbles and murders in Northern Ireland led people to search for 'spirituality' rather than follow the Christian religion and they turned to more touchy-feely New Age spirituality. While eastern religions have had their adherents for many years, in Britain there has been unprecedented opportunity to explore different faiths, with the immigration of Muslims, Buddhists, Hindus and others in the latter half of the century.

Decline in church membership does not appear to correlate with lack of concern for ethical and spiritual matters. There are signs that as dissatisfaction with technological fixes increases, so people turn again to Christianity and other religions for answers to our problems.

Before we look at ways in which both science and religion can work together for the greater good, we will examine some of the challenges the sciences still raise for worldwide religions.

IDEAS FOR DISCUSSION

1 Heresy and witchcraft. What were the reasons for the wars of religion and the witch hunts in early modern Europe? Compare beliefs about witches of this period with today's beliefs.

2 How objective is science? Can scientists set all presuppositions aside? Should they try to do so? Look into the theories of Popper, Kuhn, Lakatos, Feyerabend and Duhem-Quine (see Richardson and Wildman; also Southgate, in Chapter 7).

3 Find historical examples that show the use of selective scientific facts and sacred writings to support a presupposition (e.g. racism, sexism, homophobia). Take a current area of debate and argue alternative views using selected scientific and biblical statements for both.

4 Read Gould and discuss the misappliance of scientific facts and the skewing of research

5 Some Christians understand that scientific philosophy suggests science can never give an objective view of the 'real world', because it is only based on probabilities. Therefore any view is equally legitimate (such as the 6,000-year-old universe). What is your opinion?

6 Scientific method includes induction, deduction, inference and assessment. Can scientific method be used in theology?

7 Look up the Farming and Wildlife Advisory Group website. How have farmers addressed environmental problems? What proportion of our food should come from British farms? Should we import more?

8 Nuclear power. Energy to support our lifestyle does not come cost-free. Why could nuclear power be an answer to the problem of human-based global warming? Consider this in relation to a large developing economy like that of China.

9 Discuss the effects of the industrial revolution on people in all walks of life. How did scientists and Christians work together to find solutions to poverty and disease? Read some novels dating from this period (e.g. Dickens, Eliot, Gaskell).

10 Rights of women. Using texts like Armstrong, Davies, and Hufton, consider the position of women during the period covered by this chapter.

11 How have technological achievements in the twentieth century affected our views about planet earth (e.g. the effect of space travel, atomic power and discovery of the double helix DNA)? Has new technology had this effect historically? (For example, minds were compared to telephone exchanges at the beginning of the twentieth century.)

12 Ethical approach to environmental problems. Who should decide how scientific knowledge is used? Is there a case for banning some research? See Southgate (Chapter 7) and Barbour, for example.

REFERENCES AND FURTHER READING

Website

www.fwag.org.uk   Farming and Wildlife Advisory Group

Books

Karen Armstrong, 1986, *The Gospel According to Woman*, London: Hamish Hamilton

Ian Barbour, 1992, *Ethics in an Age of Technology*, London: SCM Press

John Hedley Brooke, 1991, *Science and Religion: Some Historical Perspectives*, Cambridge: Cambridge University Press

Charles Darwin, 1859, *The Origin of Species*, ed. J W Burrow, 1968, Harmondsworth: Penguin

Angela Davies, 1981, *Women, Race and Class*, London: Women's Press

Stephen Jay Gould, 1981, *The Mismeasure of Man*, Harmondsworth: Penguin

John Gribbin, 2003, *Science: A History*, Harmondsworth: Penguin

Christopher Hill, 1972, *The World Turned Upside Down*, Harmondsworth: Penguin

Henry Hobhouse, 1985, *Seeds of Change*, revised edition 1999, London: Macmillan

Olwen Hufton, 1995, *The Prospect Before Her*, vol. 1, London: HarperCollins

Brian P Levack, 1987, *The Witch-hunt in Early Modern Europe*, Harlow: Longman

John McManners, 1990, *Oxford Illustrated History of Christianity*, Oxford: Oxford University Press

James R Moore, 1979, *The Post Darwinian Controversies*, Cambridge: Cambridge University Press

W Mark Richardson and Wesley J. Wildman, eds, 1996, *Religion and Science: History, Method, Dialogue*, London: Routledge

Andrew Rowell, 2003, *Don't Worry, It's Safe to Eat: The True Story of GM Food, BSE and Foot and Mouth*, London: Earthscan

Quentin Seddon, 1989, *The Silent Revolution*, London: BBC Books

Keith Thomas, 1971, *Religion and the Decline of Magic*, Harmondsworth: Penguin

E P Thompson, 1963, *The Making of the English Working Class*, Pelican Books

Gilbert White, 1788, *The Natural History of Selborne*, edited by Richard Mabey, 1987, Harmondsworth: Penguin

7

Re-Imaging a Faith

In the previous chapter we saw how science and technology have eroded the Christian position. This development is being watched with alarm by other world religions. In this chapter we will examine some of the problems for Christianity in particular and how they are being tackled. Basically the problems fall into two categories.

- **Loss of belief**
- **Loss of status**
- **Responses to these**

LOSS OF BELIEF

Since the days of Galileo God has lost his traditional job of keeping the universe on track. He may have made the initial firework and lit it, but nothing that follows requires his input. He no longer breathes a life force into inanimate matter or makes individual species. Humans are not his special creation. He seems unnecessary.

In the past religions were believed to control natural events. The Pharaohs, God's sons, thought their prayers brought the Nile floods, and the downfall of one dynasty correlates with climate changes in central Africa when reduced rainfall over the Abyssinian Highlands, the Nile's source, affected the annual floods. Roman emperors also laid claim to godly status. Priests accessed the powerful spirit world that encompassed life and death, and, as they often managed the legal system too, their domination was colossal. Priests controlled tribal history, writing, education, mathematics and the use of technology. The latter was employed to beautify the dwelling of the god and the palaces of his or her priests and kings. Administration and taxation were often priestly functions, and priests rarely suffered from food shortages. This authority has gradually been eroded away as we saw in the last chapter.

LOSS OF STATUS

The Christian Church has lost status in three ways.

Biblical authority is reduced. Its history is unreliable in many areas. It is widely seen as ambiguous on such issues as slavery, war and human rights. It is seen as illiberal in its belittling of women, homosexuals and other religions.

In many countries the Church has lost its traditional roles of education and help for the sick and unfortunate, as the state has taken on these roles in a more comprehensive manner. Although it is exemplary in its charitable work in Britain, it has been reduced to begging money for the upkeep of buildings containing our rich historical heritage. Its evangelism has often degenerated into an emotional appeal to the individual to seek personal salvation and happiness.

It has lost relevance. Though it claims to be the way to true happiness, technology is seen as superior in practice, because it improves general health and comfort. The contented Christian peasant of medieval Christian Europe is known to be a myth. Christianity has often been allied with oppressive regimes so its ethical commitment is doubted. People now have more information and the leisure to enquire into other religions or ethical systems like humanism.

RESPONSES TO THESE

The churches have responded by reaffirming basic truths, developing new roles and redefining theology in the light of scientific discoveries.

One basic truth is the supremacy of God. This defines our proper position in the universe and is the foundation for ethical behaviour. Others include the importance of Christ as exemplar and saviour and the Holy Spirit as indwelling guide to truth in both individual and church.

New roles involve a reemphasis of longstanding doctrines. Our human role as stewards of the earth is pointed out during discussions on environmental degradation and the fairer use of resources. When considering the effect of the new genetics, Christians stress the value of the human person and his or her relationship to God. The Church highlights its commitment to equitable dealing in all human situations.

For the past forty years a number of Christians have searched for scientifically sensitive models and theologies. Some theologians are unhappy with this approach. Broadly speaking there are three positions.

- **Only God can reveal himself to us**
- **Scientific models have some relevance**
- **The universe reaffirms God's self-revealed nature**

Only God can reveal himself to us

As discoveries made by science and reason are merely the findings of fallible humans, they cannot have anything to add to God's self-revelation made through Bible, Church doctrine and tradition. Natural theology is idolatry for it puts nature before God. Sin has made a gulf between God and us that can never be bridged from our side. The whole universe is corrupt, so the image it gives us of God is inaccurate.

Scientific models have some relevance

A more amenable view is that, yes, scientific method can usefully test out new possibilities and scientific models can be helpful. However, theology is not merely acquisition of knowledge like the sciences. It includes practical experience of God, while religious tradition guides our ethical behaviour. Christianity's ultimate aim is to assist the believer to love Christ and conform to him, so that he or she may achieve fellowship with God and resurrection from the dead.

The universe reaffirms God's self-revealed nature

A number of trained scientist theologians support the old scientific view held by Boyle and Newton among others. Since God created the universe and gave humans the gift of reason, it must be possible to find insights through the natural world. They criticize the circularity of the current theological approach, such as the statement, 'The Bible and tradition guide us to the truth because they have been revealed by God.' A number are *process theologians* who take a more evolutionary approach than traditional orthodoxy, while stressing that God has certain enduring qualities.

Process Theologians	God presents new possibilities but leaves alternatives open to permit response by the created universe. God works through the slow emergence of new forms, and his power over world events is limited. He is still transcendent, all-knowing and omnipresent.

The rest of this chapter explores five examples that exemplify these different approaches.

- How not to use the Bible – Creationism
- Fruitful discussion – Divine action
- 'Teach us to order our days rightly . . .' – Christian teaching
- A positive revolution – Feminism
- A divided Church – Homosexuality

HOW NOT TO USE THE BIBLE – CREATIONISM

Creationists take the literalist approach, treating the Bible as a scientific textbook revealed by the God of Truth. Since the 1960s their organizations have been increasingly active in North America and Australia with a lesser presence in the UK. Their universe history includes a hot Big Bang about 6,000 years ago, a special creation of humans and other life forms, and a worldwide flood caused when a passing comet destroyed a water vapour canopy fixed above the earth (Genesis 1.6–8). During the flood year all sedimentary rocks were laid down and extinct creatures, including sea creatures, drowned and became fossilized. The Institute of Creation Research in the USA searches for evidence to disprove historical sciences like cosmology, geology and biology.

The scientific community viewed such beliefs with various degrees of amusement, but it became downright angry in the 1980s when the creationist lobby succeeded in introducing educational legislation in some 35 American states. If passed this would have legalized their teachings alongside evolution, but they were unsuccessful. However, continual lobbying of textbook publishers and state education committees curtailed the teaching of evolution. In 1996 statistics from questionnaires showed that 65% of American college students believed in a worldwide flood and 41% thought humans and dinosaurs were contemporary. Was this just a student scam? No, for apparently there are similar belief levels among newspaper editors.

The Creationists' appeal lies in their aim to provide a safe and moral society in a difficult world by retreating to past securities. Their contempt for the historical sciences probably stems from rightful abhorrence of social

Darwinism popular in the late nineteenth and early twentieth centuries. They have deduced from this that evolutionary theory is a conspiracy of atheistic and amoral scientists aiming to brainwash the public into denying God and morality. Since people are basically sinful they will relish freedom from moral control. Statistics on divorce and crime show that immorality is increasing. QED.

The result has been to antagonize many scientists against Christianity in general. They feel insulted by the creationist assumption that only Christians have ethical standards. And they assume that as Christianity is based on the Bible, then the creationist version of history is acceptable to all Christians, which it is not.

FRUITFUL DISCUSSION – DIVINE ACTION

- **How does God act within the universe? General and Special Divine Action**
- **Defining miracles, natural law and their relationship**
- **Four possibilities for Special Divine Action**

How does God act within the universe? General and Special Divine Action

There are two ways God may act. One is through the initial creation and active support for the laws of the universe, known as General Divine Action (GDA). It is easy to say this; more difficult to specify what is meant. Special Divine Actions (SDAs) are God's actions at a particular time and place. These include religious experiences, miracles and response to prayer. At the moment religious experiences provide the main confirmation of SDA, though their position is weakened by the latest research on consciousness. Miracles and response to prayer have long been questioned. Events like the resurrection are foundational for Christianity, so it is vitally important to get a handle on SDA.

Currently there is a promising liaison between theologians and a number of scientists with theological interests at the Vatican Observatory and the Center for Research into Theology and the Natural Sciences at the University of Berkeley. For more than a decade researchers have studied the vast literature covering such diverse areas as quantum cosmology and mechanics, chaos and complexity, evolution and the neurosciences.

One of the problems of relating natural science to theology is that the theoretical assertions made by the two disciplines are very different. It is probably not possible to place the biblical accounts of miracles into a scientific framework, though many attempts have been made. The simple question is: 'How do we describe SDA in this current scientifically based world?' The answer of course is not so easy. First we must define miracle and natural law before we can begin to decide which events are miraculous and which natural.

Defining miracles, natural law and their relationship

The following is necessarily a simplification of many sophisticated arguments.

- Miracles
- Natural law
- The relationship between SDA and natural law

Miracles

We need to define what sort of event we can consider miraculous. Perhaps it is something positive and personal like the healing of the sick. Do miracles have to include a spiritual message? Is it still a miracle if unobserved by a human? Can other animals observe miracles, like Balaam's ass who saw an angel with drawn sword standing in Balaam's path while her master was blind to the vision (Numbers 22)? Do particular historical events clearly show God at work among the nations, or are other explanations equally likely?

We believe God to be the upholder of law and order, so would it be morally right or feasible for God to break those laws? What sort of 'law' does a miracle imply? If there is a remarkable situation (virgin birth or resurrection) then what does this tell us about the way the universe works? In what other situations would such a law be applicable?

If religious experiences are God's chief method of communication, then we must look closely at the way the human brain might be affected. We have to decide which particular brain/body events God alters so that we may hear or feel or perceive God and respond. And what about those whose religious experience is negative (possibly an under-reported area), or malignant? Perhaps there are strong psychological and cultural components. How do we evaluate their effect?

We have to clarify questions like these before we can start to decide their relationship with natural events.

Natural law

For at least two centuries accounts of nature have been replacing God's role with physical laws. During this period, theologians have used any gap in human ability to explain the cause of an event as evidence for God's action. Gradually the gaps have diminished until very few are left. For a number of scientist-theologians, it is now axiomatic that God does not interfere in the physical laws of the universe. Laplace would approve.

This is not quite so decisive as it appears. What are the natural laws? The world appears deterministic in the sense that a ball released at the top of a slope will always roll to the bottom. God is not required to give it a push or guide its route. But what these physical laws entail is not so easily defined and unless we know all laws of nature, we can't determine whether an event is miraculous or not. Today we know the universe is so vast it's impossible to prove that it is wholly determinate or that each part can communicate fully with all the rest. Laws of nature do not necessarily apply on all scales and in all domains across the universe. It's a matter of faith based on the history of technology and observation in our small backyard in space. If our human world behaved in a totally indeterminate manner, no plant could expand its roots into the soil and there could be no inventions of wheel and printing or any journeys to the moon. But, beyond the stars or deep in the heart of an atom, who can be certain?

To make matters more difficult, the concept of indeterminism is embedded in quantum and chaos theories. You will recall Heisenberg uncertainty at the subatomic level, and non-linear dynamic systems at the macroscopic level like weather prediction. Just as the ancient idea of causality (interference by spirits and heavenly beings) gave way to a clockwork universe, so that too has yielded to a more open-ended model.

The relationship between SDA and natural Law

It's difficult to find room for God's action in any deterministic system. A car that won't start needs a mechanic, not a prayer. But the indeterminate model has novel implications for philosophy and theology. Some theologians have used a wave/particle analogy for Jesus' human/divine nature, but it is not enough to slot God's actions so simply into current theories. One needs to show how they fit together. Indeterminism allows gaps and ambiguity, but raises the question of God's knowledge, if the future is basically unknowable.

Four possibilities for Special Divine Action

To give some idea of the complexity involved when we try to understand SDA's relationship with the natural world we will look briefly at four areas.

- Probability
- Quantum SDA
- Chaotic SDA
- Top-down SDA

Probability

Scientific method is largely based on probabilities. Consider an actual experiment. Ragwort (*Senecio jacobaea*) on a sand dune is growing in a highly risky environment, and by careful observation we can calculate that fewer than 2% of seedlings become established. We can work out that the chance of a young plant growing to maturity and setting seed is only 0.25%. But we can't know which plant is going to germinate, mature and send off its seed parachutes into the great unknown. We can only calculate the probability and there is never enough data to prove every part of a theory. Even measurements like those above are theory-laden. We are theorizing that the sand dune environment will restrict the growth of ragwort before we start to count the plants.

Sometimes people put forward the simplistic view that if scientific knowledge is based merely on the probability of a certain event taking place, then there are no real *laws* of nature. Anything we imagine to be possible is possible somewhere on earth. This can generally be refuted on practical grounds, but those who believe in magic – and they are many – are unlikely to be convinced, however often their spells fail.

So science cannot prove there was no resurrection of Jesus from death some time close to 30 CE near Jerusalem. It can only note the level of probability by comparing it with all other known resurrections of living things from the dead.

However, statistical analyses have altered our perception of miracles today. If 76% of people die from a particular dread disease, a survivor may claim a miracle. But they are merely one of the fortunate 24% and their survival may be related to genetic differences or their general level of health.

Statistics and probability don't rule out SDA, but neither do they support it.

Quantum SDA

Here we must consider whether God is active in all subatomic events, choosing directly from the available possibilities. God could alter wave-function between measurements, alter probabilities or determine the result of each measurement, but these are all highly interventionist.

There is then the difficulty of how such events relate to the macroscopic world. God's alteration of the outcome of a quantum event might eventually alter an asteroid's path so that it collides with earth and extinguishes the dinosaurs. Species of ancient mammals could then multiply to utilise the vacant habitats and humans would develop. A mathematician has actually calculated God would have to make his modification three million years before the asteroid's impact. But how could one ever prove God adjusts evolution in this way? If one of the functions of miracle is to reveal God's nature to humans, then an event which may or may not be due to God is hardly convincing. And how could something as stupendously complicated as a mammalian virgin birth or the resurrection of a dead human body be accomplished in this fashion?

Though humans have discovered a basic indeterminism at subatomic level, maybe God's perception is different. Perhaps God controls all quantum events, not just some. If so, we are back in a fully determined clockwork universe with all our actions and thoughts predetermined. There is no room for creatures to explore freely.

To date theologians have not been able to develop a model for quantum SDA that correlates fully with current scientific understanding.

Chaotic SDA

Chaos theory provides us with a law-like framework which supports open-endedness and flexibility. But it is a catch-all phrase for different types of phenomena using different mathematical models. The mathematics is deterministic and does not introduce new postulates in the way quantum theory has done.

One of these models is used to predict movements in large-scale physical systems (see Chapter 1, under 'Chaos, ruler of the Evil Empire'). In the natural world chaos does not necessarily involve large changes. Chaotic fluctuations in heartbeat are background, not always complete disorder. Population crashes are not necessarily extinctions. If God uses chaos to make intervention in the world's affairs, very little can be achieved by this route.

Another idea is that God acts in the quantum world, and uses chaotic means to amplify the effects. Flexibility in the real world possibly allows God to put in active information (information in the scientific sense). Information input requires both physical input and expenditure of energy, but perhaps if God is present everywhere no extra energy would be required. If this tiny energy input produced a very large change in a system, and if God is aware of all the possibilities, then perhaps God acts in this way. But the miracle is now a statistical possibility, so unrecognizable.

Some theologians suggest that God, like humans, can't foresee the results of a chaotic system. The theory of kenosis (voluntary renunciation of divine power) suggests God may sanction such ignorance in Godself. But this doesn't help us find SDAs either.

There is considerable discussion over the possibility of non-interventionist chaotic SDA but currently there seems little possibility of using it as a basis for miracles like the resurrection.

Top-down SDA

Could mind be analogous to God and the universe be the physical expression of God? Some religions interpret the universe as the body of God. This scenario is not available to Christianity, which is based on revelation of a creator God greater than and different from the material world. Nor does the universe as a whole have anything comparable to a strongly coordinating organ like the human brain. It isn't organized like a human body. It is a network of many interconnected systems which influence one another. They exchange energy, matter and information. The laws governing the systems are based on probability and statistics.

Recall the section on emergence in Chapter 2, under 'Self-consciousness and creativity – I'm only human'. A system can be more than the sum of its parts. It can impose certain limitations on the lower-level systems. God might affect the overall state of our universe as a dynamic flow of information without invalidating any laws relevant in the subsystems. God knows everything it is possible to know about the whole network and its inter-relationships, and so could produce particular patterns of events that would affect each level down through the natural hierarchies. This pattern might appear as a personal communication within the human brain/body/society system. It might issue as a desire to search for the way God acts, or as concern for another human being which results in taking action. Meditation could be a way of developing awareness of God through a person's memories and experiences of their society and world. Any action taken 'in obedience to the perceived will of God' is then cooperation between God and the person. It is not enforced from above and it involves moral judgement by the human being, so that freedom of action and personal integrity are maintained. Because humans misunderstand situations, a particular action will not necessarily bring about the anticipated result. This leads to reinterpretation of a situation and improved proposals. In this way God 'speaks' through the results of an action.

Human ideas are very dependent on images. Images are more ancient than words and our problem is that of imaging God's action. We generally use a mechanistic image, like a potter at his or her wheel moulding clay, where God behaves like a superhuman. This creates all kinds of problems, some listed above, whenever we try to explain how God acts or why God has created or permitted evil. So another possible image is that of God as spirit where spirit means influence or bias. Consider a picture of God as a loving influence, the flow of love between humans within a society or the bias of the universe towards life, consciousness and love, justice and mercy.

The statement 'we believe God acts in the world' is not enough without some explanation of *how* God acts. The possibilities discussed above hardly allow for the sort of SDA that requires direct physical action like resurrection or virgin birth. So the current conclusion reached by the researchers at the Vatican and the University of Berkeley is that the traditional views of SDA cannot be supported by contemporary science. They observe that contemporary theology is in crisis over this matter, for so many doctrines rely on a consistent and verifiable description of God's actions. However, as we are always discovering new possibilities within the universe, other options may arise in the future.

'TEACH US TO ORDER OUR DAYS RIGHTLY THAT WE MAY ENTER THE GATE OF WISDOM' (PSALM 90.12) – CHRISTIAN TEACHING

Much of the religious education in British state schools is not specifically Christian. It includes comparative religion and discussion of ethical standards such as teenage sexual behaviour, family problems and concern for others. Doctrinal teaching is left to any religious organization attended by the pupil outside school.

The churches have risen to this challenge by producing quantities of quality literature on matters of belief, doctrine and spirituality. There are Bible study aids, modernized liturgies and new hymns. At the academic level there are many modern reaffirmations of core Christian doctrine, though wide divergences in belief make for difficulties (such as the division between Unitarian and Trinitarian doctrines). One successful and popular course is the Alpha course, started in Holy Trinity, Brompton, London, and now used in churches in many countries. It aims to convert interested non-Christians and to provide them and existing church members with a better grounding in the faith. While not everyone is happy with the implementation or content of the course, it has certainly proved successful over the twenty-odd years since its inception.

In this section we shall look briefly at some common Christian beliefs acquired by believers through church attendance, discussion groups and general reading of popular literature. We will also consider some of the confusions arising from teaching an ancient tradition with its pre-scientific bias. Finally we look at some scientific perspectives which may help to lessen the perplexity felt by many Christians and agnostics.

- **What is in the teaching?**
- **Some difficulties**
- **Scientific perspectives**

What is in the teaching?

The emphasis is on our need of God to give meaning and inner peace to our lives. We have been specially created for fellowship with God who is both holy and perfect. Our sins have separated us from God and we can never cross the gulf that separates us without aid, which Christ supplies.

For Western Christians this sinfulness is due to a Fall from a previous state of grace caused by deliberate rebelliousness. The Orthodox churches put more stress on the inevitability of the Fall. The first humans were like little children, bound to stumble rather than being wilfully disobedient.

The actual time of the Fall is disputed. One concept is that it happened about 6,000 years ago, well after the first modern humans appeared. Another idea is that God made special humans, spiritual founders of a new race of *Homo sapiens* at some much more distant moment. They refused God's offer of friendship and deliberately alienated themselves from love. All their offspring are similarly tainted, and evidence that some antisocial behaviours may have a genetic component is used to support this idea. A third view sees the Fall in terms of the individual. Babies are selfish, an indication that humans are imperfect from birth. Yet we have a certain innocence from which we fall as we gradually conform to our society which is inherently sinful.

It is quite common for Christian teaching to take a negative view of the living world, even while stating that God made the earth good. Some influential theologians in the last century like Paul Tillich believed that the natural world itself is basically evil because all organisms live through the assimilation of other organisms. God cursed the earth because of us (Genesis 3.17–19), so nature itself is out of joint and our every action pollutes and destroys it still further. Nature is in bondage to decay (Romans 8.19–23); a butcher rather than a mother. Death, pain and suffering are abnormal events; they are reminders that we have gone terribly wrong. Some theologians believe that our faults have infected the whole universe and it will never be whole until it is destroyed and recreated as a spiritual cosmos.

Over the past two thousand years Christianity has honed its description of sin by considering its results – wars, crime, pollution, destruction of the earth's resources. Socially we have inherited the corrupt values of our forefathers so that modern society is biased towards greed and selfishness. We forge groups like family and nation to promote our own self-interest at the expense of others.

As individuals we are egoistic, putting our own concerns first. Many are sexually depraved. Anger often rules our decisions. Fear and anxiety are the root cause of many sins but our pride prevents us from relying fully on God, so we can never be completely at peace. We suffer from hubris, excessive ambition that aspires to God-like knowledge. Even our best motives are mixed, never wholly good or honest. We are all 'chief of sinners' like St Paul. Our sin and immorality, said the Pope in a recent Easter message quoting the authority of Scripture, give rise to much ill-health.

Morality covers more than societies and the interactions between individuals. At its most profound it includes reflection on the meaning of one's life in relationship to God. We all have an inner law deep within our essential nature. This law is found within all humans and is God-given – it is not based on upbringing. Disregarding it is the moral equivalent of ignoring the laws of gravity – disaster ensues. We inevitably become guilt-ridden. A depressed person is possibly disobeying God somewhere in their lives.

Having analysed the human situation, Christianity then provides solutions. Christ's redeeming work is one of the most important and distinctive ideas of Christianity. God's creation of the inner law and ancient sacrifices for sin is to prepare the way for Christ who will make a bridge by his once-for-all sacrifice. To reject Jesus is tantamount to rejecting the love of God, a personal vote for evil. Some believe that eventually God will redeem us all, but others take the view that refusal to accept God's solution to our alienation leads to eternal punishment.

Theologians once emphasized that a perfect God can't have passions and emotions like ours. More recently it has been proposed that God can and indeed does suffer with the universe as it develops over time. The unfolding of the creativity inherent in the universe is continuously costly to God. God is not person-out-there observing us, but feels the pain of all who suffer. Christ is Emmanuel, God with us. So on the cross God in Christ takes the power of nothingness and evil that control the world into himself. Christ's resurrection is proof of the victory of incarnate and infinite love over infinite loss.

By accepting the Spirit of Christ freely into our lives we are forgiven and empowered to overcome our fears and selfishness. We are no longer alienated from God, our fellow humans and the rest of the living world. We can live full, free and happy lives in the knowledge that our future is secure. The fellowship of the Church, Christ's mystic body on earth, welcomes and strengthens us in our task of growing nearer God and our fellow humans. One day when world suffering is at its worst, Christ will return to overcome all evil for ever.

Some difficulties

For biologists the negative views of our living world are difficult to substantiate and seem to rest on a misunderstanding of the necessity of recycling resources. Evolution could not take place without death and decay and the claim that these are corrupt forces is debatable.

There are uncertainties about the Christian analysis of history. How likely is the return of Christ after two thousand years of eager but continually disappointed anticipation? A related anxiety is the fear that a Christian political leader in a highly militarized country might actively aim to hasten Christ's return. Some literal interpretations of the book of Revelation promote Armageddon as the forerunner to eternal happiness.

There are moral considerations of long standing. In the nineteenth century the Russian novelist Dostoyevsky raised one such conundrum in *The Brothers Karamazov*. Whatever the cause of misery in the world, how could an almighty God who permits it be good? If God has created a world of pain and evil so we can develop our souls through the use of free will, can this ever justify the suffering of an innocent child?

The idea that sacrifice by another should lead us to remorse and then love has been criticized as a form of brainwashing. Arousing guilt feelings by emphasizing a daily search for inner faults and failures has also been questioned. Do such methods give the required results in the long term?

Another difficulty is that the Christian explanation can be the reverse of helpful when someone is actually suffering. Clinical depression can be increased by fear of hell. Though hell is rarely mentioned today, the concept of eternal suffering is still evident in Christian teaching. The Son of God him-self has to suffer torture, death and separation from the love of God to save us from this appalling fate. John Donne, Dean of St Paul's, wrote in 1624, 'I have a sin of fear, that when I have spun/ My last thread, I shall perish on the shore' ('A Hymn to God the Father'). That gentle Christian William Cowper was maddened by his fears:

> Me miserable! How could I escape
> Infinite wrath and infinite despair!
> Whom Death, Earth, Heaven and Hell consigned to ruin,
> Whose friend was God, but God swore not to aid me!
> (Lines written on a window-shutter at Weston, 1795, during his final
> period of madness.)

Depression is compounded by fear of eternal rejection.

For many, bereavement is one of the most agonizing situations they will ever face. If those they love are not saved, then eternal bereavement is on the cards. Christian friends and books often provide spurious comfort by saying that God in his mercy will blot out the loved one rather than let him or her suffer for ever. There is not much the bereaved can say to such an insensitive solution.

Then there is the perception that Christianity itself accepts it has failed. Yes, there are many successes. It has held society together for centuries and strongly influenced our law and culture. It has spread widely and contin-ues to convert people to its message. But Christians themselves maintain the world has not improved since the Holy Spirit was poured upon human-ity after Christ's death. In fact they paint an unhappy picture of increasing corruption. Even those societies that have had a continuous Christian presence for centuries are troubled by civil war and sectarian hatreds. Few people turn from their egoistic desires to the call of God's love, and those who do tell us they are unable to reach the perfection they desire. Though love is said to dispel all fear, they are still anxious and fearful. They still put their own needs first. Even senior clergy seem to have a slim hold on moral-ity when they put the welfare of unmarried priests before their illegitimate children or paedophile priests before the damaged child.

Scientific perspectives

The remit of science is quite different from that of Christianity, and the sciences can in no way trespass on this territory. However, they can add some new perspectives.

Archaeology and historians give greater accuracy to biblical history and a broader outlook on early societies. Strange concepts about sacrifices and other rituals become clearer. Such ideas no longer resonate with us, and we can take a fresh look at how to interpret them today as we learn to understand the aims of the original writers.

Psychology and the neurological sciences indicate that a number of illnesses, depressions, guilt feelings and phobias are due to causes other than hidden sin. This relieves any sufferer who has been agitatedly hunting in their inner lives for faults that might have caused their illness or depression.

Sin is essentially a fault that Christianity alone can solve, not science, but the biological sciences explain that not all human problems are due to disobedience to God. There are natural causes for famine, disease and war as well as sin.

Psychology and evolutionary theory give us a further chance to reassess our ideas about sin. A number of faults like fear and selfishness are essential to the well-being of all creatures. They are ancient traits, and eradication is neither possible nor beneficial to life. Many faults have a positive side that would also be lost if we tried to remove them. The selfishness of babies mentioned earlier is a sign not of sin but of dependence and need, for it takes time for many young animals to find confidence to manage alone. A young blackbird as large as its weary bedraggled parent is well able to find worms for itself. It will still gape at the parents for food and peck them when their response is slow. We also know now that a number of our faults have both genetic and social components, though we cannot disentangle their effects in any particular case. With these and other facts in mind we may be able to improve ways of dealing with natural desires so they are satisfied without inflicting damage on the wider community.

Sociology, anthropology and the increasing availability of information enable us to be more sympathetic towards other religions. For reasons that seemed good at the time, the ancient Israelites found other religions abhorrent. We can overcome religious intolerance by developing a more sensitive understanding of other cultures.

A POSITIVE REVOLUTION – FEMINISM

Women have always had difficulty dealing with the Christian approach to their sex, but for centuries their voice was too weak to be heard. Gradually old ideas faded away as improved tools like better microscopes extended scientific knowledge. One example is the belief that men impregnated women with a human 'seed', which she must then nurture like mother earth. Abortion or still-birth resulted from her failure to care, and inability to conceive was due to some deep inner sin. Scientists actually saw the little homunculus in the head of male sperm under early microscopes. It is now known that women provide more than half the genetic component, while infertility can be a male problem.

The new confidence felt by women resulted from universal suffrage and university education, better health care, the contraceptive pill and safer, legalized abortion. A number of people, men as well as women, now recognized some of the problems for women raised by Christianity. Many resulted from the tradition that a woman's natural career choice should be marriage with children. As women worked towards greater parity in all careers a number began to scour the Bible for theological answers to male-orientated Christianity. By the 1970s many new ideas were being proposed.

Resistance was strong. Senior churchmen abhorred attempts to eliminate male language and thinking from Christianity, claiming that the damage would be irreversible. Women, they said, should accept that God himself had subordinated them to men. Women are designed to be helpers and mothers, and God's dispositions should be humbly accepted for what they are, pure goodness and truth. They dismissed radical thinking as resentment and spite. At this point some women decided Christianity was so sexist a religion it would always distort relations between men and women, and they left. Others continued to struggle within the system to extract images of God from the Bible acceptable to women as well as men.

The concerns of traditionalists were not without foundation. Society has indeed altered radically. While a number of men and women have always lived together without marriage, the numbers cohabiting have risen considerably. Women were now living outside the legal protection provided by both religious and civil marriage for mothers during childbirth and rearing. It takes time to readjust the legal system, and a number suffered as a result. Marriage has also been tied in to much-loved religious ceremonies full of beauty and historical meaning. These are performed within a supportive group, concerned for stability in marriage for the sake of any children. Such tradition and support are rarely incorporated in many of the attractive new ceremonies devised by participants.

Another dilemma for some churches is the issue of women priests and bishops. The traditional view (held by feminists also) is that the Church is primarily not an organization but the mystical body of Christ. So can its God-given laws be changed? Those opposed to women priests agree the Church can be reformed under the Holy Spirit, but feminism itself is merely a small and recent movement opposing centuries of Church practice. How can it claim to be the Spirit's messenger and guide to the whole Church under such circumstances?

In spite of opposition feminism has had its successes and many Christians now claim that the emphasis on God as mother, lover and helper has enriched their lives. But the opposition alienated women. Generally in the past it was the women – mothers, aunts and grandmothers – who taught young children the way of the Lord, supplemented by church or chapel attendance. As women became disenchanted with the traditionalist view their enthusiasm for this role waned. This has had a serious effect on church attendance.

A DIVIDED CHURCH – HOMOSEXUALITY

The difficulties faced by feminism are small compared to the issue of homosexuality.

Gender relies on those X and Y chromosomes we inherit. Or does it? There are a number of births where sex chromosomes are at odds with anatomy (intersex). Boys with an extra X chromosome have male genitals but develop some female characteristics at puberty. A baby's genotype may be XY (male) but it sometimes has ambiguous internal and external anatomy. The expression of sex hormones in the womb affects both foetal brains and sex organs in very complicated ways. Some 1 in 10,000 women are naturally exposed to high levels of male hormone before birth, but they rarely *feel* male. They may be born with a larger than normal clitoris, and sometimes doctors recommend surgery to reduce it. The parents must decide and the baby cannot give or withhold consent. Is this pandering to social prejudice?

The jury is still out on the question of genes for homosexuality. Behavioural genes are notoriously difficult to detect. If they vary in the way they express themselves and only affect an unknown number of their carriers, it is impossible to confirm their existence. It is difficult enough to conduct experiments on sexuality in laboratory conditions. How could one ever analyse human behaviour adequately? For a start, not all homosexuals are childless or live with someone of the same sex.

Nor should we forget other groupings that do not conform to the standard norms of two completely distinct sexes. Transgendered people encompass transvestites and the surgically sex-changed (transsexuals). There are about 40,000 male to female transsexuals in the USA, and even though many are comfortable with their identity the condition is still listed as a psychiatric disorder. Apart from genetics we need to consider the effect of upbringing. Some boys who suffer serious genital injury when circumcised have been surgically remodelled and reared as girls. In one case the boy retained his original sexual identity and at fourteen declared himself male. In another the boy was convinced s/he was female. Reasons for all these differences are unclear, as they may be genetic, hormonal or due to nurture and culture. Or interactions between all of them.

There are other possibilities arising from genetic modification. In some situations a three-parent solution is suggested for an infertility problem, namely, egg, nucleus and sperm from different people. Experiments in Japan recently gave rise to Kaguya, a mouse with two female parents. This is unlikely to be performed in humans because of the technical difficulties and ethical concerns, but, if they were overcome, how would Christianity classify such a child?

Homosexuality is almost lost within this sexual variability, yet for Christianity it is a major problem splitting the worldwide Anglican communion. Many bishops believe homosexuality is sinful behaviour. Humans have been created either male or female, and active homosexuality is condemned by Bible and tradition. So homosexuals must earnestly repent and seek the redemptive power of Christ. They must change. Others take a liberal approach invoking scientific findings. On the issue of morality they ask whether there is any evidence that a different sexuality results in less-loving relationships or reduced concern for the wider community. It seems unlikely there will be any easy answer to this issue, and other religions too find it difficult to give guidance on this point.

IDEAS FOR DISCUSSION

1 Check out the Creationist websites and compare with standard scientific approach using the websites for *New Scientist* (Chapter 1) and CSICOP and *Skeptic* (Chapter 4)
2 Atonement. This is based on a pre-scientific understanding of cause and effect. How would you express it today? See Leviticus, Old Testament, for example.
3 Women's position in the religions of the world. Compare several traditions. What important roles do women play in these religions?
4 Read the science fiction of Tim Lahaye and Jerry B. Jenkins – a series based on a literal interpretation of the book of Revelation, in the New Testament. This series is very popular in the USA. Give a critique of the ideas expressed. What are the dangers in taking the Bible literally?
5 Human conscience. Compare the opposing views of religion and science, e.g. Keith Ward (*In Defence of the Soul*, Chapter 4) and Dennett or Wright (Chapter 3).
6 How would you express the idea behind the Fall of Man in modern terms? See Berry.
7 Death. Investigate the explanations for death in Christian thinking. How do these differ from the scientific approach? Death is the great unmentionable in modern society, but

earlier generations were more open. (See the Brontes, Dickens, but also Samuel Johnson who rejected all mention of the word. Some church monuments to the dead are carved with skulls and skeletons. At what period was this fashionable?) What reasons can you find for modern reserve?

8   Investigate the arguments for Special Divine Action, in Saunders. How do you personally interpret the belief that God answers prayer?

9   Sin. What scientific evidence is there for an evolutionary component? Does this indicate that other animals are sinful?

10   Read Dostoyevsky's *Brothers Karamazov* and discuss the moral issues he raises.

11   Discuss evidence for the view: 'Religion is a social adaptation which requires a large amount of mental power. It is only found among animals which can understand "I think that you believe in a supernatural being who knows that we both want to behave well." Probably such mental agility was not available among hominids until language evolved, about 200,000 years ago.'

12   Research the issue of sexual differences and consider your view of homosexuality.

13   Read one or more of Alexander, Barbour, Deane-Drummond, Peacocke, Richardson and Wildman, Ruse, Southgate. Is a natural theology possible?

14   Read Richardson et al. and consider the different approaches to religious belief made by the scientists represented.

REFERENCES AND FURTHER READING

Journals

Science and Christian Belief
Zygon

Website Resources for science and religion

www.counterbalance.org   Counterbalance
www.creationresearch.org   Creation Research Society US
www.creationsciencemovement.com   Creation Science Movement UK
www.esssat.org   European Society for the Study of Science and Theology
www.metanexus.net   Metanexus Institute
www.stnews.org   *Science and Theology News*
www.science-spirit.org   *Science and Spirit* journal
www.srforum.org   Science and Religion Forum
www.ukia.co.uk   UK Intersex Association
www.templeton.org   Templeton Foundation

Books

Denis Alexander, 2001, *Rebuilding the Matrix*, Oxford: Lion
Peter Baelz, 1982, *Does God Answer Prayer?*, London: Darton, Longman & Todd
Ian Barbour, 2002, *Nature, Human Nature and God*, London: SPCK
R J Berry, 1984, *God and Evolution*, London: Hodder and Stoughton
Celia E Deane-Drummond, 2001, *Biology and Theology Today*, London: SCM Press
Paul Fiddes, 1988, *The Creative Suffering of God*, Oxford: Clarendon Press
Daphne Hampson, 1990, *Theology and Feminism*, London: Basil Blackwell
Richard Harries, 2002, *God outside the Box*, London: SPCK
John Hick, 1966, *Evil and the God of Love*, San Francisco: Harper & Row
Peter C Hodgson, 1994, *Winds of the Spirit*, London: SCM Press

Robin Keeley, ed., 1982, *An Introduction to the Christian Faith*, new edition 1992, Oxford: Lynx Communications

Alistair E McGrath, 2004, *The Science of God*, London: T&T Clark

William Oddie, 1984, *What Will Happen to God?: Feminism and the Reconstruction of Christian Belief*, London: SPCK

Arthur Peacocke, 1990, *Theology for a Scientific Age*, 2nd edition 1993, London: SCM Press

W Mark Richardson, Robert John Russell, Philip Clayton and Kirk Wegter-McNelly, eds, 2002, *Science and the Spiritual Quest*, London: Routledge

W Mark Richardson and Wesley J Wildman, eds, 1996, *Religion and Science: History, Method, Dialogue*, London: Routledge

Rosemary Radford Ruether, 1983, *Sexism and God-Talk*, London: SCM Press

Michael Ruse, 2001, *Can a Christian be a Darwinian?*, Cambridge: Cambridge University Press

Nicholas Saunders, 2002, *Divine Action and Modern Science*, Cambridge: Cambridge University Press

Christopher Southgate, ed., 1999, *God, Humanity and the Cosmos*, London: T&T Clark

Keith Ward, 2000, *Christianity: A Short Introduction*, Oxford: One World

8

The Samson Effect

The Philistines lived on the rich coastal plain of Palestine. They were far more successful than the hill tribes to the east. Their farmers grew pomegranates, grapes, figs and new varieties of wheat and barley. They cornered the market in iron goods using the latest technology. Armour of bronze scales and iron weapons made them almost invincible in battle. Their buildings were superior, designed in the style of their Aegean ancestors, and their pottery was a triumph of beauty and colour, nothing like the drab earthenware of their neighbours. They were exceptional traders, bartering highly valuable goods along the sea routes of the eastern Mediterranean.

The hill tribes observed their expansion eastward with alarm. Would these powerful neighbours with their advanced technology and mighty gods overrun the hills and take control of the inland trade routes? They did. And they ruled over the hill country for forty years, taking its produce in taxation and oppressing its people.

Samson was a hero-judge who ruled some of the hill tribes for twenty years. He was especially fond of the beautiful wealthy Philistine women. He won great battles for Israel over the invading Philistines, until at last they took him prisoner with the help of Delilah. They blinded him, bound him with bronze chains and forced him to grind corn. Then they celebrated the power of Dagon over the God of the hill tribes with a great feast in their largest temple.

Samson was dragged in to fight and make sport for them. He was enraged at their treatment of him, his tribes and his God and he despised their wealth and superior technology. Grasping the two central pillars of the temple he pulled it crashing down, killing those within and three thousand on the roof. 'So the dead whom he killed at his death were more than those he had killed in his life,' says the chronicler approvingly of this first suicide killer.

It's a response chillingly familiar to us. Can we devise better solutions to the world's current problems?

- **Technology – solution or problem?**
- **Tackling current issues**

TECHNOLOGY – SOLUTION OR PROBLEM?

Technology has come to our aid so often, but it has never been neutral in use. In ancient Palestine the poor farmer's family dug the hard stony soil with hand picks. The wealthier farmer walked past with his new wooden plough over one shoulder and his hand guiding his ox. Together they turned the soil quickly and efficiently, digging deeper so that the plant roots could penetrate to moisture further down. His crop flourished and he laughed when the poor farmer lost all his seed and feed corn in taxes and was forced to beg. He took over the poor man's land.

Technology, according to a number of people (such as Ellul), is a group of solutions without an overall goal. It looks for solutions to current problems and can't easily predict future drawbacks. The internal combustion engine solved problems of conveying goods around the country and increased our options for work and leisure. When the first vehicles were constructed, it was impossible to see problems caused by future mass-marketing. Technology has a number of unrelated suppositions, such as: the requirement for universal standardization; that change is good for change's sake; that increased power and speed are usually beneficial. Its rationale is based on scientific logic. It can be used either to help people improve their lives or to increase profit and growth at their expense.

Global warming, ozone holes, modern extinctions, pollution, more savage wars and novel diseases have been created or exacerbated by human technology. We can't be certain it will improve our situation in the long term, and science and technology are no longer seen in such a positive light.

The precautionary principle suggests ways of tackling these issues. We need to inspect any new technology for the possibility of irreversible accidents, and ask what new forms of dependency and power will arise from it and how we may avoid inequalities in its use. We must look dispassionately at technologies on offer and decide which are the most important and beneficial to humans and other living things over the long term. Then we need to direct finance for research and development into these areas. Both scientific and ethical discernment are required. Such principles are easy to list, more difficult to implement.

For historical reasons the Western world has cornered political power and technological advances. The countries involved have used their trading power to access resources across the globe. They are democratically run and their governments must accede to popular demands for better food, health and general welfare, and creative leisure opportunities for all.

Now we need to spread these gains far more widely, but no democratically elected government is able to propose a reduction in lifestyle at home in order to finance overseas prosperity. So can we improve conditions worldwide without further overuse of the world's limited resources? Can we increase benefits and at the same time reduce harmful side effects?

TACKLING CURRENT ISSUES

- **Population**
- **Energy and use of resources**
- **Medical advances and concerns**
- **Human futures**
- **Things that we don't know we don't know**

Population

- Overcrowding
- Trade – God speed plough and boat, perhaps?

Overcrowding

Success in capturing energy for growth and reproduction has led to an explosive expansion of the human population, particularly over the last two centuries. Now we are surveying ruefully the damage we inflict. Life's traditional answers to overcrowding are at work – continual warfare, famine and disease.

An obvious solution would be to encourage reduction in the birth rate. In countries with care for the elderly and good insurance in place, we no longer have to obey the old evolutionary stimulus to breed. Life can be wholly productive without children. World population growth has actually slowed since the 1960s from just over 2% per year to about 1.3%. It may even level off by the end of this century. But the decline is greatest in wealthier countries and growth is still high in many of the world's poorest regions. The sub-Saharan population is estimated at two-thirds of a billion, but may well top the billion mark by 2025, though the inroads of HIV/Aids will reduce numbers. This is an appalling and distressing solution – a non-solution in fact.

In large poor families the parents struggle to provide adequate nourishment to maintain health and growth, let alone education. The need for food and demand for wood for cooking impoverishes soils and destroys forests. Many areas with increasing populations are tropical and their ancient soils have already been heavily leached. Rainforest soils are particularly poor in nutrients so their productivity is low after clearance.

The United Nations Population Fund has shown how effective family planning can be in improving lifestyles, especially when combined with improved healthcare and better education and empowerment for women. But such planning receives decreasing financial support from the USA, and one of the reasons is strong religious opposition to birth control.

Trade – God speed plough and boat, perhaps?

So population will continue to increase along with its associated poverty. The economies of many developing countries rely on selling surplus foods worldwide, but farming is always subject to large swings in price and production. There are also huge imbalances between the price paid for the crop and that paid by the consumer. A number of organizations have been set up to encourage fairer trade so that the producer receives a better deal.

Another solution suggested is control of trade agreements so that poorer countries receive a higher reward for the labour of their people. Currently the impact of US and EU agricultural and fishing subsidies is under discussion. Developing countries have complained for years about the dumping of subsidized food on the world market. The EU fishing industry is estimated by the World Bank to receive about one-fifth of the value of the catch in subsidies, so driving down prices worldwide and encouraging EU fishermen to build fleets of large factory ships. These access the fishing grounds of other countries once their own have collapsed due to intensive trawling. The International Council for the Exploration of the Seas, the body which overlooks EU fishery management, and the UN Food and Agriculture Organization are in agreement that subsidies are the main cause of worldwide overfishing and the reduction in fish stocks.

It all looks rather simple. But no. We will look at the comparatively straightforward example of reducing subsidies to British farmers.

It isn't possible to calculate the average farming income in the UK, as comparing farm enterprises like dairying or arable is like comparing computer chip manufacturers with car factories. And the range of farm income is wide because farms are so variable in size. However, it is not a luxury income, and currently many farmers are selling up or starting non-farming enterprises. The public meanwhile believe that farmers are feather-bedded and inefficient, requiring massive subsidies from the taxpayer.

What is going on? Government money is used within the farm to pay for a plethora of paperwork in order to receive the subsidy. Numerous new regulations must be observed as well, all costly – after all, food must be hygienically produced and free from infectious disease. At the same time, money goes out of the farm in two directions. It is spent on expensive but essential input – labour, feed, medicines, seed, fertilizer, machinery and advice. In effect it supports agricultural research, development and manufacturing. The sale price (farmgate price) is also affected because it is kept down, often below the cost of production, by powerful food purchasers and cheap imports from countries with fewer regulations. Here subsidies support food safety requirements in the food manufacturing industry, and keep the price for consumers low at point of purchase so that cheap food is available for all. So subsidies skew the market, but simple withdrawal is not the answer, for it will merely result in the failure of more farm enterprises.

Governments are not particularly enthusiastic to reduce subsidies because they are a useful, though ponderous, means of controlling agricultural production. So these considerations and many more must be taken into account when we try to solve trade problems worldwide.

Energy and use of resources

- Energy for industry and home
- Waste and pollution
- Global concerns
- Photosynthetic energy, extinctions and biocontrol
- Genetic engineering solutions
- Concerns over genetic modification
- A cautionary tale – GM soya in Argentina

Energy for industry and home

Energy, we all agree, is required to support modern lifestyles. Use of ancient stores of energy, such as coal, gas, oil, has increased carbon dioxide in the atmosphere and is contributing to the greenhouse effect. This has led to development of renewables, the capturing of energy from wind, water and sun. But as world energy demands shoot up, the proportion of electricity from renewables has shrunk from 24% in 1970 to 15% today. And energy from renewables is more expensive than that from coal or gas resources – in Britain offshore windfarm electricity is about twice as expensive as that from coal. This reduces enthusiasm for private investment in such enterprises, so taxpayers will have to commit more money.

There are already improved methods for reducing harmful emissions from coal-fired power stations, and other possibilities include growing oilseed crops for biofuel. There is no net increase in atmospheric carbon dioxide, a greenhouse gas, from such crops because the gas they emit on burning is equal to the gas they use during photosynthesis for growth. The farming community in Britain supports this idea and biofuels are already in use in vehicles. Some London buses are using hydrogen as a fuel. There are innovative systems using advanced ceramics which concentrate the sun's energy and produce electricity. Such systems can be used in hot dry conditions like Spain or North Africa.

Research continues into nuclear fusion, which has a better public image than fission as it doesn't produce problematical waste products. Since research began in the 1960s the obstacle has been that reactors consume more energy than they produce. The international community is collaborating to crack this one (the International Tokamak Experimental Reactor). And the gradual unlocking of the secrets of photosynthesis raises the possibility of using one of life's own solutions to the energy problem.

Many developing countries employ a whole host of small effective remedies from clockwork radios to the use of geo-thermal heat from hot water in deep rock formations. Remote islands on Lake Titicaca on the Peruvian border have erected solar panels on house roofs to power their communities.

While it looks as if the world community may be able to produce essential energy without increasing global warming, the process is excruciatingly slow.

Waste and pollution

Waste increases as improvements to lifestyle spread through the population. Mass industrial production has spread robotic servants – washing machines, hoovers and many others – throughout society. The UK's waste burden of tens of thousands of cars and domestic appliances every week is causing huge recycling problems. Much of the iron is returned to steel plants, but only specialized landfill tips can take toxic waste, and stricter regulation has reduced their number. No government can take the option of taxing such items heavily because the poorest suffer most.

Particulates from fuel burning and other chemical processes can damage lungs. A new concern is nanotechnology, which produces useful items like non-scratch self-cleaning glass, but in some applications produces free particles, such as nanotubules. Current discussions focus on extending the regulations for novel chemicals to nanotechnology which also include protection for those working with the materials.

Global concerns

Global approaches are hampered by our inability to understand the complexities of the total environment. Holes in the ozone layer, global warming, the possibility of Gulf Stream shutdown, Asian brown smoke haze and intensified Australian droughts are too vast to succumb to small technological fixes. The International Geosphere-Biosphere Program is a worldwide scientific network studying Gaian-style feedback between biosphere and geosphere. The Gaian hypothesis maintains that these earth systems preserve a habitable planet, but the IGBP is less positive, surmising that they may be heading into a chaotic mode.

Unfortunately governments are generally more concerned with current energy problems at home, rather than global problems. Anxious climate scientists have suggested some really wacky-sounding quick fixes, using current technology. Mega-engineering solutions include the extraction of the greenhouse gas carbon dioxide from powerplant chimneys or stripping it from natural gas. It could then be injected into deep impenetrable sedimentary rocks under the oceans. Norway's Statoil company is already doing this in a small way, checking for possible leakage with seismic surveys.

Another mega-proposition is to reflect the sun's heat by a giant mirror or mirrors parked between earth and sun. Tiny aluminium balloons floated into the stratosphere could perform the same function. These are last-ditch solutions that no-one would want to attempt except in dire situations.

Photosynthetic energy, extinctions and biocontrol

Food energy derived from photosynthesis flows through interlocked living systems affecting them all. Humans seem to enjoy covering large areas with materials that are photosynthetically barren. We also take up to one-fifth of all available food energy and still suffer from famines and food shortages in many parts of the world.

Evidence mounts that this ever-increasing impact on other life is responsible for the sixth mass-extinction of species, comparable to the five previous ones. The fifth one occurred as long ago as the Cretaceous period when the dinosaurs died out. This is not an achievement humans can be proud of.

It is difficult to calculate how widespread extinctions are. Not all species are classified and only a few people can distinguish finely between different species of obscure insects, plants or fungi. For some species there's only one such person in the world, yet an extinction of one creature affects all the others in the ecosystem. Reliable data is hard to collect across earth's ecosystems, which vary from high-mountain to deep-sea and tropical to arctic. Extinctions of unknown species are probably extremely serious in the underrecorded tropical forests which are under considerable threat in the Amazon. Worldwide scares about mad cow disease in the UK and poultry flu have increased the demand for Brazilian beef, and ranchers have taken government land illegally. They destroy the forest faster than the logging industry or soybean business, increasing beef exports fivefold between 1997 and 2003. Falling beef production in the UK is expected to increase this demand.

We don't know the relative importance of different species within a particular ecosystem (see Figure 8.1). It's hard to decide which we should support with our limited resources. Should it be human-size furry or friendly animals like bears and dolphins? Should we save fragments from algae or spores from fungi? Even large collections like those of the Royal Botanic Gardens based in Kew, London, can't hold samples from all seed-bearing plants.

We may joke that the only creature that would miss humans is our body flea, but the point is serious. The douc langurs are some of the world's most endangered primates, likely to become extinct in ten years. Zoo breeding programmes are hampered by their digestive problems, which include

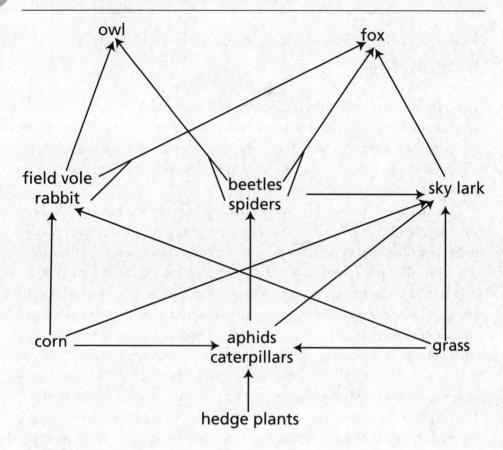

Figure 8.1   Simplified field food web
Which species is the most important?

constant vomiting and diarrhoea. Their gut microbes are being compared with those of healthy wild communities in the hopes of isolating beneficial microbes missing in the captive animals. Perhaps this is utopian, but all the same let's hear it for microbes and fleas!

In Britain we are moving land from food production into wildlife areas by channelling subsidies away from food. A return to the methods used before the green revolution is also advocated – organic farming. These schemes will reduce the food produced per hectare and increase reliance on imported food from the rest of Europe, America or developing countries. Our suppliers must then plough and drain more land to feed our population. Whether it is right to export our food and wildlife problems in this way has not yet been considered.

Biocontrol of harmful insects sounds a great solution to the use of pesticides which kill harmful and beneficial insects alike. Since the 1880s some 1,780 different animal species have been moved round the world. This is potentially dangerous as some have become ineradicable pests themselves. Recently Eurasian weevils were released by the US Department of Agriculture to remove non-native thistle from grassland. By the 1990s they had spread to the Arapaho Prairie wilderness in the central plains, where they are devouring seeds of rare native plants. This is all the more disconcerting because such releases are not authorized until strict analyses of possible damage take place.

Genetic engineering solutions

In the 1960s scientists began to publicize the possibilities of new techniques of genetic engineering – movement of genes between species, cloning, elimination of defects in the foetus, plant and animal breeding, medical possibilities, making viruses, gene warfare. They were anxious that this new godlike knowledge should be subject to wide discussion. Possible escape of a dangerous human-designed mutant virus from the laboratory, the sanctity of life and the status of species were particular concerns. They predicted that although the general public was not particularly interested, the time would come when they too would ask, 'Will these discoveries cause us problems that annul the advantages?'

In the 1970s genetic engineering was being developed in the USA with eventual huge commercial and social success. At the same time Health and Safety bodies here and in several other countries were looking at the implications of procedures and risk in laboratories working with microbes, and they implemented strict containment procedures. By 1982 cheaper insulin and the long-sought vaccine against hepatitis B were in use. In Britain the Genetic Manipulation Advisory Group approved research and development projects. By the 1980s environmental hazards were being considered like dealing with possible transfer of genetically modified plant genes carrying insect toxicity from crop to weed via pollen.

Genetic engineering is basically a cut, paste and copy operation (see Figure 8.2). Gene transfer occurs naturally in bacteria and through the actions of bacterial viruses (bacteriophages), so these are often used to transfer genes.

To feed everyone at the level of the Western world, we need to increase food production sixfold. Several possibilities are being researched. One is improvement of the rather low efficiency of photosynthesis, which could then be transferred to food plants. Another is to add the legume's ability to fix nitrogen to other food plants. They would then grow successfully in countries which can't afford the nitrogen fertilizer essential to improve their impoverished soils. Biotechnology can also boost yields by reducing the effects of weeds, pests and climate problems. Pesticides are expensive and the problems of environmental harm haven't been completely overcome, so one line of research involves inserting natural bacterial insecticides into food plants. Genetic engineering can also increase the range of a food crop by adding novel genes that confer resistance to drought, waterlogging or salty conditions.

Biopharming is the breeding of plants and animals to produce medicines or add food value. Examples are rice with Vitamin A, bananas which contain hepatitis B vaccine, or potatoes with vaccine against cholera. These will be specially valuable in Third World countries that can't store traditional vaccines safely. Scottish researchers have combined two genes from algae and one from a fungus, and transferred them to a common weed. It now produces fish style fatty acids so essential to human diet, so their next step is to transfer the system to a field crop so we can save our dwindling fish stocks. Currently hundreds of biopharming field trials are taking place in the USA. Of course seeds for these crops are expensive to produce so must be developed by large companies, a solution that doesn't appeal to everyone.

Animals too are engineered to produce greater quantities of important medicines. Modified sheep's milk provides human blood clotting protein Factor IX for haemophiliacs which is always in short supply.

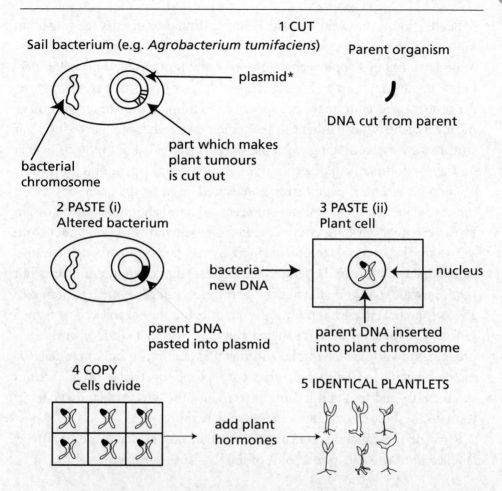

note: ***Plasmid** A piece of symbiotic DNA, not part of the bacterial chromosome. Found mainly in bacteria and yeasts.

Figure 8.2   One method of making transgenic plants.

Concerns over genetic modification

The scientific community is well aware of the risks and ethical implications of their work and are generally in a good position to judge them, but they are concerned that society as a whole must assess the ramifications. Not all scientists are happy with the use of biotechnology to help solve our food problems and there is deep suspicion among environmental activists which has been widely publicized.

Focus groups set up in the late 1990s in Britain to discuss the impact of biotechnology have found very negative attitudes and considerable poverty of understanding. People seemed unaware that humans have been 'tampering' with 'nature' from prehistory. They didn't see humans as part of nature. A number believed humans are special and completely distinct from other life forms. The value of other species in their own right is not part of popular culture. More encouragingly, people were concerned about biotech's effect on the environment and the condition of people in the developing world.

Yet not all genetic engineering is censured, even by the green parties. In the case of vegetarian cheese no-one seems to mind about the genetic origin of the essential curdling enzyme, chymosin. Chymosin is an extract from calf stomachs, so it is unacceptable to many vegetarians, depriving them of a valuable food resource. Different curdling enzymes are found in plants but don't provide such good flavour and texture. So calf genes are transferred to a yeast, and the cheese has traditional qualities but the enzyme comes from a yeast. Then there are bacteria engineered to perform all kinds of work from breaking down toxic chemicals and metal extraction to bulk manufacturing of medicine in fermenters. Viruses are spliced together to make vaccines against HIV and foot and mouth or to reduce the effects of faulty genes in humans. In these cases genetic engineering is approved.

Most of the concerns are directed at food crops, which are emotively labelled Frankenstein foods. Some of the issues are considered below.

- Superweeds
- Side effects
- Gene transfer between unrelated species
- Biopiracy
- Other objections

Superweeds

Gene transfer from crop to wild plants may create superweeds. These are not triffid monsters that will take over our countryside. If resistance to herbicide passes via pollen from the engineered crop to the related wild plant, then the wild one will survive the herbicide used by the farmer just as the crop plant does. They are an annoyance to the farmer within the field and along hedgerows, but it is not at all certain that they will be successful within a wild habitat. Resistance to a herbicide is not a useful trait here, so they tend to die out.

Superweeds will only be found where local weeds include the wild variety of the domesticated crop, so it isn't a problem in Britain when growing maize (origin USA) or wheat (origin Middle East). It affects field cultivation of plants derived from our wild cabbage – the brassica family which includes oilseed rape, cabbage, cauliflower, sprouts and broccoli. A related concern is whether genes inserted into crops for biopharming could contaminate food crops of the same species. Medicines in our cornflakes is not an attractive idea and this possibility has to be strictly monitored. Sterile pollen is one obvious solution, though not a complete one. Another one is to engineer the required gene into chloroplast DNA. Chloroplasts are inherited maternally in many species so there will be no genetic escape via pollen.

Side effects

Could these be caused by the interaction of novel genes with the original ones producing new toxins and allergens? In conventional breeding just as in bio-engineering, genetic variation changes biochemistry and physiology. Much more in fact. New varieties produced this way are rarely if ever tested for possible harmful effects on the consumer. A gardener will happily buy new non-GM carrot seed that promises resistance to carrot fly without querying the effect on family health. GM targets the alteration required much more precisely and the end-product is more easily controlled. Millions of people eat GM foods and the scary predictions of a huge rise in allergy-related deaths have not materialized.

To calm the fears some governments have demanded testing of GM food. Recently the European Union discussed the importation and selling of a genetically modified sweetcorn. Sweetcorn is badly affected by the corn borer moth and the new variety has a gene added from a soil bacterium that will protect it against the larvae. The EU decided in early 2004 that this modification doesn't adversely affect the crop for human consumption. It can't be grown in the EU, but it can be imported and sold for human food as long as it is labelled.

Gene transfer between unrelated species

This concerns many people. Should animal genes be transferred to a plant? Are we turning one creature into another quite different one?

The DNA carrying the required information is made up of four chemicals called bases (*A, T, C and G*). The sequence of these bases codes for information just as sequences of letters do in this book. The 'language' of DNA is understood by all living things. So the transfer of a human gene into a sheep does not turn the sheep into a human. The sheep merely produces the substance encoded by its new gene in its milk.

Biopiracy

The search for novel genes, insects to control pests and new plant foods and medicines has led to patenting of many species from Third World countries, without recognizing the rights of the indigenous population. There is a long tradition of such biopiracy – in 1876 rubber-tree seeds were taken from Brazil and used to establish rubber plantations in Malaysia. At last it is being recognized. The new International Treaty on Plant Genetic Resources for Food and Agriculture will help to ensure that some of the profits go into a central fund to be spent in developing countries, but more needs to be done in this area.

Other objections

Feminists, especially ecofeminists, take a strong line. Patriarchal attitudes of domination and subordination have led to exploitation of the natural world by male-orientated scientific methods and technology. This is the direct cause of our environmental problems. Humans are caretakers of the planet and should cease from meddling. This total rejection of technology seems rather unrealistic.

In general religions have followed a similar approach to that of green organizations with added spiritual concerns. For some the world is the body of God, so domination of its creatures for human benefit is deeply impious. Many religions are not impressed by current technological solutions – since technology has caused the problem, further scientifically based solutions will only make matters worse. Some developing countries see new food technologies as neocolonialism, especially where they are supported by Western-based, multinational companies, but these fears can be addressed by encouraging home research. Many societies worldwide feel their culture and beliefs are being threatened by biotechnology.

> **A, T, C and G**   The chemicals adenine, thymine, cytosine and guanine, if you really want to know.

A cautionary tale – GM soya in Argentina

GM soya seemed a heaven-sent solution to Argentina's problems. The Pampas is suffering severe soil erosion and yields have fallen by a third. To anchor the soil farmers made sure it was covered permanently by plant roots by reducing cultivation and sowing directly onto the land. Of course, weeds choked much of the crop, so farmers had to spray herbicide five or six times a year.

Argentina's agricultural economy was depressed and soya was one of the few profitable crops, so in 1997 they authorized the use of Monsanto's GM soya. The company assembled their product as an easy-to-use package of seeds, machinery and pesticides. A less toxic chemical, glyphosphate, was now applied twice a year. By 2002 almost half of the arable land was planted with soya, mainly GM. Yields increased and soil erosion decreased using the no-till method.

But soya production increased worldwide. The price fell. Then those monitoring the Argentinian situation found that farmers were having to increase their glyphosphate usage because of tolerant weeds. There was also an increase in *volunteer soya*, and to get rid of these farmers had to return to more harmful weedkillers. In some areas the tenant farmers sprayed indiscriminately and damaged neighbouring fields. Worse, animals died or gave birth to deformed young, and fruit trees were stunted. Even court orders banning spraying were not always effective. Soil bacteria declined and slugs and fungal diseases increased.

By this time the Argentinian economy was dependent on soya production, so the government was hand tied. The GM soya area continues to expand because other products like milk, rice, potatoes and lentils are unprofitable. Hundreds of small farmers producing these staple foods leave the land, so adversely affecting diet for the whole population.

It is well known among farmers and agronomists that monoculture is not a good farming method and that reliance on one particular regime to manage weeds will fail eventually. But farmers are locked into an unsustainable system due to necessity, not greed. There is great concern because the country has neither the resources nor the expertise to deal with such a huge problem.

Volunteer soya   Volunteer plants are those which grow from resistant seeds left in the field after harvest.

Medical advances and concerns

- New medicines
- Genetic modification – Frankenstein humans?
- Human cloning – (Hitler)[99]?

New medicines

Better understanding of the chemistry of the brain has resulted in new psychiatric drugs like the antidepressant Selective Seratonin Re-takeup Inhibitors (SSRIs, e.g. Prozac, Seroxat). They have been licensed to control severe depression safely and effectively, and Prozac, licensed in 1988, has been highly effective for many patients. Some have been used as a lifestyle drug (bottled sunshine) on the assurance they are not addictive and have no serious side effects.

However, there have been increasing reports of probable SSRI-related violence and suicides and side effects like muscular spasms, fatigue, apathy, pronounced withdrawal effects and loss of libido. Some scientists have tested psychiatric drugs on themselves and have had severely bad reactions. They are concerned that though a large number of patients benefit from the medication, no-one can tell which individual will experience harmful side effects.

It now seems likely that some manufacturers have kept research secret from the regulating bodies. The regulating bodies themselves are criticized for not questioning data in their possession on possible harmful side effects. There is also criticism of doctors administering the drugs. Is their relation-ship with the pharmaceutical companies too cosy?

The use of SSRIs in children is particularly controversial. In the 1960s it was believed children rarely suffered from adult mental problems. Today about one-third are expected to struggle with obsessive compulsive disorder (like continual hand-washing), attention deficit hyperactivity disorder and anxiety and depression. They are treated with drugs that were designed for and tested on adults. Children's developing brains are profoundly different from adult ones both in the chemicals they produce and in the way the nerve receptors behave. It is feared that using these powerful drugs may cause permanent changes in the brain, and not necessarily positive ones. Legal changes may take years, but the pending lawsuits will affect the way test data is made available.

Another area of concern is freedom of thought, that hard-won basis of constitutional rights. Law on freedom of thought is important but under-developed and will be challenged by neurotechnology. Memory management drugs are already available that reduce recall of a traumatic event. Propranolol has been used on car accident victims, and compared with placebos it does reduce post-traumatic stress disorders. But should it be given automatically to victims without their acceptance? In the case of violent crime there is an obvious clash between the view of the police who need clear testimony, the victim who may or may not want to testify and the doctors who want to ease pain. Similar questions concern memory-enhancing drugs currently in the pipeline. Could victims be required by the state to take such drugs until they completed testifying?

We need to be cautious about interpreting scans. MRI scanners are being used to improve advertising and may be allowed one day as courtroom evidence. Yet those attractive brain scan pictures can be very misleading. How can we be certain that the comparison of a person's scan with those from a wide range of people shows a tendency to violence? The images are not a direct view of the brain but produced by processing raw data, and a researcher decides the way that data is processed.

These concerns shouldn't blind us to all the advantages of our increasing expertise and knowledge. A promising new medical area is proteomics, the search at molecular level for the biochemical and physiological mechanisms of diseases. This allows for personalized medicine. Currently several thousand people die annually from adverse drug reactions. These include poor prescribing and wrong drug combinations, but a number are due to genetic differences. A variation in just one gene affects warfarin use, and some people are genetically susceptible to particular anaesthetics.

Genetic modification – Frankenstein humans?

The Human Genome Project has presented us with a mass of complicated information difficult to analyse. Just one X-chromosome consists of 155 million base pairs, and 98.5% of DNA has a role in regulating how actual genes are expressed. All the same this new knowledge has improved clinical diagnosis of disease out of all recognition, because if the clinician suspects a genetic problem it can be confirmed by testing.

This is especially useful where single genes are causing the problem. Some single mutations are known to cause large malfunctions. Defects in a gene called by the imaginative name *sonic hedgehog* cause the most horrendous and deadly results in embryos, from *cyclopia*, one eye in the central forehead, to malformations in heart, lungs, kidneys and guts. Mutated *sonic hedgehog* causes numerous defects because it codes for a signalling protein that guides other cells to their final positions. Harmful mutations in other single genes may not clock in until maturity. However, attempts to reduce the effects of faulty genes haven't been as effective as originally hoped. There's still no good treatment for cystic fibrosis.

Currently the new knowledge is used extensively in prenatal diagnosis, especially for couples who have a family history of a genetic disease. Embryos are often diagnosed for genetic problems where *in vitro* fertilization (IVF) is recommended for a couple with fertility problems (preimplantation genetic diagnosis or PGD). This requires removing a cell from the cluster, not a risk-free procedure though misdiagnosis is a higher risk. Saviour siblings are those embryos specifically chosen to help an older brother or sister recover from a life-threatening genetic illness.

There are a number of concerns about this technology. One is that new techniques are continually being researched, investment decisions made and the techniques used all before public discussion. Another is the increasing use of genetic testing as a prenatal diagnostic tool. In many cases a genetic disorder is obviously harmful, but in others the bearer may be able to live a successful life with little discomfort. How serious is serious? What is normality? And who decides in any one case? Perhaps we are seeking an impossible perfection. We also know that by making genetic choices we are affecting human evolution more precisely than we have ever done before, and we have no idea how to evaluate the long-term effect of choosing only those individual embryos free from particular diseases.

How is the choice explained to patients? There are risky procedures and possible misdiagnosis. In general counsellors explain risks as a percentage, but the language of probability is not always understood by the patient. When there is a history of genetic disease in a family, such as a particular form of breast cancer, the risk to a woman can be calculated. There may be an 80% chance of contracting the disease. Should she have a double mastectomy?

There is also the issue of confidentiality. It may be in the interests of the family to know the results of a test, but the individual may not want it made public. In some cases an individual will not want to have a test. Should they be forced to have one for the sake of their family? It is becoming more likely that all babies will be genetically screened, as forewarned is forearmed. If the information shows an increased risk of heart disease, then this can be reduced by lifestyle choices. But could such information be required by life insurance companies? Will the police have access? The information will be retained on file and there are possibilities of abuse.

Gradually medical research will improve treatment for people currently suffering from diseases such as thalassaemia, a hereditary disease of red blood cells especially prevalent round the eastern Mediterranean. Gene therapy can target the individual blood cells. But wouldn't it be better to prevent the disease by repairing the gene inside the fertilized egg (*germline* gene therapy), so removing it altogether from following generations? This would be difficult because we would have to eliminate it from *carriers* as well as sufferers. It might remove benefits at the same time. Sickle cell anaemia is an extremely serious disease if inherited from both parents. In its mild form it provides protection from malaria. Currently research into germline therapy is banned in the UK.

These treatments affect single genes. It is much more difficult to know how we could alter something like intelligence where the brain's development is affected by thousands of genes. While there may be genetic tendencies in criminal behaviour and child abuse, the problem of unravelling any genetic input is vast. Remember that the actual gene on the chromosome is surrounded by genetic elements that control its level of expression and where it acts. Mutations in these regulatory sequences can radically alter where and how the gene is expressed. There are jumping genes (transposons) within the genome which can cut and paste into another part of the genome or replicate themselves thousands of times. The total character of an organism is affected by all the genes, and environmental conditions play a large part in shaping behaviour. All these considerations make it exceedingly difficult to trace any route from gene to behaviour.

We aren't even sure which behaviours are genetically supported. Genetic change is slow and much of the variation in behaviour may not be genetic, but it can swamp the effects of the genes. This is obvious in human populations. The numbers of live births per woman has declined considerably in the Western world during the last century. Cultural changes can explain the situation, while it's unlikely there is a *genetic* reason.

Carriers	Those who do not express the mutation but can pass it on to the next generation. Queen Victoria is the famous example. She passed haemophilia on to many male members of the royal families of Europe who were descended from her, but did not suffer from it herself.
Germline	Early in the development of many animals some cells become differentiated from the rest of the body (the somatic cell line). These differentiated cells are the only ones that form gametes – in humans, eggs and sperm.

Human cloning – (Hitler)[99]?

Embryo cloning has been used for a long time to produce many genetically identical animals for livestock and zoo breeding programmes (see Figure 8.3). These animals have half their genes from each parent but are clones of one another.

The famous sheep Dolly (1997–2003) – may she rest in peace – was a breakthrough in mammalian cloning techniques, but it's expensive and difficult to produce livestock by nuclear transfer (see Figure 8.4). Here the animal comes from one parent and is genetically similar to it. Highly valuable animals like racehorses are the most likely candidates.

Concern for the welfare of cloned animals is strong. Hundreds of animals have been cloned by embryonic techniques, and both the animals themselves and their offspring are healthy and normal. The newer technique of nuclear transfer is more problematical. Dolly didn't live as long as most other sheep of her breed and suffered from early arthritis, and it isn't known whether this was due to the use of adult donor cells.

Legislation in many countries forbids attempts at human implantation or reproduction using either type of cloning, and sensational stories of cloned babies have not been backed up by the necessary genetic proofs. Currently there is more freedom in the UK in this area than in the rest of the European Union and USA, but it is still tightly controlled. The UK Human Fertilization

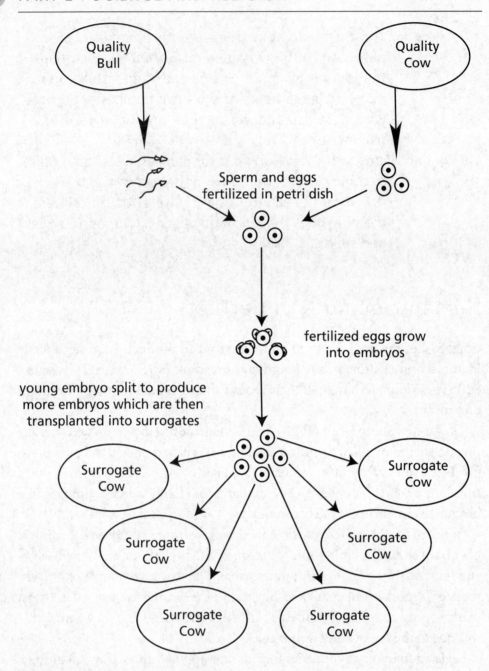

Figure 8.3 Embryo cloning.
Used in high quality farm animals and conservation
programmes.

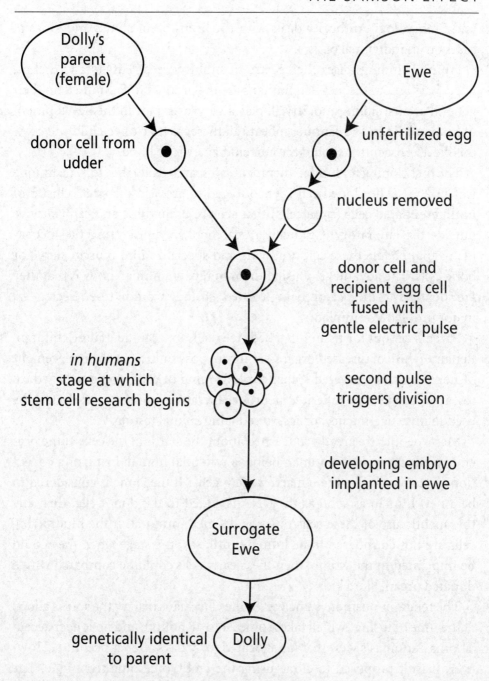

Figure 8.4 Cloning by nuclear transfer.

and Embryology Authority deals with the licensing of clinics and looks at cases on an individual basis.

Human cloning raises the spectre of multitudes of Hitlers and Stalins. Such fears ignore the fact that humans are the product of far more than their genes. Parents, siblings, society all play a very large part in the development of human beings. We cannot replicate all these, so no cloned child will grow up like its progenitor should the current ban ever be lifted.

The first cloning for human therapeutic research using the Dolly technique was in 2001. The cloned cell is encouraged to grow into a small cluster of undifferentiated cells (stem cells) that are pre-embryonic and can't survive outside the laboratory. Gradually researchers are uncovering the mechanisms that enable these cells to divide and specialize into muscle, nerve or bone cells. The advantage of using them to repair a human body is that they are identical to the person being treated, so they wouldn't be rejected – a major problem for implants.

Parents cry out for tissue-matched stem cells to treat their ailing children. Repair or cure of diseased organs are future possibilities, or the replacement of nerve cells in a severed spinal cord. Cloning of cells would aid medical research into certain inherited neurodegenerative diseases. It could also be used in investigating new drugs, so reducing animal testing.

Many people are greatly concerned about the status of the cells at the pre-embryonic stage. Is it a human being, a potential human being or a collection of stem cells like bone marrow stem cells? If the clone is considered to be a new human as soon as the DNA is added to the donor egg, then any therapeutic use of these cells must be deemed immoral. If the multiplying cells are not considered to be human until, say, the stage when they could be implanted in the womb, then these early cells could be compared with a donated organ, like a kidney.

The religious position is unclear. Some Christians believe the soul is added at the time of fusing (which takes some 24 to 48 hours), and no longer accept Thomas Aquinas's view that it's allocated forty days after conception. However, it isn't proposed to clone using the embryo cloning technique. The status of cloned cells produced by nuclear transfer, when an *adult* cell is added to an *unfertilized* egg, is ambiguous. A number of religions support the idea that the single cell with a full complement of genes is a human being, whether those genes have been supplied from one adult cell or the fusing of two sex cells.

Human futures

Science and technology are giving us greater possibilities than ever before. They have always helped us extend our reach since we learnt to knap flint and control fire. Now we can alter ourselves. What can we expect in a post-human future?

The predictions are truly marvellous. Through the internet information will become increasingly available to all in easy-to-access form. We can extend our personalities in multiple ways by the use of internet chat rooms and mobile phones, so exploring all parts of our characters. Some drugs already control concentration and mental energy, and soon mood enhancers and better psychosomatic drugs will enable us to manage emotions, so we can decide when we want to be in love or adventurous or kind. Tailored drugs will improve our health and increase our lifespan way beyond a hundred years. We are already producing designer babies by PGD, and we shall shortly be able to increase intelligence and other useful qualities. Once germline intervention is permitted we shall delete all harmful mutations and add special faculties like increased musical abilities, spirituality or eroticism. We shall improve our bodily design. Advances in computer technology will enable us to download our brains so that we never die. Space colonization will become a reality.

First we need to reject the fear of hubris that has dogged humans for so long. Our future is in our hands and we can recreate ourselves as we want. In the past evolution was blind but we can control the routes we follow. To do this successfully we need to understand and control the risks. The new technologies must be available to everyone, but we must only permit those which favour all humans – increase in height for example provides no net benefit. For safety reasons there needs to be international cooperation, tolerance and global security.

A number of these improvements may be more difficult to attain than the proponents suggest. For instance while it is possible to alter moods with drugs, can our deeper emotions of jealousy, love, greed, generosity and so on be altered in this way? They are dependent on upbringing and memory. Any attempt to remove or alter a particular emotion, say anger, may also remove desirable traits. Altering a genetic cascade would probably change personality in totally unpredictable ways, due to the complexity of genetic and environmental interactions.

Another difficulty occurs when we download our brains. The computer, however advanced, will only receive current information stored in our neurons. The whole complex person includes continual feedback from external senses and internal organs. It is constantly changing even though we are aware of central control. The atoms and molecules change, new pathways develop in the nervous system. Downloading a living personality is no simple task.

Such doubts do not mean we should ignore future possibilities, only that we should consider them very carefully before implementation.

Things that we don't know we don't know

- What is human?
- Right to procreate and rights of the child
- Sharing futures
- Wisdom

What is human?

There is a strong reductionist view embedded in the notion that we are mainly genes and chemicals which needs redressing. Human personalities, behaviours and cultures differ widely, so what is normal? If we are to alter ourselves through the use of genetic engineering and drugs we need to have some aim in mind. What exactly are these perfect humans to be like? Many answers suggest more powerful, able to control their lives and their environments for their own advancement – a recipe for more conflict, not less. Perhaps greater awareness of others' needs might be more valuable.

Genetic changes are concerned with individuals, not society, but they will still skew society in certain directions. Change doesn't occur overnight and many people will not have access to the technology. Do these aspirations hide a new eugenics – the survival of those with wealth and power, rather than those who are loving and generous?

It seems likely that we shall want to control our own evolution. Could we modify ourselves into complete reliance on machines? Computer control of many systems is already a concern in our post 9/11 situation. Could we modify ourselves out of existence? Intelligent life could turn upon itself destructively, and annihilate itself with its own technology.

Right to procreate and rights of the child

The right to procreate is seen as central to personhood, but it involves three people, parents and child. As childbirth changes from chance to choice, what are the rights of the child?

Many interests conflict. Abortion of foetuses with disabilities or threatening diseases is not approved by some religions. It is also seen as insulting and threatening by current sufferers who insist they and people like them have a right to life. But parents want their children to be as healthy and able as possible.

There are tricky situations to deal with. We need to consider how the saviour sibling will feel about his or her selection, and also the feelings of the sibling whose illness has made that birth necessary. Parents will have to explain this very sensitively. A child genetically engineered for better intelligence will be left behind when the next upgrade becomes available – not an attractive arms race. How can society make sure such children feel wanted and secure?

Sharing futures

We considered some solutions to our ever-increasing requirement for energy. How do we share that technology and medical advances equitably, taking into account the various political situations in countries worldwide?

Information access through the internet is one method, but we also need to share other resources like equipment and practical skills, and too often the benefits go in the wrong direction. There are many fine hospitals, trained personnel and research centres in developing countries, but their staffing problems are far more serious than in the West. Their trained staff are encouraged by Western governments to emigrate and the continual brain-drain depletes their resources. How can they cope with the current HIV/Aids pandemic or starvation, let alone these new technologies?

Large numbers of people view our new control over ourselves with horror as hubris of the worst kind. West Africans have a saying that the hand that reaches under the incubating hen is guilty. We are trying to steal knowledge we should never possess. They may accept blood transfusion and kidney donation as praiseworthy, but donations from dead bodies, foetus selection and stem cell research are abhorrent. Hindus and Buddhists are as anxious about cloning and genetic selection as the monotheistic religions. Abortion and planned death of early foetuses are considered murder. Are we playing God? Or are we being called by God to be co-creators? Do we really view health and intelligence as more important than our relationship to God or Brahman? Every culture has a different view, and our zeal to share needs to be tempered with understanding.

In a number of countries poverty and starvation are being tackled by boosting agricultural production, which both feeds people and increases income. Low-tech solutions rather than state-of-the-art technology reduce many problems. Many organizations concerned about the current situation are coming together to assess problems and discuss solutions, including the World Bank and a number of organizations supported by the United Nations. They can then target investment into making technology more available, improving women's access to resources, solving questions of land tenure and many other areas related to the key problems.

Wisdom

Religions are deeply associated with their society's ethical system. Scientists are often well aware of the problems their research raises. Learning to understand one another's viewpoint helps locate acceptable solutions to many problems that at first sight appear intractable.

The Christian solution requires a change of heart. It seeks Wisdom or Sophia, the third person of the Trinity, as spiritual guide towards a loving and respectful approach to the world. Sophia seeks the good of the many and the reduction of harm to all, both humans and the whole planet. It uses similar principles to those that guide parents in family matters, teachers in a classroom and conciliatory bodies in industrial disputes.

So – the future is yours – handle with care

IDEAS FOR DISCUSSION

1   Research proposed solutions to the world's energy problems from websites.

2   You are talking to a citizen of a country suffering huge deprivation due to HIV/Aids. How do you explain that your country has a right to advertise for their nurses and doctors because your country suffers from a shortage of medical personnel?

3   Consider a country whose economy is dependent on agriculture, an industry highly reliant on climate. There is low investment in farming, poor infrastructure, limited access to financial and other supporting services, a mediocre legal framework, problems with land tenure, and a poorly educated rural population (especially the women). Health services and family planning are limited. Knowledge of marketing abroad is inadequate, product quality and hygiene poor, technology and research primitive. Add to that the problems of trade barriers. Read Curtis and look at the websites. What solutions are being proposed? Note – Vietnam, Thailand and China have all managed to boost agricultural production, increase calorie intake and improve their economies. How did they manage to do this?

4   Consider the population density of the UK. What proportion of land should be allocated for improved housing, roads

and new industry, for producing food and for recreation and wildlife? What foodstuffs should we produce? Remember that large parts of the UK are unsuitable for arable crops (e.g. the mountains of Scotland, the Pennines and flood plains of rivers). The organic option reduces the arable output per hectare by about half.

5　Biocontrol. Check out the Australian cane frog problem. What legislation is in place to prevent a reoccurrence?

6　Read Shiva, Rifkin, or Lewington (Chapter 1) on GM crops and animals. Look up the Agricultural Science and Technology Assessment of the world food problem backed by major agencies like the World Bank and Food and Agriculture Organization (FAO) of the United Nations. Compare solutions.

7　What are the rights of a foetus? Does it have just a right to life, or does it have a right to as healthy a life as possible? Is it selfish for parents to want a healthy child? Increasing knowledge about genetic make-up will make it possible to discover areas of abnormality at early stages. Will this make the case for early abortion clear cut? A number of inherited problems may not appear until maturity, or may never be a problem if the parents are given advice on means of control. What is serious? (Severity creep – where do we stop testing embryos for inherited diseases?) Who should decide? What are the rights of separated parents with opposing views?

8　Who should research and develop expensive new medicines – private companies (multinationals) or governments (the taxpayer)? What precautions are currently taken to reduce possible harmful side effects?

9　Human Cloning. What is your opinion of cloning for human therapeutic research? Currently the failure rate is high, though it will fall as techniques improve. In South Korea recently 242 human eggs were used and 30 cloned eggs produced. Of these only one developed to the stem cell stage. So was this in effect the destruction of human beings to research the making of spare parts?

10 Read Kitcher, Kaku, Turkle, McKibben. What is a human person? What are your hopes and fears for the human future?

11 Germline therapy. Give the arguments for and against.

12 Discuss the precautionary principle.

13 Note how production of staple foods fell as Argentina grew more soya for export. How could proposals to remove food trade barriers between developing and affluent countries affect developing countries in the long term? How much food should affluent countries grow for their own population and how much should they rely on the developing world?

14 Some 95% of deaths from natural disasters occur in developing countries. Research the reasons. Research the international response (e.g. Hyogo Framework for Action 2005–15 agreed at the World Conference on Disaster Reduction at Kobe, January 2005; the UN International Strategy for Disaster Reduction; World Meteorological Association).

REFERENCES AND FURTHER READING

Websites

www.bbsrc.ac.uk   Biotechnology and Biological Sciences Research Council
www.bioethics.net   *Journal of Bioethics*
www.energy.usgs.gov   US website on energy resources
www.fao.org   United Nations Food and Agriculture Organization. Also www.fao.org/ethics
www.fao.org/ag/cgrfa/itpgr   International Treaty on Plant Genetic Resources
www.hfea.gov.uk   Human Fertilisation and Embryology Authority
www.ices.dk   International Council for the Exploration of the Seas
www.igbp.kva.se   International Geosphere-Biosphere Program
www.jetpress.org   *Journal of Evolution and Technology* – science and philosophy
www.ncbe.reading.ac.uk   National Centre for Biotechnical Education
www.nerc.ac.uk   National Environmental Research Council
www.nottingham.ac.uk/rbru   UK Farm Business Surveys

www.tradejusticemovement.org.uk   Trade Justice Movement
www.uea.ac.uk   Environmental Change
www.wfp.org   United Nations World Food Programme
www.worldbank.org   World Bank
www.wto.org   World Trade Organization

Books

Mark Curtis, 2001, *Trade for Life*, London: Christian Aid

Celia Deane-Drummond and Bronislaw Szersznski, eds, 2003, *Re-ordering Nature: Theology, Science and the New Genetics*, London: T&T Clark

Jacques Ellul, 1990, *The Technological Bluff*, Grand Rapids, MI: Eerdmans

Michio Kaku, 1998, *Visions*, Oxford: Oxford University Press

Philip Kitcher, 1996, *The Lives to Come*, London: Allen Lane

James Lovelock, 1988, *The Ages of Gaia*, Oxford: Oxford University Press

Sally McFague, 1997, *Super Natural Christians*, London: SCM Press

Bill McKibben, 2003, *Enough: Genetic Engineering and the End of Human Nature*, London: Bloomsbury

M Reiss and R Straughan, *Improving Nature: The Science and Ethics of Genetic Engineering*, Cambridge: Cambridge University Press

Jeremy Rifkin, 1998, *The Biotech Century*, London: Victor Gollancz

Holmes Rolston III, 1988, *Environmental Ethics: Duties to and in the Natural World*, Philadelphia: Temple University Press

Vandana Shiva, 2000, *Tomorrow's Biodiversity*, London: Thames & Hudson

Sherry Turkle, 1995, *Life on the Screen*, London: Orion

Index

Abelard, Peter, 151
Académie Royale des Sciences, 160
Age of Reason, 162
Aggression
    chimpanzees, 86
    human, 90
    vetebrates, 77
Algae, blue-green, 22, 23, 24, 25
Algorithm, 15, 16
Allergies, 225
Altruism
    insects, 72
    vertebrate, 74
American Independence, 162, 166
American Psychological
        Association, 112
Anselm, 150
Anthropic Principle, 7
Aquinas, Thomas, 69, 144, 151,
        236
Archimedes, 140
Aristotle, 140
Augustine, 12, 144
Awareness, degrees of, 41

Bacteria, 23,
Big Bang, 5, 6, 8
Binomial, 167
Biocontrol, 221
Biopharming, 222
Biopiracy, 226
Blake, William, 88, 90, 165
Bonding, 50, 79, 81, 84, 85
Boyle, Robert, 160
Brain
    consciousness, 56
    damage, 59
    ganglia, 45
    primate, 81
Bronze Age, 133
Bruno, Giordano, 158

Calvin, John, 103, 155
Capitalism, 162
Care of young, 78, 85
Catholic Church, 155, 172
Caxton, William, 155
Chaos, 14, 195
Chartists, 171

Chimpanzees, 81
Christianity
    19th century, 171
    early, 143, 144
    feminism, 204
    homosexuality, 205
    loss of belief and status, 185
    middle ages, 147, 150
    scientific theology, 188, 190
    teaching, 198
    worldwide, 180
Christian Science, 173
Civil War, 14, 157
Clone, 28
    embryo, 233
    therapeutic research, 236
Cobbett, William, 168
Communal living, 50
Competition, 32
Computer, 52, 239
    brain, 56
    human, 54
    interaction with the environment,
        42
    recognition of others, 42
    self-consciousness, 54, 56
Conscience, 69, 87, 89
Consciousness, 40
Cooperation, 32
Copernicus, Nicolaus, 158, 159
Counting, 51
Creationism, 189
Creativity
    animals, 64
    human, 61
    Cromwell, Oliver, 157

Darwin, Charles
    evolution, 175, 189
Darwinism
    eugenics, 175
    social, 189
Disease
    Bronze Age, 134, 139
    classical Greece and Rome, 142
    Islam, 145
    Middle Ages, 148
    New Stone Age, 131
    nineteenth century, 171, 172
    plants, 30, 130, 147, 221
Dissent, 149, 151, 163
Divine Action
    General, 190
    Special, 190
DNA, 25, 26, 30, 32, 33
    discovery, 179
    genetic modification, 221, 230
Dynamic relationships, 34

Ecofeminism, 226
Einstein, Albert, 174
Emergence, 53, 55, 110, 196
Emotion, 57, 63, 77
Empathy, 77
    chimpanzees, 85
    humans, 88
    vertebrates, 77
Energy
    food, 219
    for life, 27, 32, 214
    industry, 216
    nuclear fusion, 217
    plants, 27, 28

renewable, 216
Enlightenment, 161
Entanglement, 11, 115
Environment, 34, 63, 213, 216
Eugenics, 175
Evolution, 20, 25
    Darwin, 175, 189
Extinction,
Extra-sensory perception, 113
Eyes, 43

Falsification, 179
Famine, 31, 131, 214
Faraday, Michael, 174
Farming
    Bronze Age, 133
    classical Greece and Rome, 140
    eighteenth century, 163
    Middle Ages, 147
    nineteenth century, 168
    Stone Age, 129
    twentieth century, 176, 214, 215,
        219, 224, 227
Fear, 59
Feminism, 204
Fertile Crescent, 130
Feudalism, 147
Fire, 127
Fishing, 126, 215
Free will, 91
French Revolution, 41, 162, 166, 170
Freud, Sigmund, 173
Friendly Societies, 165

Gaia, 34, 218
Galileo, 158

Game theory, 74
Ganglia and brains, 45
Gaskell, Elizabeth, 170
GDA see Divine Action, General
Gene,
    gene therapy, 232
    jumping gene. 232
    selfish gene, 72, 74
Gene transfer, 226
Genetic engineering, 221
    Argentina, 227
    concerns, 223, 237, 239
    human, 230
    plants, 222, 224
Genius, 61
Genome, 26
Global Warming, 218
Goldsmith, Oliver, 163
Grafting, 140
Greeks, 140
Grief, 78, 90
    chimpanzees, 86
Growth, 28

Harvey, William, 161
Heisenberg Uncertainty Principle,
    11, 193
Heresy, 155
Hierarchies
    chimpanzees, 83
    scientific, 54
Homo sapiens, 127, 199
Homosexuality, 50, 84, 205
Human cloning, 233
Human Genome Project, 230
Hunting, 126

In vitro fertilization, 231
Indeterminism, 193
Industrial Revolution, 162, 168, 170
Inquisition, 104, 156
Insects, 72
Ireland
    potato famine, 169
Iron Age, 136
Islam, 145
Israel, 135
    classical era, 142
    exile, 136

James, William, 99, 103
Jefferson, Thomas, 165, 166
Jericho, 132
Jesus Christ, 143, 144, 150, 200, 202

King, Martin Luther, 181
Kuhn, Thomas, 179

Labour Party, 171
Langland, Will, 147
Laplace, Pierre, 167
Lavoisier, Antoine Laurent, 167
Laws
    gods, 69
    human, 70
    universal, 71
Life, 19
Linnaeus, Carl, 167
Lollards, 151
Luddites, 170
Luther, Martin, 155, 158

Maccabees, 142

Malthus, Thomas Robert, 169, 175
Marx, Karl, 70, 173
Medicine, 128, 142, 145, 156, 171,
    228
Memory, 46, 58
Methodism, 166
Middle Ages, 147
Miracles see Religion
Momentum, 11
Moods, 59, 98
Muhammad, 145
Multi-universes, 7, 11
Music, 97

Napoleon, 41, 162, 167, 171, 174
Natural philosophers, 154, 157
Neanderthals, 128
Near-Death experiences, 117
Near East, 129, 133
Neurosensory systems
    neurons, 45
    sight, 43
Newton, Isaac, 9, 140, 160

Old Testament, 135, 138
Open field system, 163
Out-of-Body experience, 117

Pain, 47, 60
Palestine, 132, 134, 142, 221
Paradigm shift, 179
Paranormal, 111
Parasites, 33, 48
Pavlov fashion, 52
Pecking order, 51, 77
Peterloo massacre, 171

Pharisees, 143

Philistines 136, 211

Philo, 141

Photosynthesis, 25, 27, 219

Piers Plowman, 147, 180

Plato, 109, 141

Play, 79, 85

Psychical Research, Society for, 111

Pleasure, 47, 59

Politics
  eighteenth century, 165
  English Commonwealth, 157
  nineteenth century, 170, 172
  socialism, 171, 178

Popper, Karl, 179

Population, 213

Precautionary principle, 213

Predation, 29

Predestination, 91

Prediction, 15, 92, 196

Preimplantation genetic diagnosis,
  231, 237

Priestley, Joseph, 166

Probability, 17, 194

Proteomics, 230

Psychokinesis, 12, 114

Ptolemy, 158, 159

Punishment, 73, 77, 80, 103, 163
  cheating, 75

Quantum Theory, 9, 17, 115, 195

Qumran, 143

Racism, 175

Recognition, 42, 50, 73

Reconcilation, 77, 85, 89

Recycling, 35

Reduction, 55, 238

Reform Acts, 171

Reformation, 103, 144, 154, 155, 161

Relativity, 12

Religion
  beauty and mystery, 104
  believers, 102
  Buddhism, 107, 181
  comparison with music, 97
  death, 106
  downside, 103
  early Christianity, 141, 143, 144
  early Israel, 135, 138
  ecology, 227
  education, 198
  eighteenth century, 166
  experience, 116
  fellowship, 103
  Hinduism, 107, 181
  Islam , 106, 145, 148, 181
  Judaism, 106
  Middle Ages, 147, 150
  miracles, xii, 107, 190
  nineteenth century, 171
  ritual, 101, 156
  sociology, 99
  spiritual powers, 101
  Stone Age, 129
  suffering, 106
  tolerance, 157, 171
  tradition and sacred knowledge,
    100, 102
  twentieth century, 180

Religious Experiences Research
    Centre, 116

Renaissance, 140, 146, 154
Rights of Man, 162
Romans, 140
    end of empire, 144
Royal Agricultural Society of
        England, 168
Royal Society of London, 160
Rules
    chimpanzees, 83
    human teachers, 80
    internalized in chimpanzees, 87
    internalized in vertebrates, 80
    learning in vertebrates, 79

Samson,
Schistosomiasis, 131
Scientific method, 125, 140, 146,
        151, 154, 157, 161, 179
SDA see Divine Action, Special
Second law of thermodynamics, 8
Selfconsciousness see Consciousness
Selfish genes see Gene
Sex
    behaviour differences, 84
    homosexuality, 205
    selection, 50
    why?, 30
Shaftesbury, Lord, 172
Sharing
    chimpanzees, 85
    humans, 88
    vertebrates, 76
Signals, animal, 49
Slavery, 134, 141, 163
Society
    bronze age, 134

chimpanzee, 81
friendly, 165
insect, 72
Iron Age, 136
religious, 99, 165
Stone Age, 128, 129
vertebrate, 74
Soul, 69, 108, 116
Spirit, 108
    bias, 109
    concepts, 110
    emergent, 110
    ghosts, 111
Spiritualism, 173
SPR see Psychical Research, Society
        for
Stem cells, 236
Storing information, 32
Supernova, 6
Superweeds, 224
Symbiosis, 33

Taxonomy, 167
Technology
    Bronze Age, 133
    classical Greece and Rome, 140
    eighteenth century, 164
    human future, 21, 216, 217, 221,
        239
    Iron Age, 136
    Islam, 145
    Middle Ages, 147
    nineteenth century, 170, 174
    Old Testament, 138
    seventeenth ceentury, 157
    Stone Age, 127, 129

twentieth century, 176

Telekinesis, 116

Teleportation, 12

Tillich, Paul, 199

Time, relative, 12

Tithing, 168

Tolpuddle Martyrs, 171

Toolmaking, 51, 64

Trade
Bronze Age, 133
classical Greece and Rome, 141
eighteenth century, 162
Iron Age, 136, 139
Islam, 145
Middle Ages, 147
nineteenth century, 174
Stone Age, 131
twenty-first century, 215

Transhumance, 133

Transubstantiation, 151

Tsunami, 35, 93, 243

Twenty-first century
energy, 216

global concerns, 214, 218

pollution, 217

waste, 217

Tyndale, William, 156

Unitarian, 166

War, 136, 162, 164, 176
English Civil, 14, 157
religious, 143, 145, 148, 156

Waste
humans, 217
plants, 28

Wesleys, John and Charles,
166

White, Gilbert, 167

Wisdom/Sophia, 240

Witchcraft, 156

Women, 156, 178
feminism, 181, 204
Middle Ages, 148
suffragettes, 178

Wyclif, John, 151